Descriptosaurus Grammar Companion Ages 9 to 12

Descriptosaurus Grammar Companion Ages 9 to 12 is a flexible grammar toolkit based on current research about effective strategies for teaching grammar tools and sentence construction (investigation, imitation, combining and expansion). It includes guidelines, exercises, scaffolds and models, and by showing a clear progression route to the acquisition and consolidation of increasingly more complex grammar tools it provides teachers and students with a road map that makes learning about sentence construction and revision visible.

This book is a collection of connected resources that can be used as and when required and it provides an easily accessible differentiation resource for each student based on their current stage of development, not the age-related targets and expectations. It enables the learning process for grammar tools to be recursive rather than linear: to be regularly revisited in short bursts to consolidate students' knowledge and usage, or to correct any misconceptions or problem areas without impeding any writing activities already planned. Chapters focus on four main points:

- ★ Investigation
- ★ Imitation
- ★ Combining
- ★ Expansion

This Grammar Companion supports the main *Descriptosaurus* book and scaffolds students in their journey through the world of language. This essential resource will strengthen their language muscles and build confidence with sentence manipulation when revising their own texts, thus freeing their minds to think about the important issues of writing: content, audience and purpose, and organisation and structure.

Alison Wilcox has extensive teaching experience in schools in England and Scotland. Colleagues describe her methods as "innovative and inspirational to even the most reluctant of writers".

Descriptosaurus Grammar Companion Ages 9 to 12

A Language Toolkit and Support for Creative Writing

Alison Wilcox

Routledge
Taylor & Francis Group

LONDON AND NEW YORK

Designed cover image: © Dani Pasteau

First published 2024
by Routledge
4 Park Square, Milton Park, Abingdon, Oxon, OX14 4RN

and by Routledge
605 Third Avenue, New York, NY 10158

Routledge is an imprint of the Taylor & Francis Group, an informa business

British Library Cataloguing-in-Publication Data
A catalogue record for this book is available from the British Library

ISBN: 978-1-032-66285-5 (hbk)
ISBN: 978-1-032-66283-1 (pbk)
ISBN: 978-1-032-66286-2 (ebk)

DOI: 10.4324/9781032662862

Typeset in Myriad Pro
by Deanta Global Publishing Services, Chennai, India

Printed in Great Britain by Bell & Bain Ltd, Glasgow.

"Writing is hard work. A clear sentence is no accident. Very few sentences come out right the first time, or even the third time. Remember this in moments of despair. If you find that writing is hard, it's because it is hard."

— **William Zinsser, *On Writing Well: The Classic Guide to Writing Nonfiction***

Contents

Acknowledgements

Thank you to all the students I have had the pleasure to work with over the years who have patiently and enthusiastically explored with me the many strategies for learning about sentence construction and revising a text. It has given me immense pleasure to watch those students transform into competent, confident and creative writers.

Introduction

The aim of the *Descriptosaurus Grammar Companion Ages 9 to 12* is to provide a resource that supports and improves the teaching of two of the fundamental building blocks of good writing, the ability to:

1. write clear, precise and complete sentences
2. revise a first draft for syntactic accuracy and fluency.

Mastering these elements of writing are vital in enabling students to:

★ demonstrate their talent and knowledge in all subjects
★ reach their full potential both in education and their future career prospects.

The goal of writing instruction should be to help students to cope with the onerous cognitive demands imposed by writing. E. W. Nold (1981) suggests that one way in which young and developing writers can exercise better control over the composing process is by making various elements of the process automatic. Building a bank of vocabulary, phrases and clauses; understanding the function, construction, position and punctuation of grammar tools; and practising and experimenting with sentence construction and revision will build confidence and automaticity with sentence construction and manipulation. This will greatly reduce the onerous cognitive demands of writing and leave more processing space available for consideration of purpose, content and text cohesion.

A FLEXIBLE GRAMMAR TOOLKIT

The *Descriptosaurus Grammar Companion Ages 9 to 12* is a flexible grammar toolkit based on current research about the effective strategies for writing instruction (investigation, imitation, combining and expansion). It includes guidelines, scaffolds and models, and by showing a clear progression route to the acquisition and consolidation of increasingly more complex grammar tools it provides teachers and students with a road map that makes learning about sentence construction and revision visible. The handbook helps students to identify where they are at, what knowledge and skills they need to acquire and what they are aiming to achieve. It is designed to support student writers according to their current stage of development rather than to age-related targets and expectations. The handbook is a resource that can be used not only to teach a new grammar tool but to return to a tool previously studied, allowing either a group or an individual student to consolidate their knowledge and usage or to correct any misconceptions.

It is an easily accessible resource for students, enabling them to practise expressing ideas using different grammar tools without the additional cognitive demands of having to develop their own content. The focus is purely on using the content provided to construct and experiment with different grammar tools and sentence structures.

Currently, the teaching of grammar tools and sentence constructions is too often a modular, linear process based on age-related writing targets and the grammar strands of individual national or state curricula; however, to be effective, consistent revision of the 'grammar tools' available is vital. Whilst a student might be taught about relative (adjective clauses) at the age of ten, this does not guarantee that they have a secure understanding of how and when to use them, their function and position, and how they are punctuated. Extensive research supports scheduling a time delay between learning sessions, as this forces students to work harder to retrieve the information, process or strategy. This helps to consolidate it into their long-term memory, leading to automaticity and mastery of the skill or strategy – in this case sentence construction.

As well as introducing the phrases and clauses required for each age group and key stage, it is important to see each of the grammar tools as building blocks that are added gradually to the foundations and base structure. These building blocks improve the effectiveness of the original design, resulting in a unique and elaborate design. Starting initially with a one-storey basic construction, with knowledge and experience new layers and designs are added until students can construct their own 'grand edifices'; these are always built on solid foundations, with each layer being reinforced and any gaps cemented. Adding more complex designs without first developing structural knowledge will result in half-remembered rules and techniques; a confused design will cause the construction to become a tangle of different rules that are ineffectually applied. It will also prohibit the acquisition of an essential component of developing writing skills – automaticity in sentence construction, ultimately leading to structures that do not achieve their purpose, are overly complicated and confusing, and do not satisfy the needs of the audience (or external examiner). Before adding extensions and new designs, it is therefore essential to revisit and assess the solidity of the foundations. Writing progression and the acquisition of grammar tools should be tackled as a recursive rather than linear process, one which considers students' experience, knowledge and understanding, and makes connections to the grammar tools that have already been learned and mastered.

The design of this handbook enables the learning process for grammar tools to be recursive rather than linear. It allows for grammar tools to be regularly revisited in short bursts without impeding the writing activities already planned. This approach allows problem areas to be addressed that have become evident from assessing a group or individual's writing progress.

EFFECTIVE METHODS

There is overwhelming evidence that teaching traditional grammar by labelling, identifying and parsing sentences in isolated grammar exercises does not transfer to students' own writing. However, extensive evidence suggests that there are three effective contexualised methods which facilitate students' understanding and application of grammar in terms of sentence construction, modification and revision, and which do transfer to their own writing.

1. Sentence imitation.
2. Sentence combining.
3. Sentence expansion.

Although each method should be modelled and practised separately, the processes are complementary. They should be used together to consolidate knowledge of the 'grammar tools' available as well as developing automaticity in sentence construction, experimentation, evaluation and the revision of a text.

Based on the work of Don and Jenny Killgallon (see the Bibliography for further details), several scaffolds can be used to explore the function, construction, position and punctuation of grammar (modification) tools in a sentence:

*   chunking
*   modelling
*   matching
*   unscrambling
*   combining
*   imitating
*   creating.

These methods are demonstrated in Part 1 for:

*   prepositional phrases
*   adverb clauses
*   relative (adjective) clauses
*   participial phrases.

CHUNKING A SENTENCE

Learning to construct sentences is based on the same concept as learning to comprehend what we have read: phrase by phrase not word by word. We divide a sentence into meaningful 'chunks', which allows us to read more effectively to understand, or to write more concisely and clearly to make a point. Phrases and clauses are the building blocks of language, the craft (grammar) tools of writing, and we naturally divide sentences into these meaningful chunks.

The grammar tools (word, phrases and clauses) demonstrated in this book include:

*   expanded noun phrases
*   prepositional phrases

* adverb clauses
* relative (adjective) clauses
* opening and delayed adjectives
* opening and delayed adverbs
* participial phrases.

When modelling and exploring a new tool or revisiting one already studied, an effective approach for struggling or inexperienced writers is to pare back the model to a kernel (base) sentence and isolate the grammar tool. You can then examine, discuss, explore and experiment with:

* the function and effect (cohesion, clarity, precision and emphasis) of using that particular phrase, clause or technique, comparing it with other variations
* the construction of the phrase or clause
* how the grammar tool is embedded or added to the kernel sentence, including punctuation
* where the grammar tool can be positioned in a sentence: beginning, middle (between the subject and verb) or end, and how the position impacts on the flow, emphasis and clarity of the sentence.

It is also important to:

* make explicit any links with similar grammar tools, for example, coordinating conjunctions and semi-colons, expanded noun phrases, relative clauses and participial phrases
* experiment with changing word order, for example, using delayed adjectives to improve a long list of adjectives preceding the noun, and how this changes the emphasis and creates a different rhythm.

Once students have developed their knowledge of the various phrases and clauses at their disposal and gained confidence with using and experimenting with these sentence parts, work on sentence variety, manipulation and length, as well as combining and connecting ideas and images becomes more effective. This is a useful technique to imitate sentence constructions and to elicit the main points when paraphrasing a text.

Chapters 3 and 23 include a detailed breakdown of the grammar tools, which:

1. defines and illustrates the construction of subject and predicate phrases and subordinate clauses, and demonstrates what each adds to a writer's toolkit
2. demonstrates progression and variation by taking a simple kernel sentence

    A snake slithered slowly through the grass.

    and, using the various grammar tools, expands and varies its construction, rhythm and emphasis.

WHAT DO STUDENTS NEED?

STUDENTS NEED TO KNOW:

★ what 'grammar tools' are available
★ what they add to a sentence
★ how to use them in their own writing.

STUDENTS NEED TO:

★ have excellent models
★ link writing to reading.

To widen their repertoire of phrases and clauses, students should collect models by professional authors found in class texts (fiction or non-fiction) or from their personal reading. These models will illustrate different constructions that create a variety of rhythms and emphasis.

REVISING A TEXT

Effective teaching of writing includes working on sentence construction and manipulation during the revision stage of the writing process, in order to explore and experiment with different constructions.

Researching and writing *Descriptosaurus Personal Writing: The Writing Process in Action* (2022) highlighted the lack of attention by students to the revision process, who were instead committed to a one-draft method with varying degrees of 'proofreading'. And even when time was allocated for revising a text, the amendments made were surface-level changes, focusing on word choice, spelling, punctuation and capitalisation. There was a failure to appreciate that it is at the revision stage of the process that sentence construction work proves to be the most effective: expanding sentences, combining them, reformulating them; changing constructions for rhythm, effect and emphasis in the context of the whole passage. There was a lack of understanding that experienced writers work from a first draft, and then during the revision stage rearrange the structure of the content, develop description and detail, and craft powerful, interesting and vivid sentences. Well-structured, developed, descriptive writing and original sentences rarely emerge from a pen or keyboard without extensive work and a willingness to experiment, add, delete or substitute in the revision stage of the writing process. But to be able to do this effectively, students need to know what grammar tools (writing craft tools) are available and to have practised using them.

SENTENCE COMBINING

Research by Saddler and Graham (2005) provided evidence that the ability to construct grammatically correct and syntactically mature sentences and to revise a text improved after learning and practising **sentence combining** in a peer-assisted arrangement. Many studies have agreed on the positive effects of sentence combining practice to enhance syntactic fluency and improve the quality of students' writing.

The goal of sentence combining practice is to improve students' fluency in sentence construction and their proficiency in moving sentence parts around when revising their texts. This is achieved by providing structured practice in manipulating and rewriting basic and kernel sentences into more syntactically mature and varied forms.

This system can be taught and practised alongside a writing process approach and can be easily tailored to meet the needs and skill levels of individual students. Exercises can be introduced at any time and can be developed from class texts or *Descriptosaurus*. Using students' own writing is also beneficial as it engages them at their level of understanding and makes their progress visible. This shows them where they currently are, where they are aiming and the steps they need to take to improve. For example, this approach would help students who are currently:

*   writing in short, choppy sentences
*   creating sentences that are connected by a series of 'ands'
*   comma splicing
*   developing many of their sentences in the same way
*   writing a series of long, complex and confusing sentences.

These exercises can be done orally or in writing as an independent consolidation or a revision activity. However, whichever method is used, it is important to provide opportunities for discussion as this is vital to developing students' knowledge, understanding and confidence with language. Acquiring the 'technical' knowledge of how to construct, position and punctuate a grammar tool is only a small part of ensuring its accurate and effective use in students' own writing. It is important to use these exercises to discuss what a grammar tool adds to a sentence in terms of detail, clarity and cohesion, rhythm and emphasis, which will hopefully lead to students spotting similar techniques in their own reading and imitating them in their writing.

The exercises in this book are designed to provide a template that can be easily adapted for models selected from a class or student's text.

Whilst grammar tools have been examined in isolation in this section, authors often use a range of grammar tools in a sentence to achieve a certain effect, impact or rhythm. It is always exciting and useful to examine how an author has created a particular effect in their writing by ordering words, phrases and clauses in new and creative ways. With a working knowledge of the grammar tools, this makes this process more accessible to students.

GUIDELINES, EXERCISES AND MODELS (FICTION AND NON-FICTION)

Apart from using the language toolkit provided in *Descriptosaurus (Fourth Edition)* to create the models and exercises for descriptive writing, this book also includes guidelines, exercises, resources and models to support using the same techniques to learn about non-fiction topics, such as the Great Fire of London. This process is also useful for

* revising subject content
* providing a revision outline for a topic
* crafting a paragraph.

Using authentic class texts (fiction or non-fiction) is invaluable to learning about sentence construction, so Chapter 20 provides guidelines on how to construct a sentence combining exercise from a class text.

A sample sentence de-combining exercise is also included in Chapter 25 as this is a useful tool for teachers to be able to use in the context of students' own writing to de-combine overly complex and confused sentences into a series of base (kernel) sentences, before then working on recombining them for greater clarity and precision.

EXPERIMENTING WITH DIFFERENT GRAMMAR TOOLS

It is important to make explicit any links between grammar tools to enable students to experiment with the use of a variety of phrases and clauses. They can also discuss which grammar tool is the most effective in the context of their text in terms of clarity, precision, emphasis and cohesion.

EXAMPLE 1: MAKING CONNECTIONS WITH OTHER GRAMMAR TOOLS

Introducing the semi-colon

* Demystify the semi-colon by making connections with what students already know and understand.
* Demonstrate **how a semi-colon** can be **used instead of a coordinating conjunction**.
* Demonstrate how a comma cannot be used to join two independent clauses.

Students experiment with the semi-colon using their own writing.

* ⋆ Find sentences joined by coordinating conjunctions.
* ⋆ Substitute coordinating conjunctions with a semi-colon.

Discuss which is more effective in the context of the text and why.

Example:

1. Two simple sentences

The crunching had stopped. The cave fell silent.

2. Join using a coordinating conjunction

The crunching had stopped, and the cave fell silent.

3. Semi-colon

The crunching had stopped; the cave fell silent.

The cave fell silent; the crunching had stopped.

4. Comma splice

The crunching had stopped, the cave fell silent.

(Examining the run-on sentences is useful when investigating semi-colons as it gives students another tool to use when editing their work.)

Other grammar tools

1. Subordinating conjunction

When the crunching had stopped, the cave fell silent.

2. Colon

The crunching had stopped: silence.

EXAMPLE 2: EXPERIMENTING WITH THE POSITION OF A GRAMMAR TOOL

Experiment with positioning the participial phrases at the opening, middle and end of a sentence and discuss which option is preferred and why.

1a. ^, James stepped up onto the stage.
1b He **clutched** his hands together to stop them shaking. (**-ING**)
   clutched > clutch > clutch**ing**

i. <u>Clutching his hands together to stop them shaking</u>, James stepped up onto the stage.
ii. James, <u>clutching his hands together to stop them shaking</u>, stepped up onto the stage.
iii. James stepped up onto the stage, <u>clutching his hands together to stop them shaking</u>.

Other grammar tools

1. A coordinating conjunction

James clutched his hands together to stop them shaking **and** stepped up onto the stage.

2. A relative (adjective) clause

James, **who was clutching his hands together to stop them shaking**, stepped up onto the stage.

3. An adverb clause

As he stepped up onto the stage, James clutched his hands together to stop them shaking.

James clutched his hands together to stop them shaking **as he stepped up onto the stage.**

Compare which grammar tool is more effective in the context of each sentence and discuss why (clarity, cohesion, rhythm, emphasis).

CONCLUSION

An extensive vocabulary is a necessary starting point, but it is by paying attention to language as modelled in the fourth edition of *Descriptosaurus* or class texts, by identifying an author's craft and using the *Descriptosaurus Grammar Companion Ages 9–12* to learn how to use words, to combine them, and to rearrange them for effect that turns an apprentice writer into a master. Chunking sentences into meaningful parts, imitating those parts, expanding sentences according to models and combining kernel sentences are all complementary processes. When used in tandem they can consolidate students' understanding of different sentence types and arrangements and how they are constructed. They provide contextualised methods for students to practise and experiment with imitating model sentences and paragraphs. Students can then use that knowledge to develop automaticity in sentence writing when composing their own texts, and to gain independence in experimenting and evaluating different constructions and amendments in the revision stage of the writing process.

The goal must be to ensure that students understand that grammar is a tool to help communicate meaning clearly, precisely and effectively and to improve writing; to ensure that the focus is on the codes and structures of written language; to encourage students to take risks; to understand that errors are welcomed as a learning opportunity; and to try out and evaluate new sentence patterns to enable them to make informed choices in their own writing. Building knowledge of grammar tools and automaticity in sentence construction increases confidence with language, and, with practice and motivation, creates flair and individuality.

This language toolkit is a resource that supports students on their journey towards automaticity in sentence construction. It does so by training their 'automatic pilot', strengthening their language muscles and building confidence with sentence manipulation when revising their own texts, thus freeing their minds to think about the important issues of writing: content, audience and purpose, organisation and structure.

Mastering the craft of writing is a long and difficult journey and, at times, students can feel like they are navigating their way through a strange and noisy landscape without a clearly labelled map. The fourth edition of *Descriptosaurus* and its *Grammar Companion* aim to provide student writers with the vocabulary, tools, scaffolds and models to help them discover routes through the world of language. Students are provided with a visual map to help them develop their vocabulary and automaticity in sentence construction, as well as to have a variety of options in their writing toolkit. The resources also provide ideas, models and activities to enable teachers to construct maps and routes appropriate to the needs of their students.

Part 1
Investigations

1

Chunking into meaningful sentence parts

When we read a sentence, we automatically break it down into chunks of meaning. Reading aloud and dividing the model sentences into chunks (as they would naturally do when reading) helps students to become aware that authors compose their sentences one 'chunk' (meaningful sentence part) at a time. This knowledge is important for students as they learn to imitate model sentences and to use them in their own writing.

Reading the sentence aloud taps into students' linguistic experience gained through speaking and reading, and they begin to automatically 'chunk' the sentence parts meaningfully and grammatically. At this stage, do not insist on chunking according to grammatical divisions or identifying the terms for those sentence parts. This knowledge is built up in the context of these exercises by discussing:

★ why students have divided up the sentence in the way they have
★ what information each sentence part tells the reader.

FOR EXAMPLE

1. The massive waves crashed mercilessly onto the side of the boat.
   i. The massive/ waves crashed/ mercilessly onto/ the side of the boat.
   ii. The massive waves/ crashed/mercilessly/ onto the side of the boat.

DOI: 10.4324/9781032662862-2

The massive waves	What does this tell us?
Crashed	What does this tell us?
Relentlessly	What does this tell us?
onto the side of the boat	What does this tell us?
a. What is the subject of the sentence?	the massive waves
b. What did they do?	crashed
c. How did they do it?	relentlessly
d. Where did they crash?	onto the side of the boat

Reading aloud each of the sentences that have already been chunked will help students to 'hear' the chunks that have not been divided into meaningful sentence parts.

FOR EXAMPLE

1. The massive/ waves crashed/ mercilessly onto/ the side of the boat.
   i. Discussing why this sentence has not been divided into meaningful chunks will elicit, for example, that *the massive* is incomplete. It does not tell the reader what was *massive* and therefore is not a meaningful sentence part.

As with development in reading comprehension (where students progress from reading a sentence word by word to being able to group words together in chunks of meaning which gradually increase in size), when students gain more experience and knowledge of writing conventions, and more automaticity with sentence construction, they also develop the ability to hold larger chunks of meaning in their working memory as they chunk or construct sentences.

EXERCISE 1

INSTRUCTIONS

1. In pairs, take turns to read each of the sentences aloud.
2. Decide which of the sentences is divided into meaningful chunks.

EXAMPLE

The monstrous wave reared up menacingly over the top of the boat.

i. The monstrous/ wave reared up/ menacingly over/ the top of the boat.
ii. The monstrous wave/ reared up/ menacingly/ over the top of the boat. √

1. *A strange, swirling mist shrouded the old house.*

i. A strange/ swirling mist shrouded/ the old house.
ii. A strange swirling mist/ shrouded the old house.

2. *The horror of what she had just seen hit her like a hammer blow in the chest.*

i. The horror/ of what she had just seen/ hit her like a hammer blow/ in the chest.
ii. The horror/ of what she/ had just seen/ hit her like a hammer/ blow in the chest.

3. *The billowing curtains fluttered towards the light and brushed against her face like rippling silk.*

i. The billowing curtains/ fluttered towards the/ light and brushed against her/ face like rippling silk.
ii. The billowing curtains/ fluttered towards the light/ and/ brushed against her face/ like rippling silk.

4. *The breeze which hissed through the gap in the door sounded like whispered threats.*

i. The breeze which/ hissed through the gap/ in the door sounded/ like whispered threats.
ii. The breeze/ which hissed through the gap in the door/ sounded like whispered threats.

5. *In the middle of the night she was woken by a piercing spine-chilling scream.*

i.   In the middle of the night/ she was woken/ by a piercing spine-chilling scream.

ii. In the middle/ of the night she was/ woken by a piercing /spine-chilling scream.

EXERCISE 2

Punctuation has been removed for this exercise.

INSTRUCTIONS

1. In pairs, read each sentence aloud.
2. Chunk sentences (i) and (ii) using a slash between sentence parts.
3. Mark the sentence which matches the sentence division in the model.
4. Write your own imitation of the model sentence.

EXAMPLE

Mercilessly/ the massive waves/ crashed onto the side/ of the boat.

i.   Rising higher and higher/ in an arch/ above the boat/ was a monstrous wave.

ii. Slowly/ the venomous snake/ slithered through the gap/ between the railings. √

Imitation: *Alarmingly/ the heavy rain/ seeped through the cracks/ in the thatched roof.*

1. *Later that day/ she searched/ through the internet/ for any news stories/ about the hotel.*

i. Nervously she scanned the street for any sign of her pursuer.
ii. In the middle of the night she woke to the sound of smashing glass outside her house.

Imitation:

_____

_____

2. *A blast of cold air/ a savage icy chill/ whipped around her shoulders.*

i. A blood-curdling shriek which came from the locked room made every nerve in her body prickle.
ii. The light from the fire a flickering red ember quivered against the wall.

Imitation:

_____

_____

3. *An icy dread/ spread through her veins/ as the clock struck midnight.*

i. A swirling mist loomed ahead of her as she entered the forest.
ii. When she entered the room she was met by a wizened old man with huge hollow black eyes.

Imitation:

_____

_____

4. *Dark and narrow/ damp and uneven/ the alley/ was a treacherous route.*

i. Across the floor up the walls and over the ceiling the beam from the torch flashed.

ii. Tangled and twisted prickly and needle-sharp the undergrowth was a spiked spider's web.

Imitation:

_____

_____

5. *She swung her legs/ wrapped them around the branch/ and pulled herself up onto it.*

i. It gripped her clothes trapped her legs in its tangled web and scratched her face with its claws.

ii. From every branch hung frozen crystals that glittered in the bright morning sunlight.

Imitation:

_____

_____

EXERCISE 3

Punctuation has been removed for this exercise.

INSTRUCTIONS

★ Using a slash (/) divide the following sentences into meaningful sentence parts.

1. The monstrous wave with its fringe of boiling white foam reared up in an arch above the boat.
2. The cone-shaped dormant volcano had a snow-capped peak.

3. Above the town the towering mountains dusty blue and white created a dramatic scene.
4. A magical world of shimmering snow and ice towered above the wooden chalets of the alpine village.
5. Beneath their feet an unstable subterranean world hid beneath the slopes of the dormant volcano.
6. A thundering torrent of water thundered down the rock-face and hurtled over the edge of the canyon into the swirling mist below.
7. Freezing fog like ghostly arms wrapped around the slopes of the mountain.
8. The old haunted house on the edge of the lake was slowly crumbling.
9. Curious she zoomed in to have a closer look at the photo she had taken on the front steps of the hotel.
10. Below them a silver river threaded the hills and wound around the bends as it swooped down the slopes until it disappeared into the horizon near the foot of the mountain.

EXERCISE 4

Punctuation has been removed for this exercise.

INSTRUCTIONS

1. Divide the following sentences into meaningful chunks.
2. Write your own sentences by imitating the structure of the model sentence (as shown in the above example).

1. Scarlett was hungry exhausted and desperate.

Imitation:

_____

_____

2. A narrow twisting alley led off to the right.

Imitation:

_____

_____

3. A high brick wall blocked the way.

Imitation:

_____

_____

4. To her right she spotted a row of enormous rubbish bins.

Imitation:

_____

_____

5. Beneath her feet she could feel the slime of rotting rubbish.

Imitation:

_____

_____

6. For the hundredth time she glanced over her shoulder.

Imitation:

_____

_____

7. Nervously she peered through the gap between the bins and scanned the alley.

Imitation:

_____

_____

8. The cobbles were damp and slippery and she kept sliding and stumbling.

Imitation:

_____

_____

9. They had found a path but their progress was slow.

Imitation:

_____

_____

10. He quickened his pace but the ground was uneven and he stumbled frequently.

Imitation:

_____

_____

11. If he stopped and listened he could hear the branches rattling in the wind.

Imitation:

_____

_____

12. When winter came icy frosts coated the trees the bushes the undergrowth.

Imitation:

_____

_____

13. After the sun had spread its glittering rays the forest was bathed in a hazy golden light.

Imitation:

_____

_____

14. She followed the passage until she came to a low metal gate.

Imitation:

_____

_____

15. She crouched under the stairs where the shadows concealed her presence.

Imitation:

_____

_____

16. Sprinting wildly down the corridor Kitty tugged at every door.

Imitation:

_____

_____

17. When she closed the door the room was plunged into darkness.

Imitation:

_____

_____

18. She glanced at her watch and her heart sank: less than an hour left.

Imitation:

_____

_____

19. She peered through the hanging branches: still no sign of them.

Imitation:

_____

_____

20. Within moments they were buried in boiling swirling foam.

Imitation:

_____

_____

21. Relentless and merciless the massive waves crashed onto the side of the boat.

Imitation:

_____

_____

22. Around and around the leaves swirled as the frosty gusts chased them along the ground.

Imitation:

_____

_____

23. Soon the gusts of frosty air would arrive to steal the leaves from the branches.

Imitation:

_____

_____

24. The stinking stench of damp and decay seeped under the door curled around the room and filled the air.

Imitation:

_____

_____

25. Before she had found that envelope she had been a normal eleven-year-old girl.

Imitation:

_____

_____

2

Subject and predicate

To develop a secure knowledge of sentence construction, to understand (and avoid) run-on sentences and unintentional sentence fragments (minor sentences), it is essential that students understand:

★ the component parts of a sentence – words, phrases and clauses
★ how a sentence is divided into a subject and predicate.

This gives students not only a firm foundation of how a sentence is constructed but also how it can be used to

★ modify with words, phrases and clauses to provide extra detail, description, clarification and explanation
★ convey complicated information clearly and precisely
★ achieve a desired effect or create a rhythm or emphasis in a text.

MAIN POINTS

A sentence is built around **SUBJECTS** and **PREDICATES**.

1. A subject (noun) – who or what the sentence is about.
2. A predicate (verb) – what the subject is or does.
3. It cannot be a complete sentence without both a subject and a predicate.

DOI: 10.4324/9781032662862-3

SUBJECTS: WHO OR WHAT THE SENTENCE IS ABOUT

FACTS

A. Position

Subjects can be:

- ★ at the very <u>beginning</u> of the sentence
- ★ at the <u>end</u> of the sentence.

FOR EXAMPLE

a. Bottles, cans and broken glass/ <u>were strewn</u> across the pavement.
b. *There were* bottles, cans and broken glass <u>strewn</u> across the pavement.
c. Across the pavement <u>were strewn</u>/ bottles, cans and broken glass.
d. <u>Strewn</u> across the pavement <u>were</u> **bottles, cans and broken glass.**

Usually, the subject of the sentence comes before the verb. Positioning the subject at the end of the sentence is an effective technique to delay the information about the subject of a sentence to build tension or for emphasis.

There are four ways of changing the position of the subject.

1. *There is/was* to introduce the subject

There <u>were</u> a group of photographers <u>heading</u> in her direction.

There <u>was</u> an enormous venomous snake in the tangled undergrowth.

There <u>was</u> a stack of glossy magazines <u>piled</u> high on the table.

2. Prepositional phrases

An enormous venomous cobra *slithered* **out of the tangled undergrowth.**

Out of the tangled undergrowth **slithered** **an enormous venomous cobra.**

3. Verb (past tense ending in -ed/-en)

A group of photographers are headed in her direction.

Headed in her direction are a group of photographers.

A stack of glossy magazines was piled high on the table.

Piled high on the table was a stack of glossy magazines.

4. Participial phrases

   a.   Shimmering stalactites hung from the roof.

   b.   From the roof hung shimmering stalactites.

       Convert the verb into a participle by adding -ing to the root verb.

       For example:

            hung – to hang (root verb) – hang**ing** (participle)

   c.   Hanging from the roof were shimmering stalactites.

EXERCISE 1

INSTRUCTIONS

For each of the sentences below:

★   Circle or highlight the subject of the sentence.

★   Underline the predicate (verb).

★   Rewrite the sentence with the subject at the end of the sentence.

★   Discuss which sentence construction is preferred and why.

EXAMPLE

A blood-curdling shriek came from the locked room.

There was a blood-curdling shriek from the locked room.

From the locked room came a blood-curdling shriek.

Coming from the locked room was a blood-curdling shriek.

1. A tramp crouched behind the door.

   _____

2. A snake was hidden under a pile of shavings.

   _____

3. An ancient gravestone was wrapped in a veil of swirling mist.

   _____

4. The snow-capped mountains soared above them.

   _____

5. A faint silver moonlight peeked through the window.

   _____

Note: Questions 4 and 5: when 'there is/was' is used to introduce the subject, read the sentences aloud to decide which verb ending is the most appropriate (-ed or -ing).

B. Length

Subjects can be:

★ short (a single word) – **simple subject** – the core idea/subject of the sentence without all the description

★ long (all the words that tell you who or what the sentence is about) – **complete subject** – the subject and all its modifiers (determiners, adjectives, prepositions etc.).

FOR EXAMPLE

a. The light/ spread across the wall. (simple subject)
b. The bright light/ spread across the wall above her head. (complete subject)
c. The bright light, a wide circular bream from a torch, which moved up and down the alley,/ spread across the wall above her head. (complete subject)

EXERCISE 2

INSTRUCTIONS

For each of the sentences below:

- ★ Circle or highlight the simple subject of the sentence
- ★ Underline the complete subject.

1. The hissing whispers made her scalp prickle.
2. The old haunted house on the edge of the lake was slowly crumbling.
3. A row of rusty medieval swords hung from the wall above the entrance.
4. Ferocious, remorseless gusts of wind pounded on the door.
5. The semi-circle of ancient, cracked gravestones with their blanket of moss and lichen leaned together as if whispering secrets of the past.
6. The dark gloomy staircase on the second floor spiralled steeply upwards into the shadows of the attic floor.

C. Action(s)

Subjects can do:

- ★ one thing
- ★ more than one thing.

FOR EXAMPLE

He/ moved off to the end of the alley.

He/ moved off to the end of the alley and kicked the empty bottles and cans in his way.

He/ moved off to the end of the alley, crunched over the breaking glass, and kicked the empty bottles and cans in his way.

EXERCISE 3

INSTRUCTIONS

For each of the sentences below:

 ★ Underline the subject of the sentence
 ★ Circle or highlight each of the verbs which describes what the sub-
    ject is or does.

1. He slithered to a halt and stood as still as a statue.
2. She peered round the door and shone her torch down the passage.
3. Her mobile phone fell out of her pocket and clattered to the ground.
4. The torchlight flickered and cast dancing shadows in front of her.
5. The icy wind burned her cheeks and blistered her lips.
6. A fist-sized chunk of rock slammed into the side of the cliff and thudded
    down the side of the gorge.
7. The wintry storm had buried the mountain in its icy grip, turned its
    slopes into icy treacherous paths and frozen its waterfalls into rippling
    sheets of ice.
8. The eagle rose from the side of the cliff in a majestic spiral and then
    soared above their heads.
9. The snow burst through the trees and barrelled down the mountain,
    shattering the silence as it snapped and splintered the trees in its path.
10. Holding both reins in her left hand, she lifted her foot into the stirrup,
    grabbed the cantle with her right hand, and levered herself into the
    saddle.

D. Sentences can have:

* one subject
* more than one subject.

FOR EXAMPLE

Shards of broken glass were strewn across the pavements.
Shards of broken glass, piles of bin bags, food cartons and plastic wrappers, bottles and cans were strewn across the pavements.

EXERCISE 4

INSTRUCTIONS

For each of the sentences below:

★ Circle or highlight each of the subjects in the sentence.

1. Antarctica and the Arctic are both polar deserts.
2. Only mosses, lichen and algae can survive its harsh climate, and these occur mainly along its warmer coastlines.
3. Snow-capped peaks and cloud-piercing crags gleamed spectrally above them.
4. There were lines of battlements and towering cliffs, castles, towers and spires.
5. The distant thunder and lightning warned of the imminent arrival of a storm.
6. Decaying leaves and rotting branches covered the trail.
7. Plastic bags and crisp packets flapped like streamers from the trees.
8. The sweet, succulent smell of mangoes and papayas filled the air.
9. Belching tongues of fire and thick yellow smoke spouted from the volcano.
10. A cacophony of chirrups and tweets, whistles and shrieks greeted them as the sun rose.

SENTENCES MUST HAVE SUBJECTS OR THEY WON'T MAKE SENSE.

> **FOR EXAMPLE**
>
> i.   **Dropped to her knees and searched for a gap between the bins**
>   This doesn't tell the reader **who dropped to her knees**, so it doesn't make sense.
> ii. **Spread across the wall above her head**
>   This doesn't tell the reader **what spread across the wall**, so it doesn't make sense.

PREDICATES: COMMENT ON WHAT THE SUBJECT IS OR DOES

FACTS

A. Position

Predicates can:

* come after the subject (usual position)
* come before the subject.

> **FOR EXAMPLE**
>
> A series of narrow twisting alleys/ led off to the right.
> Off to the right led/ a series of narrow twisting alleys.

B. Length

Predicates can be:

* short
* long.

FOR EXAMPLE

She/ slipped further into the shadows.
She/ slipped further into the shadows between the bins and the wall.

C. Action

Predicates can tell:

* ★ just one thing.
* ★ more than one thing.

FOR EXAMPLE

She/ slipped further into the shadows.
She/ slipped further into the shadows, flattened herself against the wall and held her breath.

SENTENCES MUST HAVE PREDICATES OR THEY DON'T MAKE SENSE.

FOR EXAMPLE

A series of narrow, twisting alleyways

Whilst information is supplied about the topic (the alleyways), there is no information about **what the alleys are or do**, so the sentence doesn't make sense and is incomplete. To complete the sentence the reader needs to know what the alleys are or do.

EXERCISE 5

INSTRUCTIONS

★ In the table below, match the subjects with their predicates to complete the sentences.

Subject	Predicate
1. Enormous snow-capped mountains	a. cascaded down the side of the cliff
2. The narrow winding track	b. blew through the window
3. The bubbling mountain streams	c. was a welcome relief from the scorching heat
4. A wild frothing waterfall	d. pierced the silence of the icy wilderness
5. The first rays of morning sunlight	e. trickled down the slopes
6. A welcome breeze	f. dipped and climbed up the side of the mountain
7. The enticing smell of roasting vegetables	g. came from the attic
8. The cold water of the swimming pool	h. cast a golden light over the wood
9. A loud crack	i. towered above the alpine village
10. The creak of a floorboard	j. wafted from the kitchen

As students develop their reading and writing skills, identifying subject and predicate can become more complex, so at this stage it is worth considering additional guidelines. This is usually where students run into problems proofreading their work and spotting run-on sentences or sentence fragments, particularly when their sentences advance to learning about active and passive voice and multiple clauses (coordinating and subordinating).

SIMPLE DEFINITION OF A SUBECT

★ **Who or what the sentence is about.**

A more precise definition is that:

★ The subject is the part of the sentence that is **doing the action of the main verb** (usually a **noun or pronoun or noun phrase**).

FOR EXAMPLE

a. **The frozen Weddell Sea surrounded the Endurance in all directions.**
b. **The Endurance was surrounded in all directions by the frozen Weddell Sea.**

In the above examples there are two nouns: the Weddell Sea and the Endurance. How do you decide which is the subject of the sentence?

ACTIVE VOICE

A sentence is written in the **active voice** when **the subject** of the sentence is **performing the action**.

> The frozen Weddell Sea surrounded the Endurance in all directions.

Step 1: Find the main verb – **surrounded**

Step 2: Ask who or what is doing the surrounding?

Step 3: The frozen Weddell Sea is surrounding the Endurance. The subject is therefore the frozen Weddell Sea.

PASSIVE VOICE

A sentence is written in the **passive voice** when the **subject** of the sentence **has something done to it** by someone or something.

> The Endurance was surrounded in all directions by the frozen Weddell Sea.

Step 1: Find the verb.

Step 2: Who or what is being surrounded?

The **Endurance** is having the 'surrounding' done to it and so is the subject of this sentence, which is written in the passive voice.

To gain a greater understanding of active and passive voice, practising converting active sentences into the passive voice (and vice versa) is a useful exercise and gives students confidence in manipulating sentences when revising their texts. The sentences in the exercise below can be used or those from a class text. Why is this important? For every grammar tool, it is important to consider its effect on the text. Whilst students will be familiar with the active voice from conversations and reading, they will increasingly encounter the passive voice in non-fiction texts. What are the perceived benefits?

1. Emphasises the action.
2. Creates an emotional distance with the text.
3. Regarded as providing a more authoritative tone.

EXERCISE 6

INSTRUCTIONS

For each of the sentences below:

★ Circle or highlight the verb
★ Underline who or what is doing the action (verb) or (as in example b) is having something done to it.

EXAMPLE

a. A cluster of wheelie bins lined the wall to the right.
b. The wall to the right was lined by a cluster of wheelie bins.

1a. The house was shielded from the road by a high red-brick wall.
1b. A high red-brick wall shielded the house from the road.
2a. Over the years the windows in the roof of the attic had been smeared by layers of dust and dirt.
2b. Layers of dust and dirt had smeared the windows in the roof of the attic over the years.
3a. Her scent had been detected by the wolves.
3b. The wolves had detected her scent.
4a. The chilly air froze his breath in clouds in front of his mouth.
4b. His breath was frozen in clouds in front of his mouth by the chilly air.
5a. The beach was sheltered by large dunes.
5b. Large dunes sheltered the beach.

EXERCISE 7

INSTRUCTIONS

For each of the sentences below:

★ Convert the passive voice into the active voice.

EXAMPLE

To convert into the active voice, find out who or what is doing the action of the sentence.

His feet were <u>trapped</u> by the oozing mud of the swamp.

What <u>trapped</u> his feet – **the oozing mud of the swamp**.

Position the subject that is doing the action at the beginning of the sentence.

The oozing mud of the swamp <u>trapped</u> his feet.

1. The windows were rattled by the wind.

   _____

2. The door was blocked by a wooden chest wrapped in chains.

   _____

3. His face was lit up by a huge smile

   _____

4. The dense tangled canopy was penetrated by beams of bright sunlight.

   _____

5. They had been tracked through the city by two furtive figures.

   _____

MULTIPLE CLAUSES

★ A sentence can have multiple clauses.
★ Every clause has its own subject and verb.
★ A multi-clause sentence can have more than one subject.

Example: coordinating conjunction (and)

A door opened down the passage,[1] and a cold draught rushed towards her.[2]

Sentences [1] and [2] are independent clauses linked by **and**. Each has its own subject.

Subjects: [1]door; [2]draught

Subordinate (dependent) clauses

As the footsteps came closer and closer,[1] she desperately tried to slow her breathing.[2]

Dependent clause[1]: As the footsteps came closer and closer,

Main clause[2]: she desperately tried to slow her breathing.

Subjects: footsteps[1]; she[2]

EXERCISE 8

INSTRUCTIONS

For each of the sentences below:

★ Underline the main clause (if a coordinating conjunction is used, underline both clauses).
★ Highlight the dependent clause (if a subordinating conjunction is used).
★ Circle or highlight the subject and verb in each clause.

EXAMPLE

[1]If she waited any longer, [2]it would be too late.

[1]subject = she; verb = waited

[2]subject = it; verb = would be

1. She whipped her head over her shoulder when she heard the thudding of footsteps.

i.   Subject = ; verb =
ii. Subject = ; verb =

2. Slowly she lifted her head above the windowsill, and she peered out from behind the curtain.

i. Subject = ; verb =

ii. Subject = ; verb =

3. She had no choice because time was running out.

i. Subject = ; verb =

ii. Subject = ; verb =

4. Although she was in the middle of the city, the streets were deserted.

i. Subject = ; verb =

ii. Subject = ; verb =

5. When night came, a black cloak was drawn across the sky.

i. Subject = ; verb =

ii. Subject = ; verb =

6. As she whirled around, her mobile phone fell out of her pocket.

i. Subject = ; verb =

ii. Subject = ; verb =

7. As the volcano erupted, the ground shook.

i. Subject = ; verb =

ii. Subject = ; verb =

8. Before she could take a step into the room, there was a sudden thud on the floorboards upstairs.

i. Subject = ; verb =

ii. Subject = ; verb =

9. While he waited for the phone to ring, the hours seemed endless.

i. Subject = ; verb =

ii. Subject = ; verb =

10. Where the corridor ended, a padlocked metal gate blocked the exit.

i. Subject = ; verb =

ii. Subject = ; verb =

Dividing sentences into subjects and predicates is a useful exercise when teaching students how to identify incomplete or run-on sentences when proofreading their own work.

1. Collect examples of sentence fragments and run-on sentences from students' writing (past or present).
2. Model how to identify the subject and predicate.
3. Elicit why they are not complete sentences.
4. Encourage suggestions about how the sentences should/could be edited.
   Students can use the same process when editing their own writing and make the necessary corrections.

ANSWERS

EXERCISE 1

1. **A tramp crouched behind the door.**
   There was a tramp crouched behind the door.
   Behind the door was crouched a tramp.
   Crouched behind the door was a tramp.
   Crouching behind the door was a tramp.

2. **A snake was hidden under a pile of shavings.**
   There was a snake hidden under a pile of shavings.
   Under a pile of shavings was hidden a snake.
   Hidden under a pile of shavings was a snake.
   Hiding under a pile of shavings was a snake.

3. **An ancient gravestone was wrapped in a swirling veil of mist.**
   There was an ancient gravestone wrapped in a swirling veil of mist.
   In a swirling veil of mist was wrapped an ancient gravestone.

Wrapped in a swirling veil of mist was an ancient gravestone.

4. **The snow-capped mountains soared above them.**
    There were snow-capped mountains soaring above them.
    Above them soared snow-capped mountains.
    Soaring above them were snow-capped mountains.

5. **A faint silver moonlight peeked through the window.**
    There was a faint silver moonlight peeking through the window.
    Through the window peeked a faint silver moonlight.
    Peeking through the window was a faint silver moonlight.

EXERCISE 2

1. The hissing whispers made her scalp prickle.
2. The old haunted house on the edge of the lake was slowly crumbling.
3. A row of rusty medieval swords hung from the wall above the entrance.
4. Ferocious, remorseless gusts of wind pounded on the door.
5. The semi-circle of ancient, cracked gravestones with their blanket of moss and lichen leaned together as if whispering secrets of the past.
6. The dark gloomy staircase on the second floor spiralled steeply upwards into the shadows of the attic floor.

EXERCISE 3

1. He slithered to a halt and stood as still as a statue.
2. She peered round the door and shone her torch down the passage.
3. Her mobile phone fell out of her pocket and clattered to the ground.
4. The torchlight flickered and cast dancing shadows in front of her.
5. The icy wind burned her cheeks and blistered her lips.

6. <u>A fist-sized chunk of rock</u> slammed into the side of the cliff and thudded down the side of the gorge.
7. <u>The wintry storm</u> had buried the mountain in its icy grip, turned its slopes into icy treacherous paths and frozen its waterfalls into rippling sheets of ice.
8. <u>The eagle</u> rose from the side of the cliff in a majestic spiral and then soared above their heads.
9. <u>The snow</u> burst through the trees and barrelled down the mountain, shattering the silence as it snapped and splintered the trees in its path.
10. Holding both reins in her left hand, <u>she</u> lifted her foot into the stirrup, grabbed the cantle with her right hand, and levered herself into the saddle.

EXERCISE 4

1. Antarctica and the Arctic are both polar deserts.
2. Only mosses, lichen and algae can survive its harsh climate, and these occur mainly along its warmer coastlines.
3. Snow-capped peaks and cloud-piercing crags gleamed spectrally above them.
4. There were lines of battlements and towering cliffs, castles, towers and spires.
5. The distant thunder and lightning warned of the imminent arrival of a storm.
6. Decaying leaves and rotting branches covered the trail.
7. Plastic bags and crisp packets flapped like streamers from the trees.
8. The sweet, succulent smell of mangoes and papayas filled the air.
9. Belching tongues of fire and thick yellow smoke spouted from the volcano.
10. A cacophony of chirrups and tweets, whistles and shrieks greeted them as the sun rose.

EXERCISE 5

1.i. Enormous snow-capped mountains <u>towered above the alpine village</u>.
2.f. The narrow winding track <u>dipped and climbed up the side of the mountain</u>.
3.e. The bubbling mountain streams <u>trickled down the slopes</u>.
4.a. A wild frothing waterfall <u>cascaded down the side of the cliff</u>.
5.h. The first rays of morning sunlight <u>cast a golden light over the wood</u>.
6.b. A welcome breeze <u>blew through the window</u>.
7.j. The enticing smell of roasting vegetables <u>wafted from the kitchen</u>.
8.c. The cold water of the swimming pool <u>was a welcome relief from the scorching heat.</u>
9.d. A loud crack <u>pierced the silence of the icy wilderness</u>.
10.g. The creak of a floorboard <u>came from the attic</u>.

EXERCISE 6

1a. <u>The house</u> was shielded from the road by a high red-brick wall.
1b. <u>A high red-brick wall</u> shielded the house from the road.
2a. Over the years <u>the windows in the roof of the attic</u> had been smeared by layers of dust and dirt.
2b. <u>Layers of dust and dirt</u> had smeared the windows in the roof of the attic over the years.
3a. <u>Her scent</u> had been detected by the wolves.
3b. <u>The wolves</u> had detected her scent.
4a. <u>The chilly air</u> froze his breath in clouds in front of his mouth.
4b. <u>His breath</u> was frozen in clouds in front of his mouth by the chilly air.
5a. <u>The beach</u> was sheltered by large dunes.
5b. <u>Large dunes</u> sheltered the beach.

EXERCISE 7

1.   Passive: The windows were rattled by the wind.
     Active: The wind rattled the windows.
2.   Passive: The door was blocked by a wooden chest wrapped in chains.
     Active: A wooden chest wrapped in chains blocked the door.
3.   Passive: His face was lit up by a huge smile
     Active: A huge smile lit up his face.
4.   Passive: The dense tangled canopy was penetrated by beams of bright sunlight.
     Active: Beams of bright sunlight penetrated the dense tangled canopy.
5.   Passive: They had been tracked through the city by two furtive figures.
     Active: Two furtive figures had been tracking them through the city.

EXERCISE 8

1.   She whipped her head over her shoulder when she heard the thudding of footsteps.

i.   Subject = SHE; verb = WHIPPED
ii.   Subject = SHE; verb = HEARD

2.   Slowly she lifted her head above the windowsill, and she peered out from behind the curtain.

i.   Subject = SHE; verb = LIFTED
ii.   Subject = SHE; verb = PEERED

3.   She had no choice because time was running out.

i.   Subject = SHE; verb = HAD
ii.   Subject = TIME; verb = WAS RUNNING OUT

4.   Although she was in the middle of the city, the streets were deserted.

i.   Subject = SHE; verb = WAS
ii.   Subject = STREETS; verb = WERE

5.   When night came, a black cloak was drawn across the sky.

i.   Subject = NIGHT; verb = CAME
ii.   Subject = CLOAK; verb = WAS DRAWN

6.   As she whirled around, her mobile phone fell out of her pocket.

i.   Subject = SHE; verb = WHIRLED AROUND
ii.   Subject = PHONE; verb = FELL OUT

7.   As the volcano erupted, the ground shook.

i.   Subject = VOLCANO; verb = ERUPTED
ii.   Subject = GROUND; verb = SHOOK

8.   Before she could take a step into the room, there was a sudden thud on the floorboards upstairs.

i.   Subject = SHE; verb = COULD TAKE
ii.   Subject = THUD; verb = WAS

9.   While he waited for the phone to ring, the hours seemed endless.

i.   Subject = HE; verb = WAITED
ii.   Subject = HOURS; verb = SEEMED

10.   Where the corridor ended, a padlocked metal gate blocked the exit.

i.   Subject = CORRIDOR; verb = ENDED
ii.   Subject =GATE; verb = BLOCKED

3

Writing craft tools

Who or what the sentence is about.

It tells the reader something about the topic of the sentence – in this case a snake.

Subjects can be:

★ short (a single word)
★ long (all words that tell you who or what the sentence is about).

PREDICATE (VERB)

Comments on what the subject is or does.

Predicates can tell:

★ just one thing
★ more than one thing.

Experimenting and evaluating

1. Collect information about the subject.
2. Experiment with combining the information using the grammar tools demonstrated below.
3. Discuss which combination is preferred.

DOI: 10.4324/9781032662862-4

It is important that students have plenty of opportunities to:

* experiment with the construction of a subject using several grammar tools
* evaluate the most effective constructions
* consider whether shorter constructions are clearer, more precise and effective.

<table>
<tr><td colspan="6" align="center">**SUBJECT**</td></tr>
<tr><td colspan="6">**Information:** There was a snake. It was in the long grass. It was between Joe and the tree. It was a green and yellow cobra. It was enormous and venomous.</td></tr>
<tr><td colspan="6" align="center">**EXPANDED NOUN PHRASES**
(adjective, preposition or adverb modifies a noun)</td></tr>
<tr><td colspan="6" align="center">**Level 1**</td></tr>
<tr><td>**Determiner**</td><td colspan="2">**Adjective**</td><td>**Noun**</td><td colspan="2">**Prepositional phrase**</td></tr>
<tr><td>A</td><td colspan="2">big</td><td>snake</td><td colspan="2">in the long grass</td></tr>
<tr><td>An</td><td>enormous venomous</td><td>green, yellow, striped</td><td>snake stripes</td><td>in the long grass</td><td>between Joe and the tree</td></tr>
<tr><td>An</td><td>enormous</td><td>venomous</td><td>snake</td><td>with green and yellow stripes</td><td>in the long grass between Joe and the tree</td></tr>
<tr><td colspan="6">
1. A big snake in the long grass …
2. An enormous venomous green and yellow striped snake in the long grass between Joe and the tree ….
3. An enormous venomous snake with green and yellow stripes in the long grass between Joe and the tree …
4. An enormous venomous green and yellow striped snake in the long grass between Joe and the tree …
5. In the long grass between Joe and the tree, an enormous venomous snake with green and yellow stripes …
</td></tr>
</table>

SUBJECT			
Information: There was a snake. It rose in the long grass between Joe and the tree. It was a cobra. It had green and yellow stripes. It was enormous and venomous. It had a black forked tongue. Its tongue flicked from side to side. It had two needle-sharp fangs.			
Level 2			
Noun phrase	**Prepositional phrase**	**Prepositional phrase**	**Prepositional phrase**
An enormous venomous snake A black forked tongue Two needle-sharp fangs	with green and yellow stripes	in the long grass	between Joe and the tree
Noun phrase	**Delayed adjectives**	**Prepositional phrase**	**Prepositional phrase**
A green and yellow striped snake	enormous and venomous,	with a black forked tongue	in the long grass between Joe and the tree

1. An enormous venomous snake with green and yellow stripes in the long grass between Joe and the tree …
2. An enormous venomous snake with green and yellow stripes and a black forked tongue in the long grass between Joe and the tree …
3. A green and yellow striped snake, enormous and venomous, with a black forked tongue and two needle-sharp fangs in the long grass between Joe and the tree …
4. In the long grass between Joe and the tree, a green and yellow striped snake, enormous and venomous, with a black forked tongue and two needle-sharp fangs …

SUBJECT			
Information: There was a snake. It rose in the long grass between Joe and the tree. It was a cobra. It had green and yellow stripes. It was enormous and venomous. It had a black forked tongue. Its tongue flicked from side to side. It had needle-sharp fangs. They dripped with venom.			
Level 3 Relative (adjective) clauses			
Expanded noun phrase	**Relative (adjective) clause**	**Prepositional phrase**	**Prepositional phrase**
An enormous venomous snake,	which was a green and yellow striped cobra,	with a black forked tongue and two needle-sharp fangs	in the long grass between Joe and the tree
An enormous snake,	which was a venomous cobra with green and yellow stripes, a black forked tongue and two needle-sharp fangs,	in the long grass	between Joe and the tree
Expanded noun phrase	**Relative (adjective) clause**	**Relative clause**	**Relative clause**
A green and yellow striped snake, enormous and venomous,	whose black forked tongue flicked from side to side,	whose needle-sharp fangs dripped with venom,	which had risen suddenly out of the long grass directly in front of Joe,
Expanded noun phrase	**Prepositional phrase**	**Relative clause**	**Relative clause**
An enormous venomous snake	in the long grass between Joe and the tree,	which was a green and yellow striped cobra with a black forked tongue … that flicked from side to side,	which had needle-sharp fangs, that dripped with venom,

(Continued)

1. An enormous venomous snake, which was a green and yellow striped cobra with a black forked tongue and two needle-sharp fangs, in the long grass between Joe and the tree …
2. In the long grass between Joe and the tree, an enormous venomous snake, which was a green and yellow striped cobra with a black forked tongue and two needle-sharp fangs, ….
3. An enormous snake, which was a venomous cobra with green and yellow stripes, a black forked tongue and two needle-sharp fangs, …
4. A green and yellow striped snake, enormous and venomous, whose black forked tongue flicked from side to side, …
5. An enormous venomous green and yellow striped snake, which had a black forked tongue that flicked from side to side, …
6. An enormous green and yellow snake, whose needle-sharp fangs dripped with venom, ….
7. An enormous green and yellow striped snake, which had needle-sharp fangs that dripped with venom, …

PREDICATE			
Information: There was a snake. It slithered slowly. It moved through the long grass. The long grass was between Joe and the tree.			
Level 1			
Verb (verb phrase)	**Adverb (adverb phrase)**	**Adverb (adverb phrase)**	**Adverb (adverb phrase)**
slithered	slowly	through the long grass	between Joe and the tree
must have slithered could have slithered	towards Joe	through the long grass	between him and the tree

Information: There was a snake. It was almost invisible. It was in the long grass. The long grass was between Joe and the tree.

Level 2			
Verb (verb phrase)	**Adverb (adverb phrase)**	**Adverb (adverb phrase)**	**Adverb (adverb phrase)**
was	almost invisible	in the long grass	between Joe and the tree

Information: There was a snake. It was almost invisible. It reared suddenly into the air in the long grass between Joe and the tree. It flared its neck. It displayed its black banded hood.

Level 3				
Verb (verb phrase)	**Adverb (adverb phrase)**	**Adverb phrase**	**Conjunction**	**Predicate (2)**
reared	suddenly	into the air in the long grass between Joe and the tree	and	flared its neck displayed its black banded hood

(Continued)

Information: There was a snake. It reared suddenly high into the air in the long grass between Joe and the tree. It flared its neck. It displayed its black banded hood.

Level 4			
Verb (verb phrase)	**Adverb (adverb phrase)**	**Adverb phrase**	**Participial phrase**
reared	suddenly	high into the air in the long grass between Joe and the tree	flaring its neck displaying its black banded hood

1. … slithered slowly through the long grass between Joe and the tree
2. … must have slithered towards Joe through the long grass between him and the tree
3. … could have slithered towards Joe through the long grass between him and the tree
4. … was almost invisible in the long grass between him and the tree
5. … reared suddenly into the air and flared its neck.
6. … reared suddenly into the air, flared its neck and displayed its black banded hood
7. … reared suddenly into the air, flaring its neck and displaying its black banded hood

SENTENCE MODIFICATION

Information: There was a snake. It reared high into the air. It was directly in front of Joe in the long grass between Joe and the tree. He didn't have time to react.

Level 1			
Subordinate clause (dependent)	**Main clause (independent)**		**Subordinate clause (dependent)**
	Subject	**Predicate**	
Before he had time to react,	an enormous snake, which was a green and yellow striped cobra,	reared high into the air directly in front of Joe.	
	An enormous snake, which was a green and yellow striped cobra,	reared high into the air directly in front of Joe	before he had time to react.
Subordinate clause (dependent)	**Main clause (independent)**		**Subordinate clause (dependent)**
	Subject	**Predicate**	
Even though he had remained motionless,	the enormous green and yellow striped cobra,	reared high into the air directly in front of Joe with its black forked tongue flicking from side to side and venom dripping from its needle-sharp fangs.	
Subject		**Subordinate Clause (dependent)**	**Predicate**
The enormous green and yellow striped cobra,		even though he had remained motionless,	reared high into the air directly in front of Joe, flicking its tongue from side to side and dripping venom from its needle-sharp fangs.

(Continued)

Subject	Relative clause	Predicate	Subordinate Clause (dependent)
The enormous green and yellow striped cobra,	which had reared high into the air directly in front of Joe,	flicked its tongue from side to side and dripped venom from its needle-sharp fangs	even though he had remained motionless.

1. Before he had time to react, an enormous snake, which was a green and yellow striped cobra, reared high into the air directly in front of Joe.
2. An enormous snake, which was a green and yellow striped cobra, reared high into the air directly in front of Joe before he had time to react.
3. Even though he had remained motionless, the green and yellow striped snake, which was an enormous venomous cobra, reared high into the air directly in front of Joe.
4. The enormous green and yellow striped cobra, even though he had remained motionless, reared high into the air directly in front of Joe.
5. Even though he had remained motionless, the enormous green and yellow striped cobra, which had reared high into the air directly in front of Joe, flicked its tongue from side to side and dripped venom from its needle-sharp fangs.

Information: There was a snake. It reared high into the air. It was directly in front of Joe in the long grass between Joe and the tree. It flattened its neck. It displayed its black banded hood. Venom dripped from its needle-sharp fangs.

Level 2				
Participial phrase	**Subject**	**Compound verbs**		
Rearing into the air directly in front of Joe,	the green and yellow striped cobra with venom dripping from its needle-sharp fangs	flattened its neck	and	displayed its black banded hood.
Subject	**Predicate**	**Participial phrase**		**Participial phrase**
With venom dripping from its needle-sharp fangs, the green and yellow striped cobra	reared into the air directly in front of Joe,	flattening its neck	and	displaying its black banded hood.

1. Rearing into the air directly in front of Joe, the green and yellow striped cobra with venom dripping from its needle-sharp fangs flattened its neck and displayed its black banded hood.
2. With venom dripping from its needle-sharp fangs, the green and yellow striped cobra reared into the air directly in front of Joe, flattening its neck and displaying its black banded hood.

WHAT DOES EACH TOOL ADD TO THE WRITER'S TOOLKIT?

To become more confident and adept at constructing and revising sentences, understanding what tools are available and what they add to a sentence is important.

When revising a draft text to assess its clarity, precision, effectiveness, flow, rhythm and cohesion, consider the following questions in respect of sentence construction:

* Has the message been communicated clearly and concisely?
* Have the ideas and details been clearly linked?
* Is the emphasis in the right place?
* Does the sentence flow? Has it achieved the desired rhythm?
* How does changing the position and order of the words, phrases and clauses in the sentence affect the emphasis, impact or rhythm?
* How does each sentence connect with the preceding and subsequent sentences?
* Consider the effect of sentence length:
  a. short sentences: emphasise a point; add drama, tension and suspense
  b. long sentences: link ideas; delay revealing information
  c. read sentences aloud so that you can hear the rhythm and emphasis.
* Experiment with other tools (words, phrases and clauses) to improve the current construction, sentence order and text cohesion.
* Make a note of effective and interesting constructions in literature (fiction and non-fiction) and practise imitating their constructions using a different subject.

1. Determiners – add precision and clarity to a sentence by specifying:

* whether the noun is **general/generic** or **specific/already known**
  For example: a building; the building
* the quantity (**how many**)
  For example: one, many, several
* **where the nouns (pronouns) are in relation to the writer** (distance, time emotionally)

For example:
- ☆ this, these (close)
- ☆ that, those (at a distance)
- ★ **who or what owns the noun (pronoun)**
  For example: my, your, his, her, its, our, their, whose

2. Nouns: general versus specific

Specific nouns **name a particular person, place, thing or idea** and:

- ★ add clarity
- ★ create a more vivid image.

For example: the cobra rather than **the snake** gives the reader a clearer and more vivid image of the snake.

3. Adjectives

- ★ expand what is known of the noun (pronoun)
- ★ add depth and colour to a description or explanation
- ★ add more detail to a description or explanation
- ★ add more detail about:
  - ☆ size, shape, colour
  - ☆ texture, sound, smell, taste
  - ☆ age, style, condition
  - ☆ origin, nationality, ethnicity
  - ☆ characteristics and traits.

4. Delayed adjectives

- ★ amplify and emphasise the details of an image by spotlighting them
- ★ create a different rhythm to the basic sentence construction
- ★ are an alternative to overloaded descriptions using a long list of adjectives.

FOR EXAMPLE

a. The enormous green and yellow striped venomous snake …

b. The green and yellow striped snake, enormous and venomous, …

5. Relative (adjective) clauses

★ identify, clarify

★ describe, modify or adapt a noun (pronoun)

★ add precision and clarity.

Relative (adjective) clauses are useful subordinate clauses that can be embedded into a main clause to enable a writer to **construct tighter sentences** which show a **clearer connection** between the noun (pronoun) and the detail modifying and clarifying it.

They are useful tools to construct more **precise** complex sentences by combining what would otherwise have been two separate sentences into one connected multi-clause sentence.

FOR EXAMPLE

1a. The teenage girl was lurking on the corner of the street. She had handed Scarlett the package.

1b. The teenage girl **who had handed Scarlett the package** was lurking on the corner of the street.

2a. The creature charged into the door. It rocked back and forth with each assault.

2b. The creature charged into the **door, which rocked back and forth with each assault**.

In 2a it isn't entirely clear if it was the door or the creature rocking back and forth with each assault. Combining the two sentences using a relative clause allows the writer to establish the connection between the two events and clarify that it is the door that rocked back and forth, not the creature.

6. Prepositional phrases

★ identify the relationship between one noun in relation to another, for example, location

★ are important to clarify the time period in which an event occurred

★ modify nouns and verbs by indicating various relationships between subjects and verbs.

For example:

☆ the enormous cobra **with green and yellow stripes**

☆ the enormous cobra **in front of him**

☆ **during the night,** the cobra slithered into the camp.

☆ the enormous cobra **with its neck flared**

★ add a more vivid image

★ improve clarity and precision

★ can be used instead of relative clauses to create a different emphasis and rhythm.

FOR EXAMPLE

The cobra, whose neck was flared to display its black banded hood, reared into the air directly in front of him.

The cobra, with a flared neck displaying its black banded hood, reared into the air directly in front of him.

7. Adverbs and adverb phrases

★ modify verbs, adjectives and other adverbs.

Strong adverbs:

★ aid description of how things appear and where and how things happen

★ help to visualise an action with an appropriate degree of intensity (slightly, absolutely)

- ★ show how regularly an event happens (daily, rarely)
- ★ can add an energy and intensity to writing if used sparingly and only if they add something to the writing
- ★ add more precision to the message (strengthening or weaking it).

FOR EXAMPLE

The cobra hissed **viciously**.

Before Joe had time to react, the cobra reared into the air **directly** in front of him.

The cobra reared into the air **directly** in front of Joe before he had time to react.

---

8. Participial phrases (present -ing; past -ed)

- ★ bring the descriptions to life
- ★ add movement
- ★ single participial phrases create rapid movement.
- ★ a series of participial phrases add details at a slower rate but still create a more intense pace.

4

An investigative approach

Using an investigative approach to identify sentence parts helps students to understand and imitate a sentence in terms of:

* function
* construction
* position
* punctuation.

Give students plenty of opportunities to investigate the grammar tool, including:

* how it functions in a sentence
* the questions it answers
* what additional details, description or explanation it provides.
* what the grammar tool adds to sentence in terms of clarity, precision, flow and rhythm.

Opportunities should always be provided that enable students to

* imitate the grammar tool
* experiment with its use.

DOI: 10.4324/9781032662862-5

INVESTIGATION SEQUENCE

1. Chunk sentences into meaningful sentence parts to isolate the grammar tool.
2. Use sentences where the grammar tools are already underlined to complete the table provided and identify the construction of the grammar tool, its position, punctuation, and the information it provides.
3. Identify the grammar tool in a series of sentences.
4. Match the grammar tool with the appropriate main clause.
5. Experiment with the position of the grammar tool.
6. Unscramble and reconstruct sentences.
7. Combine two sentences to include the grammar tool (cued).
8. Combine two or more sentences to include the grammar tool (open).
9. Imitate the use of the grammar tool.
10. Create their own examples.

These exercises expose students to a wealth of grammar tools used in different sentence constructions and locations, which they can then use in their own writing.

METHOD

These exercises have been designed to facilitate the I, WE, YOU process (which, where appropriate, has been modelled):

★ teacher modelling
★ guided
★ independent.

DISCUSSION

Discussion of preferences is an important part of learning about language, so it is important to provide ample opportunities for students to work as a class, in groups or in pairs. According to the research undertaken by Saddler and Graham

(2005), working in mixed-ability groups is an effective strategy. Discussions should involve asking the following questions:

★   What would be the impact on the sentence if the grammar tool was moved to a different position in the sentence?
★   Which sentence construction do you prefer and why?
★   Would using another grammar tool be more effective in the context of the preceding or subsequent sentences?

FOR EXAMPLE

1. Experimenting with different positions in a sentence

a.   Hiding what may be concealed behind them, the trees stood silent and dark.
b.   The trees, hiding what may be concealed behind them, stood silent and dark.
c.   The trees stood silent and dark, hiding what may be concealed behind them.

2. Connecting grammar tools

Convert the sentence into two main clauses.

1.1   The trees stood silent and dark.
1.2   The trees shielded what may be concealed behind them.

What other grammar tools can be used to connect these two sentences?

i.   **Coordinating conjunction**
     The trees stood silent and dark, and they hid what may be concealed behind them.

ii.   **Relative clause**
     The trees, which stood silent and dark, hid what may be concealed behind them.
     Students could then compare the grammar tools and discuss which they prefer and why.

As well as connecting a new grammar tool with one that is already familiar, this exercise serves two purposes:

1. Revising the use of other grammar tools.
2. Engaging in a process that forms the basis for the revision stage of the writing process: evaluating the effectiveness of a sentence construction and considering alternatives.

5

Prepositional phrases

EXERCISE 1 – CHUNKING (LINKING READING AND WRITING)

Punctuation has been removed for this exercise.

INSTRUCTIONS

1. In pairs, take turns to read each of the sentences aloud.
2. Decide which of the sentences is divided into meaningful sentence parts.
3. Discuss and explain your decisions.

EXERCISE

1. **The old haunted house on the edge of the lake was slowly crumbling.**

   i.   The old haunted/ house on the edge of/ the lake was/ slowly crumbling.
   ii. The old haunted house/ on the edge/ of the lake/ was slowly crumbling.

DOI: 10.4324/9781032662862-6

2. **The panel slid back to reveal a narrow twisting staircase which wound down into the darkness of the underground passage.**

i. The panel slid back/ to reveal a narrow twisting staircase/ which wound down/ into the darkness/ of the underground passage.
ii. The panel slid back to/ reveal a narrow twisting staircase/ which wound down into/ the darkness of/ the underground passage.

3. **With his right hand he swatted the air in front of him.**

i. With his right hand/ he swatted the/ air in front of him.
ii. With his right hand/ he swatted the air/ in front of him.

4. **Out of the corner of his eye he saw a flickering movement by the window.**

i. Out of the corner of his eye/ he saw a flickering movement/ by the window.
ii. Out of the corner/ of his eye he saw/ a flickering movement/ by the window.

5. **All of a sudden everything became blurred as if a misty curtain had slithered along the floor up the walls and across the ceiling until its grey tentacles filled the room.**

i. All of a sudden everything/ became blurred as if/ a misty curtain had slithered/ along the floor up/ the walls and across/ the ceiling until its grey tentacles/ filled the room.
ii. All of a sudden/ everything became blurred/ as if a misty curtain had slithered along the floor/ up the walls/ and across the ceiling/ until its grey tentacles filled the room.

EXERCISE 2 – CHUNKING INTO MEANINGFUL SENTENCE PARTS

Punctuation has been removed for this exercise.

INSTRUCTIONS

1. In pairs, read the sentences aloud.
2. Using a slash, chunk the sentences into meaningful parts.
3. Discuss and explain your decisions.

EXERCISE

1. He flung himself down behind the tree.
2. At the end of the alley the beam from the torch created dancing shadows.
3. A strange murky fog hung like an icy breath over the graveyard.
4. The light from the torch swung over the ground and up the wall.
5. Under the floorboards by her bed she could just make out the outline of an enormous bronze key.

EXERCISE 3 – IDENTIFYING THE CONSTRUCTION, POSITION AND PUNCTUATION OF PREPOSITIONAL PHRASES

INSTRUCTIONS

1. Read each sentence. The prepositional phrases are underlined.
2. Add each prepositional phrase to the table provided.
3. What question does the prepositional phrase answer? (Which one, where, when, how?)
4. Highlight the words at the start of the prepositional phrase.
5. Make a note of where it is positioned in the sentence:
    ☆ opening
    ☆ middle (between the subject and the verb)
    ☆ at the end.

EXAMPLE 1

To her right[1], a narrow uneven path **through the trees**[2] twisted and turned **towards the house**.[3]

[1]To her right **(beginning) – where**
[2]through the trees **(middle: between the subject and the verb)** –**where**
[3]towards the house **(end) – where**

For example:

[1 & 2]location; [3]direction

EXTENSION

Identify whether the prepositional phrases are modifying the noun or the verb. (Does the prepositional phrase come after the noun or after the verb?)

EXAMPLE 2

The light **from the torch**[1] swung **over the ground**[2] and **up the wall**.[3]

[1]**from the torch** – modifies the noun (light)
[2]**over the ground** – modifies the verb (swung)
[3]**up the wall** – modifies the verb (swung)

EXERCISE

1. Kitty backed away from the mirror.
2. A huge silver mirror, like a shimmering moon, hung beside the door.
3. From below the cliffs came the sound of roaring rapids.
4. With his right hand, he swatted the air in front of him.
5. During the morning, the fire started burning out of control.
6. In the dead of night, a sudden desperate shriek from the next room woke Rob up.
7. A man with a bushy red beard stepped out of the crowd.
8. The old haunted house on the edge of the lake was slowly crumbling.
9. The heavy snow on Sunday had made all the roads treacherous.
10. At dawn, a mist crept up from the river, along the ground, around the trees and over the hedges.

EXERCISE 3 (continued)

	Prepositional phrase(s)	Position (opening, middle, end)	What question does it answer? (which one, what kind of, where, when, how?)
1.			
2.			
3.			
4.			
5.			
6.			
7.			
8.			
9.			
10.			

EXERCISE 4 – IDENTIFYING PREPOSITIONAL PHRASES

INSTRUCTIONS

1.   Underline the prepositional phrases in the following sentences.

Note: In some of the sentences, there are a series of prepositional phrases. For example: in the passage[1] on the second floor[2]

EXTENSION

1.   Complete the table below.
2.   Highlight the preposition and the object.

For example: He peered through the gap.

EXERCISE

1.   She ran up the steps and paused before the entrance.
2.   Under the floorboards, she could just make out the outline of an enormous bronze key.
3.   A strange murky fog like an icy breath hung over the graveyard.
4.   At dusk, the suits of armour looked like a row of ghostly sentinels lined up along the wall.
5.   At midday, they were ready to leave the house at a moment's notice.
6.   Vines had descended from the roof, climbed down the wall and wriggled across the floor.
7.   With the help of her brother, she located the entrance to the cellar.
8.   She lived in an old Victorian cottage at the end of the street.
9.   Down the stone steps, a long dark tunnel under the medieval church twisted and turned toward the woods.
10. The car drove at high speed down the country lane.

EXERCISE 5 – MATCHING PREPOSITIONAL PHRASES

INSTRUCTIONS

1.   Match the prepositional phrases with their respective main clauses.
2.   Write out each sentence, inserting and underlining the prepositional phrase.

EXAMPLE

1.   The tomb was hidden where the dark could hide its tragic secrets.
a.   (in the corner of the graveyard between high walls)

The tomb was hidden, in the corner of the graveyard between high walls, where the dark could hide its tragic secrets.

DIFFERENTIATION

For those students for whom this exercise could prove to be difficult, the table can be photocopied and cut into individual boxes to enable those students to physically add each prepositional phrase to individual sentences to work out which is the correct combination.

EXERCISE

Main clause	Prepositional phrases
1. As she moved across the hall, ^ she glimpsed a reflection.	a. without any warning
2. ^, They were plunged into darkness.	b. in the shadows behind the crates
3. She grasped the doorknob ^ and yanked the door open.	c. [1]at night [2]in a thick layer of glinting frost
4. She was unaware of his presence ^, watching her every movement.	d. in the long mirror by the front door
5. ^, She took off across the street.	e. [1]during the summer [2]with multi-coloured blossoms
6. ^The garden was brimming. ^	f. with a flick of a switch
7. ^, The pavements were coated ^.	g. behind his thick fleshy lips
8. They walked ^ around the lake.	h. [1]with an enormous suitcase [2]down the station platform
9. The woman ^ barged her way. ^	i. in her right hand
10. ^, She could see his stained and crooked teeth.	j. for miles

EXERCISE 6 – UNSCRAMBLING SENTENCE PARTS

INSTRUCTIONS

1.　Unscramble the list of sentence parts and write out the sentence.
2.　Underline the sentence parts that are prepositional phrases.

Clue: The capitalized sentence part begins the sentence.

EXAMPLE

a.　upon the rat
b.　On silent wings
c.　the powerful owl
d.　like a white shadow
e.　swooped down

On silent wings, the powerful owl, like a white shadow, swooped down upon the rat.

EXERCISE

1a.　she could just make out a few items of furniture
1b.　covered in white sheets
1c.　In the shadows
1d.　around the room

_____

_____

2a.　he saw a flickering movement
2b.　by the window
2c.　Out of the corner of his eye

_____

_____

3a.　the sun faded
3b.　into spidery black silhouettes
3c.　At four o'clock
3d.　and transformed the trees

_____

_____

4a. like a cold, skeletal hand
4b. on the back of his neck
4c. was pinching the nerves
4d. A shiver charged down his spine

_____

_____

5a. but had soon regretted that decision
5b. she had agreed to go back with him to the deserted house
5c. Without any hesitation
5d. to search for his phone

_____

_____

EXERCISE 7 – COMBINING SENTENCES (CUED EXERCISE)

INSTRUCTIONS

1. Combine the two sentences and write out the new sentences with the prepositional phrases underlined.

i. In sentences 1–6, the prepositional phrases are underlined and their position in the combined sentence is marked by ^.

ii. In sentences 8–12, the prepositional phrases are underlined but their position is not marked.

iii. In sentences 11–16, no clues are given.

EXAMPLE

a. The loud chimes ^ shattered the silence.
b. The loud chimes were <u>from the grandfather clock under the stairs</u>.

The loud chimes <u>from the grandfather clock under the stairs</u> shattered the silence.

EXERCISE

1.1 The path ended abruptly. ^
1.2 It ended <u>at a vertical cliff</u>.

_____

_____

2.1 She lived in a street. ^
2.2 The street was <u>of terraced Georgian townhouses</u>.

_____

_____

3.1 The house was shielded. ^ ^
3.2 It was shielded <u>from the road</u>.
3.3 It was shielded <u>by a high red-brick wall</u>.

_____

_____

4.1 ^ She felt her way. ^ ^ ^
4.2 She did this <u>with outstretched hands</u>.
4.3. She did this <u>along the corridor</u>.
4.3 She did this <u>until her fingers brushed</u> SOMETHING.
4.4 They brushed <u>against cold metal</u>.

_____

_____

5.1 ^ The door closed. ^
5.2 It closed <u>with a thud</u>.
5.3 It closed <u>behind him</u>.

_____

_____

6.1   ^ There was no sign. ^ ^ ^
6.2   There was nothing <u>during the day</u>.
6.3   There was no sign <u>of the blood-splattered knight.</u>
6.4   He <u>had prowled the corridors</u>. (**WHO**)
6.5   He had prowled the corridors <u>until dawn.</u>

_____

_____

7.1   ^The torch shone. ^ ^
7.2   It happened <u>for a brief moment</u>.
7.3   It shone <u>on the wall.</u>
7.4   The shadows were <u>above her head.</u>

_____

_____

8.1   Scarlett inched her way.
8.2   She went <u>up the alley.</u>
8.3   She went <u>towards the cluster of bins.</u>

_____

_____

9.1   She was miles from home.
9.2   She was <u>lost and hungry.</u>
9.3   She was <u>out of luck.</u>
9.4   <u>Her phone had run out of battery</u>. (**AS**)

_____

_____

10.1 The windows in the attic roof had been smeared.
10.2 This happened <u>over the years</u>.
10.3 They were smeared <u>by layers of dust and dirt.</u>

_____

_____

11.1 She had learned a lot.

11.2 She had learned <u>about rainforests</u>.

11.3 She had learned <u>from the internet</u>.

_____

_____

12.3 They followed the road.

12.2 They followed it <u>over a hump-backed bridge</u>.

12.3 They followed it <u>along a narrow track</u>. **(AND)**

12.4 The narrow track was <u>through thick woodland</u>.

_____

_____

13.1 She was terrified of walking down the corridor.

13.2 The corridor was long.

13.3 The corridor was dark.

13.4 The corridor was to her room.

13.5 She was terrified at night.

_____

_____

14.1 She knew she would have to wait.

14.2 She would have to wait until the morning.

14.3 She would have to wait to find out who had arrived.

14.4 Someone had arrived in the middle of the night.

_____

_____

15.1 She had searched in the attic.

15.2 She had done this out of curiosity.

15.3 She had searched for her grandmother's memory box.

_____

_____

16.1 She had not been back.

16.2 She had not been to the house.

16.3 She had not been since that fateful night.

_____

_____

EXERCISE 8 – CREATING PREPOSITIONAL PHRASES

1. These exercises can be done in sections as a quick warm-up activity (orally or written; modelled, guided or independent). Working orally as a class produces a greater variety of prepositional phrases and a greater understanding of how they are constructed.

2. The warm-up can be extended by using the sentences as writing prompts and asking a series of questions: who, where, when, how, why, what (happened next)?

EXERCISE

INSTRUCTIONS

A. Use as many prepositions as possible to fill in the gaps and create a list of prepositional phrases.

1. … the water
2. …. the bridge
3. … the sofa
4. … an enormous handbag
5. … the crowd
6. … the room
7. … the water
8. … his head
9. … her hand
10. … the mountain

B.   Add a noun or noun phrase (object) to the following prepositions to complete the prepositional phrase.

1.   the sound of …
2.   the smell of …
3.   the touch of …
4.   the taste of …
5.   during the …
6.   outside the …
7.   in the …
8.   searched for …
9.   walked through …
10. learned about …

C.   Complete the sentence stems by using the highlighted preposition to construct your own prepositional phrases.

EXTENSION

Innovate the sentences by substituting some of the prepositional phrases already included (which are underlined)

1.   The parcel was collected <u>by the woman</u> **with** …

_____

_____

2.   The shelf was piled high **with** …

_____

_____

3.   She lived **in** …

_____

_____

4.   <u>In the distance</u>, she saw a group **of** …

_____

_____

5. <u>For days</u> the roads had been blocked **by** …

_____

_____

6. <u>In the dead of night</u>, they had been woken **by** …

_____

_____

7. **With** <u>the help</u> **of** …, she searched **for** …

_____

_____

8. He had learned **about**… **from**…

_____

_____

9. She woke <u>from a deep sleep</u> and lay <u>for a minute or two</u> listening **to** …

_____

_____

10. **During** … the air was thick <u>with the scent</u> **of** …

_____

_____

11. She took a deep breath as the smell **of** …wafted **through** …

_____

_____

12. She drifted off to sleep, listening to the sound **of** …

_____

_____

13. She had not been back **to** the … **since** …

_____

_____

14. A secret compartment had been built **into** …

_____

_____

15. The mist had spread **across** …, and slithered **up** …

_____

_____

SECTION 2 – REVIEW

1. What information do prepositional phrases add to a sentence? What questions do they answer?
2. What words usually begin prepositional phrases?
3. What word class never appears in a prepositional phrase?
4. Where can prepositional phrases be placed in a sentence?
5. How can prepositional phrases improve your writing?

COMMON PREPOSITIONS

About, above, across, after, against, along, among, around, at

Before, behind, below, beneath, besides, between, by

Down, during, except, for, from, in, in front of, inside, instead of, into

Like, near, of, off, on, onto, on top of, out of, outside, over, past

Since, through, throughout, to, towards, under, underneath, until, up, upon, with, within, without

WHAT ARE PREPOSITIONS?

PREPOSITIONS are **linking words in a sentence**, which are used to indicate:

* what kind of
* how many
* how long
* which one
* where
* when
* how.

FOR EXAMPLE

A preposition that answers 'where' is any word that can be inserted into the gap in the sentence below to complete the sentence.

They were ---------- the door.

At the door; by the door; outside the door; below the door; behind the door; before the door; through the door; above the door; against the door; underneath the door

---

CONSTRUCTION OF A PREPOSITIONAL PHRASE

A **PREPOSITIONAL PHRASE** is constructed by combining a **PREPOSITION** with an **OBJECT**.

Examples

a. *Preposition – in*

   Object(s) – coat, water, night, spring, tree, hand, wind

   Prepositional phrase(s)

   in an orange coat; in the water; in the night; in spring; in his hand; in the wind

b. *Preposition – against*

Object(s) – hand, current, clock

Prepositional phrase(s)

against his hand; against the current; against the clock

c. *Preposition – around*

Object(s) – shoulders, neck, clock, world

Prepositional phrase(s)

around his shoulders; around her neck; around the clock; around the world

d. *Preposition – with*

Object (s) – tyre, chicken, coat, hair, grin

Prepositional phrase(s)

with a flat tyre; with spicy chicken; with a red coat; with blond hair; with a broad grin

e. *Preposition – out*

Object – breath, curiosity, room, light, time, luck

Prepositional phrase(s)

out of breath; out of curiosity; out of the room; out of the light; out of time; out of luck

f. *Preposition – at*

Object – glance, distance, door, end

Prepositional phrase(s)

at a glance; at a distance; at the door; at the end

g. *Preposition – for*

Object – time, hours, sale, lunch

Prepositional phrase(s)

for the tenth time; for three hours; for sale; for lunch

RULE FOR PREPOSITIONAL PHRASES

Preposition + object (noun, pronoun, noun phrase)

Prepositional phrases **NEVER** include a **VERB**.

(Remembering this fact will assist students in distinguishing between a preposi-tional phrase and a subordinate clause.)

WHAT DO PREPOSITIONAL PHRASES TELL US?

A. Which one; What kind of; How many?

1. Helps the reader to identify which noun is being referred to.
    She lived in the Victorian cottage **at the end of the street**.
    Identifies which cottage she lived in.
2. Provides more detail about the noun (pronoun), which tells the reader what kind of noun.
a. From below came a deadly sound **of roaring rapids**.
    *Tells the reader what kind of **sound**.*
b. Balls of flames **like fiery comets** plummeted to the ground.
    Tells the reader what kind of flames.
c. An enormous man **with a bushy red beard** stepped out of the crowd.
    Identifies which man stepped out of the crowd.
d. The dish with spicy chicken was too hot.
    Identifies which dish.

B. Where something is – *besides, under, on, in, at, against, beneath, over, above, below, inside*

*   **At a point**: at the entrance, at the corner
*   **In an enclosed space**: in the house, in the passage
*   **On a surface**: on the floor, on the wall, on her hand

C. When something happens – *until, during, before, on her birthday, at midnight, in December*

* ★ **At a precise time:** at 3:40 pm; at midnight
* ★ **In months, years, centuries:** in March; in the winter; in 1066
* ★ **On days and dates:** on Saturday, on National Poetry Day, on 14th October 1066

D. How something happens

a. The fire was burning **out of control**.
b. He rescued his rucksack **with the help of his dog**.
c. The storm descended on the forest **without any warning**.
d. The car drove **at high speed** down the country lane.
e. They were ready to leave the house **at a moment's notice**.
f. They glanced behind them **for the hundredth time**.

SECTION 3 – ANSWERS

EXERCISE 1 – CHUNKING (LINKING READING AND WRITING)

1. **The old haunted house on the edge of the lake was slowly crumbling.**

The old haunted/ house on the edge of/ the lake was/ slowly crumbling.
The old haunted house/ on the edge/ of the lake/ was slowly crumbling. √

2. **The panel slid back to reveal a narrow twisting staircase which wound down into the darkness of the underground passage.**

The panel slid back/ to reveal a narrow twisting staircase/ which wound down/ into the darkness/ of the underground passage. √
The panel slid back to/ reveal a narrow twisting staircase/ which wound down into/ the darkness of/ the underground passage.

3. **With his right hand he swatted the air in front of him.**

With his right hand/ he swatted the/ air in front of him.

With his right hand/ he swatted the air/ in front of him. √

4. **Out of the corner of his eye he saw a flickering movement by the window.**

Out of the corner of his eye/ he saw a flickering movement/ by the window. √

Out of the corner/ of his eye he saw/ a flickering movement/ by the window.

5. **All of a sudden everything became blurred as if a misty curtain had slithered along the floor up the walls and across the ceiling until its grey tentacles filled the room.**

All of a sudden everything/ became blurred as if/ a misty curtain had slithered/ along the floor up/ the walls and across/ the ceiling until its grey tentacles/ filled the room.

All of a sudden/ everything became blurred/ as if a misty curtain had slithered along the floor/ up the walls/ and across the ceiling/ until its grey tentacles filled the room. √

EXERCISE 2 – CHUNKING INTO MEANINGFUL SENTENCE PARTS

1. He flung himself down/ behind the tree.
2. At the end of the alley/ the beam from the torch/ created dancing shadows.
3. A strange murky fog/ hung like an icy breath/ over the graveyard.
4. The light from the torch/ swung over the ground/ and up the wall.
5. Under the floorboards/ by her bed/ she could just make out/ the outline of an enormous bronze key.

EXERCISE 3 – IDENTIFYING THE CONSTRUCTION, POSITION AND PUNCTUATION OF PREPOSITIONAL PHRASES

	Prepositional phrase(s)	Position in sentence (opening, middle, end)	What question does it answer? (which one, where, when, how?)
1.	from the mirror	end – after the verb	where
2.	i. like a shimmering moon ii. beside the door	i. middle (between subject and verb) ii. end after the verb	i. what kind of ii. where
3.	i. from below the cliffs ii. of roaring rapids	i. opening ii. end	where what kind of
4.	i. with his right hand ii. in front of him	i. opening ii. end	i. how ii. where
5.	i. during the morning ii. out of control	i. opening ii. end	i. when ii. how
6.	i. in the dead of night ii. from the next room	i. opening ii. middle	i. when ii. where
7.	i. with a bushy beard ii. out of the crowd	i. middle ii. end	i. which man ii. where
8.	i. on the edge ii. of the lake	i. middle ii. middle	i. which one ii. which one
9.	on Sunday	middle	when
10.	[1]at dawn [2]from the river [3]along the ground [4]around the trees [5]over the hedges	[1]opening [2-5]end – after the verb	[1]when [2-5]Describes the direction of the mist

EXERCISE 4 – IDENTIFYING PREPOSITIONAL PHRASES

	Prepositional phrase(s)	Position (opening, middle, end)	What question does it answer? (which one, what kind of, where, when, how?)
1.	i. up the steps ii. before the entrance	i. end ii. end	i. where ii. where
2.	i. under the floorboards ii. of an enormous bronze key	i. opening ii. end	i. where ii. what kind of
3.	i. like an icy breath ii. over the graveyard	i. middle ii. end	i. what kind of ii. where
4.	i. at dusk ii. like a row of ghostly sentinels iii. along the wall	i. opening ii. middle iii. end	i. when ii. what kind of iii. where
5.	i. at midday ii. at a moment's notice	i. opening ii. end	i. when ii. how long
6.	i. from the roof ii. down the wall iii. across the floor	i. end ii. end iii. end	i. where ii. where iii. where
7.	i. with the help of her brother ii. to the cellar	i. opening ii. end	i. how ii. which one
8.	i. in an old Victorian cottage ii. at the end iii. of the street	i. end ii. end iii. end	i. which one ii. which one iii. which one
9.	i. down the stone steps ii. under the medieval church iii. toward the woods	i. opening ii. middle iii. end	i. where ii. which one iii. where
10	i. at high speed ii. down the country lane	i. end ii. end	i. how ii. where

HIGHLIGHTING THE PREPOSITION AND OBJECT

1. up the steps; before the entrance
2. under the floorboards; of an enormous bronze key
3. like an icy breath; over the graveyard
4. at dusk; like a row of ghostly sentinels; along the wall
5. at midday; at a moment's notice
6. from the roof; down the wall; across the floor
7. with the help of her brother; to the cellar
8. in an old Victorian cottage; at the end of the street
9. down the stone steps; under the church; toward the woods
10. at high speed; down the country lane

EXERCISE 5 – MATCHING PREPOSITIONAL PHRASES

Combined sentences
1.d. As she moved across the hall, <u>in the long mirror by the front door</u> she glimpsed a reflection.
2.f. <u>With a flick of a switch</u>, they were plunged into darkness.
3.i. She grasped the doorknob <u>in her right hand</u> and yanked the door open.
4.b. She was unaware of his presence <u>in the shadows behind the crates</u>, watching her every movement.
5.a. <u>Without any warning</u>, she took off across the street.
6.e. <u>During the summer</u>, the garden was brimming <u>with multi-coloured blossoms</u>.
7.c. <u>At night</u>, the pavements were coated <u>in a thick layer of glinting frost</u>.
8.j. They walked <u>for miles</u> around the lake.
9.h. The woman [1]<u>with an enormous suitcase</u> barged her way [2]<u>down the station platform</u>.
10.g. <u>Behind his thick fleshy lips</u>, she could see his stained and crooked teeth.

EXERCISE 6 – UNSCRAMBLING SENTENCE PARTS

1. <u>In the shadows around the room</u>, she could just make out a few items of furniture covered <u>in white sheets</u>.
2. Out of the corner of his eye, he saw a flickering movement <u>by the window</u>.
3. <u>At four o'clock</u>, the sun faded and transformed the trees <u>into spidery black silhouettes</u>.
4. A shiver charged <u>down his spine like a cold, skeletal hand</u> was pinching the nerves <u>on the back of his neck</u>.
5. <u>Without hesitation</u>, she had agreed to go back <u>with him to the deserted house</u> to search for his phone but had soon regretted that decision.

EXERCISE 7 – COMBINING SENTENCES (CUED EXERCISE)

1. The path ended abruptly <u>at a vertical cliff</u>.
2. She lived <u>in a street of terraced Georgian townhouses</u>.
3. The house was shielded <u>from the road by a high red-brick wall</u>.
4. <u>With outstretched hands</u>, she felt her way <u>along the corridor</u> until her fingers brushed <u>against cold metal</u>.
5. <u>With a thud</u>, the door closed <u>behind him</u>.
6. <u>During the day</u>, there was no sign <u>of the blood-splattered knight</u> who had prowled the corridors <u>until dawn</u>.
7. <u>For a brief moment</u>, the torch shone <u>on the wall above her head</u>.
8. Scarlett inched her way <u>up the alley toward the cluster of bins</u>.
9. She was miles <u>from home</u>, lost and hungry, and <u>out of luck</u> as her phone had run out <u>of battery</u>.
10. <u>Over the years</u>, the windows <u>in the attic roof</u> had been smeared <u>by layers of dust and dirt</u>.
11. She had learned a lot <u>about rainforests from the internet</u>.
12. They followed the road <u>over a hump-backed bridge</u> and <u>along a narrow track through thick woodland</u>.

13. She was terrified of walking <u>down the long dark corridor to her room at night</u>.
14. She knew she would have to wait <u>until the morning</u> to find out who had arrived <u>in the middle of the night</u>.
15. <u>Out of curiosity</u>, she had searched for her grandmother's memory box <u>in the attic</u>.
16. She had not been back <u>to the house since that fateful night</u>.

6

Adverb clauses

EXERCISE 1 – CHUNKING (LINKING READING AND WRITING)

Punctuation has been removed for this exercise.

INSTRUCTIONS

1. In pairs, take turns to read each of the sentences aloud.
2. Decide which of the sentences is divided into meaningful sentence parts.
3. Discuss and explain your decisions.

EXERCISE

1. **She had to keep going because there was nowhere to hide.**

i. She had to keep going/ because there was nowhere to hide.

ii. She had to/ keep going because/ there was nowhere to hide.

DOI: 10.4324/9781032662862-7

2. **If she had known what was waiting for her she would have run the other way.**

i. If she had known what/ was waiting/ for her she/ would have run the/ other way.

ii. If she had known what was waiting for her/ she would have run the other way.

3. **When he reached the end of the wall he peered cautiously round the corner.**

i. When he reached the end of the wall/ he peered cautiously/ round the corner.

ii. When he reached/ the end of/ the wall he peered/ cautiously round the corner.

4. **After sprinting for a few minutes Scarlett began to slow down.**

i. After/ sprinting for a/ few minutes Scarlett began/ to slow down.

ii. After sprinting for a few minutes/ Scarlett began to slow down.

5. **Although the building had been deserted for some time he thought that he was being watched from one of the upper windows.**

i. Although the building had been deserted for some time /he thought that he was being watched/ from one of the upper windows.

ii. Although the building had been/ deserted for some/ time he thought that/he was/ being watched from one/ of the upper windows.

EXERCISE 2 – CHUNKING INTO MEANINGFUL SENTENCE PARTS

Punctuation has been removed for this exercise.

INSTRUCTIONS

1.   In pairs, read the sentences aloud.
2.   Using a slash, chunk the sentences into meaningful parts.
3.   Discuss and explain your decisions.

Note: The sentences can be chunked in a variety of ways. At this stage, the aim should be to guide students to chunking the adverb clause as one sentence part.

EXAMPLE

As the chilly air/ wrapped around Andrew/ like an icy blanket/ it froze his breath/ in clouds around him.

As the chilly air wrapped around Andrew/ like an icy blanket/ it froze his breath in clouds/ around him.

As the chilly air wrapped around Andrew like an icy blanket/ it froze his breath in clouds around him.

EXERCISE

1.   Before he tried inserting the key into the lock he held it in the palm of his hand and stared at the strange interlocking symbols.
2.   The puddles jumped to life as pellets of water drummed the surface.
3.   It would be too dark if he waited any longer to find the trail.
4.   When the sun sank below the horizon a black cloak was drawn across the sky.
5.   While they had been struggling through the swamp the wolves had detected their scent.

EXERCISE 3 – IDENTIFYING THE FUNCTION, CONSTRUCTION, POSITION AND PUNCTUATION OF ADVERB CLAUSES

In the following sentences, the adverb clauses have already been underlined.

Punctuation has been removed for this exercise.

INSTRUCTIONS

In the table provided:

1. Write out the adverb clauses.
2. Highlight or circle the words (subordinating conjunctions) at the start of each adverb clause.
3. Identify what additional information is provided by the adverb clause.
4. Make a note of where the adverb clause is positioned in the sentence (beginning, middle or end).
5. Make a note of the punctuation:
   - ☆ no commas
   - ☆ bracketing commas
   - ☆ one comma separating the adverb clause from the main clause.

EXTENSION

Examine why the adverb clause cannot stand alone but is dependent on being linked to the main clause. See the Review section for additional guidance.

MODEL

If they took any of the hairpin bends too quickly, a sheer drop over the side of the cliff awaited them.

Main clause:	A sheer drop over the side of the cliff awaited them.
Adverb clause:	if they took any of the hairpin bends too quickly

Position:	beginning of the sentence
Punctuation:	one comma after the adverb clause
What information is supplied?	Under what conditions a sheer drop would await them.
Dependent clause:	This is a dependent clause (needs to be combined with the main clause to make sense) because it does not tell the reader what would happen if they took any of the bends too quickly.

EXERCISE

1. Joe kept glancing at his watch <u>because he knew time was running out</u>.
2. <u>As she whirled round</u>, her mobile phone fell out of her pocket.
3. <u>Even though she was terrified</u>, she was seized with a desperate need to open the door to check if there was anyone there.
4. The sun, <u>while she had been exploring the house</u>, had fallen like a sinking stone.
5. They would have to cross the river at some stage <u>if they continued travelling south</u>.
6. She gradually, <u>after her eyes had adjusted to the dark</u>, started to pick out a few shapes scattered across the room.
7. <u>Since she had no clue where she was</u>, Kitty had no choice but to follow the main road.
8. She waited silently in the shadows <u>until she was sure that the man wasn't coming back</u>.
9. <u>Before she could stagger to her feet</u>, she heard the front door creak open.
10. <u>Whenever she looked up at the mountain</u>, the images of the day the volcano had erupted and destroyed her village replayed in her mind like a horror movie.

EXERCISE 3 (continued)

	Adverb clause	a. Position in sentence: Opening, middle (between subject and verb) or end b. Punctuation i. No commas ii. Bracketing commas iii. One comma separating the adverb clause from the main clause	What information does the adverb clause reveal?	Main clause
Model	if they took any of the hairpin bends too quickly	a. beginning b. one comma (iii)	Under what conditions a sheer drop would await them.	A sheer drop over the side of the cliff awaited them.
1.		a. b.		
2.		a. b.		
3.		a. b.		
4.		a. b.		
5.		a. b.		
6.		a. b.		
7.		a. b.		
8.		a. b.		
9.		a. b.		
10.		a. b.		

EXTENSION

	Adverb clause	Main clause	Punctuation a. No commas b. Bracketing commas c. One comma separating the relative clause from the main clause	Does the adverb clause make sense without the main clause?
Model	as the creature charged against the door	It rocked back and forth with each assault.	C	No – it doesn't tell the reader what happened when the creature charged against the door.
1.				
2.				
3.				
4.				
5.				
6.				
7.				
8.				
9.				
10.				

EXERCISE 4 – IDENTIFYING ADVERB CLAUSES

INSTRUCTIONS

1. Underline the adverb clauses in the following sentences. Highlight the words (subordinating conjunctions) that begin the adverb clauses.

EXTENSION

This can be done orally or by completing the table below.

2. Identify where the adverb clauses are positioned in the sentences:

i. Beginning
ii. Middle (between the subject and verb)
iii. End (after the main clause).

3. How are they punctuated?

i. One comma separating the adverb clause from the main clause
ii. Bracketing commas
iii. No commas.

4. What information does the adverb clause provide?
5. Is the adverb clause dependent on the main clause to make sense?
6. Experiment with the position of the adverb clause by moving it to the beginning, middle or end.

EXERCISE

1. The crater, while he was collecting fruit from the edge of the forest, had begun belching out a bubble of black smoke and gas.
2. Because the volcano continued to belch out huge clouds of black smoke, the town was covered in thick choking fumes.
3. She had to hold onto the rail to keep her balance whenever the ground vibrated.
4. Before he could warn the village, enormous fireballs had begun to rain from the volcano.
5. The fireballs, as they struck the ground, burst into clouds of sparks.

6. They made hurried preparations to evacuate the village because the volcano was showing ominous signs of awakening.

7. When the truth had finally dawned on her, she had been enveloped by a sense of horror.

8. The house, although it was the middle of the day, had become strangely dark.

9. When the volcano erupted, a hot mixture of rock, gas and ash was hurled from the vent.

10. Although the river of lava was covered in a black crust, there were still pockets of red.

EXERCISE 4 (continued)

	Adverb clause	Information supplied Position Beginning, middle, end	Punctuation a. No commas b. Bracketing commas c. One comma separating the relative clause from the main clause	Main clause
	as the creature charged against the door	Explains when the door rocked back and forth. Beginning	C	It rocked back and forth with each assault.
1.				
2.				
3.				
4.				
5.				
6.				
7.				
8.				
9.				
10.				

EXERCISE 5 – MATCHING ADVERB CLAUSES

INSTRUCTIONS

1. Match the adverb clauses with their respective main clauses.
2. Write out each sentence, inserting and underlining the adverb clause.

EXTENSION

3. Experiment with inserting the adverb clauses in different positions (beginning, middle and end).

DIFFERENTIATION

For those students for whom this exercise could prove to be difficult, the table can be photocopied and cut into individual boxes to enable those students to physically add each adverb clause to individual sentences to work out which is the correct combination.

EXERCISE

Main clause	Adverb clauses
1. ^ A large chunk of rock had slammed into the rock-face above the bridge.	a. when the fog had descended
2. She prayed that the rickety wooden bridge over the rapids would hold her weight. ^	b. because its barbed spikes were hidden by layers of dead leaves
3. ^ It had cloaked the trees in wreaths of swirling grey.	c. if they had chosen the right path
4. She did not see the trip wire that wriggled across the ground. ^	d. although it appeared dormant at the moment
5. ^ The volcano was boiling and bubbling deep underground.	e. because there was no other way to cross the rapids
6. ^ She checked the corridor.	f. even though his legs felt like rubber
7. They were forced to retrace their steps to the iron gate. ^	g. after a couple of minutes had passed
8. ^ They should be close to the entrance to the Inca city.	h. because he had heard footsteps on the stairs
9. ^ He tried to keep moving.	i. when they reached a dead end
10. Rob ^ yanked Kitty back into the room.	j. while he was crossing the bridge

TIP: This exercise requires close reading. Look for key words in the main clauses and adverb clauses that connect the two sentence parts.

EXERCISE 6 – UNSCRAMBLING SENTENCE PARTS

INSTRUCTIONS

1. Unscramble the list of sentence parts and write out the sentence.
2. Underline the sentence parts that are adverb clauses.

Clue: The capitalized sentence parts begin the sentences.

EXAMPLE

a. because she was convinced
b. She kept searching for the old tramp
c. that he was the key to solving the mystery.

She kept searching for the old tramp <u>because she was convinced that he was the key to solving the mystery</u>.

Imitation

She kept searching for the tramp <u>because she was certain that he had seen something the night of the break-in</u>.

<u>Because she was certain that he had seen something the night of the break-in</u>, she kept searching for the tramp.

EXERCISE

1a. because she was running out of time
1b. Kitty prayed
1c. that she had taken the right path

_____

_____

2a. before stopping to think
2b. Rob opened the door
2c. and slipped through into the reception area

_____

_____

3a. green shoots
3b. After spring had thawed the frosty ground
3c. started to appear in the woods

_____

_____

4a. If he had never found that chest
4b. discovered his father's secret identity
4c. Rob would not have

_____

_____

5a. Although the main exit was blocked
5b. out of the building
5c. Kitty knew there was another way

_____

_____

EXERCISE 7 – COMBINING SENTENCES (CUED EXERCISE)

INSTRUCTIONS

1. Sentences are broken down into base sentences (called kernel sentences).
2. Cross out any repeated or unnecessary words.
3. Using an adverb clause, combine the two/three base sentences into one sentence.
4. Cues provided in brackets (IF…,) go at the beginning of the clause, which is combined with the base sentence to complete the transformation. (*see example below*)
5. The punctuation to be used is indicated.
6. The position of the adverb clause is indicated by a ^.

EXAMPLE

a   ^, Kitty would have heard footsteps behind her.

b.   She had stopped and listened. (IF)

If she had stopped and listened, Kitty would have heard footsteps behind her.

Variation:

Kitty would have heard footsteps behind her if she had stopped and listened.

Kitty, if she had stopped and listened, would have heard footsteps behind her.

EXERCISE

1.1   ^ Rob had to use his staff to force a path through the undergrowth.

1.2   The trail became more difficult to follow. (**WHEN**)

_____

_____

Variation:

_____

_____

2.1   Kitty knew he was standing in front of the bins. ^

2.2   She could clearly smell the stench of his stale sweat. (**BECAUSE**)

_____

_____

Variation:

_____

_____

_____

3.1   ^, Night had fallen and blanketed the streets in darkness.
3.2   She had been on the tube. (**WHILE**)

_____

_____

Variation:

_____

_____

_____

4.1   ^, the streets were deserted.
4.2   She was in the middle of the city. (**ALTHOUGH**)

_____

_____

Variation:

_____

_____

_____

_____

5.1   Kitty waited silently in the shadows. ^
5.2   She was sure that the man wasn't coming back. (**UNTIL**)

_____

_____

Variation:

_____

_____

_____

_____

CHALLENGE

6.1 ^, Every nerve in her body urged her not to move. ^

6.2 The torch shone above her head. (**WHEN**)

6.3 Pins and needles prickled painfully in her left leg. (**EVEN THOUGH**)

_____

_____

Variation:

_____

_____

_____

EXERCISE 8 – CHOOSE THE APPROPRIATE CONJUNCTION (CUED EXERCISE)

INSTRUCTIONS

1. Choose which conjunction is appropriate to use:
    When, while, before, after, until, whenever
    Because, as, since
    If, although, even though, though

2. The position of the adverb clause is marked with ^.

3. Experiment with the adverb clauses in different positions. (*At this stage, it is probably best to focus on adverb clauses at the beginning and end of a sentence. Some examples of an adverb clause positioned between the subject and verb have been included for reference.*)

EXERCISE

1a.   They would have been lost in the swirling blizzards ^.

1b.   They had not strung guide ropes between the buildings.

_____

_____

Variation:

_____

_____

2a.   He needed to cross a narrow, knife-edged ridge. ^

2b.   He could reach the summit.

_____

_____

Variation:

_____

_____

3a.   ^, She didn't have time to answer her phone.

3b.   She was sprinting to get to the train before the doors closed.

_____

_____

Variation:

_____

_____

4a. An orange glow appeared on the horizon. ^
4b. They watched the sun set.

_____

_____

Variation:

_____

_____

5a. ^ , She eventually managed to insert the key into the lock .
5b. Her hands were trembling.

_____

_____

Variation:

_____

_____

EXERCISE 9 – COMBINING SENTENCES (CUED EXERCISE)

INSTRUCTIONS

1. Use the subordinate conjunctions (indicated in brackets) to combine the two sentences.
2. Decide where to position the adverb clause (beginning, middle or end)
3. Dependent on the position of the subordinate clause, decide how it should be punctuated (one comma, bracketing commas, no commas).

EXAMPLE

1a.   Rob would have nowhere to run.

1b.   His attacker returned. (IF)

He would have nowhere to run <u>if his attacker returned</u>.

Variation:

<u>If his attacker returned</u>, Rob would have nowhere to run.

Rob, <u>if his attacker returned</u>, would have nowhere to run.

1a.   Scientists still can't predict exactly when a volcano will erupt.

1b.   They monitor Earth's movements. (ALTHOUGH)

_____

_____

Variation:

_____

_____

_____

2a.   They had a nerve-wracking journey through dense, treacherous forests that were inhabited by outlaws.

2b.   They eventually reached their destination (BEFORE)

_____

_____

Variation:

_____

_____

_____

3a. Someone had walked into the room.

3b. He was asleep (WHEN)

_____

_____

Variation:

_____

_____

_____

4a. Rob was on edge and kept checking his watch.

4b. He waited for them to return. (WHILE)

_____

_____

Variation:

_____

_____

_____

5a. Kitty couldn't see the man's eyes.

5b. They were hidden behind a pair of silver-mirrored sunglasses. (BECAUSE)

_____

_____

Variation:

_____

_____

_____

EXERCISE 10 – COMBINING SENTENCES (OPEN EXERCISE)

INSTRUCTIONS

1.   Decide how to combine the two sentences.
2.   Choose the appropriate subordinate conjunction.
3.   Decide where to position the adverb clause (beginning, middle, end).
4.   Decide how to punctuate the clause correctly in the combined sentence.

Tips:

1.   To decide on which subordinate conjunction to use, consider what question is being answered by the second sentence (when, why, under what condition/in spite of).
2.   Choose an appropriate subordinate conjunction from the list supplied – for example, *when, while, whenever, after, before*.
3.   Experiment with positioning the adverb clause at the beginning and at the end. (*More advanced: try positioning the adverb clause between the subject and verb.*)

EXAMPLE

1.1   The grandfather clock suddenly started chiming at midnight.
1.2   It had not worked for years.

1.   What question does 1.2 answer? – when, why, or under what condition/in spite of?

a.   Does it explain when the grandfather clock started chiming? X
b.   Does it explain why? X
c.   Does it explain under what condition/in spite of? √

2.   Subordinating conjunctions: although, though, even though, despite

3. Position

i.   **Though** it had not worked for years, the grandfather clock suddenly started chiming at midnight.

ii. The grandfather clock suddenly started chiming at midnight **though** it had not worked for years.

iii. The grandfather clock, **though** it had not worked for years, suddenly started chiming at midnight.

EXERCISE

1.1 Rob paced backwards and forwards across the room.
1.2 He waited for the phone to ring.

_____

_____

Variation:

_____

_____

2.1 Rob's pulse started to race.
2.2 He realised that he had run in the wrong direction.

_____

_____

Variation:

_____

_____

3.1 His legs buckled under him.
3.2 He could get to the chair.
3.3 He fell to the floor. (AND)

_____

_____

Variation:

_____

_____

4.1   He didn't want to leave the safety of his bedroom.

4.2   Rob knew he had no choice.

_____

_____

Variation:

_____

_____

5.1   Rob couldn't see who was in the car.

5.2   The windows were tinted black.

_____

_____

Variation:

_____

_____

EXERCISE 11 – CREATING ADVERB CLAUSES BY COMPLETING SENTENCE STEMS

INSTRUCTIONS

1.   Complete the adverb clauses provided to complete the sentence.
2.   Change the nouns in brackets if necessary.

EXERCISE

SENTENCE STEMS

1.   When he reached the (river) …
2.   If she didn't leave soon …
3.   If she waited any longer …
4.   Because time was running out …
5.   When she turned off the (torch) …
6.   After she left the (shop) …

7. Before he had a chance to (move) …
8. Although he knew he was going to be late …
9. As she waited motionless in the shadows …
10. As she whirled round …
11. Until she was sure he had gone …
12. Although she had heard about the Instagram post …
13. She did not check her messages because …
14. While she waited for Rob to catch her up …
15. Before he dialled the number …
16. Whenever she looked up at Rob …
17. Joe kept glancing at his watch because …
18. Although her mobile phone was buzzing in her pocket …
19. Because he didn't have time to answer his phone …
20. While her phone had been turned off …

SECTION 2 – REVIEW

1. What information do adverb clauses reveal? What questions do they answer?
2. Which words usually begin adverb clauses?
3. What subordinate conjunctions answer the questions:
    a. when it happened
    b. why it happened
    c. under what conditions it happened.
4. Where can adverb clauses be placed in a sentence?
5. When is one comma used for an adverb clause? When are two bracketing commas used for an adverb clause? When are no commas used?
6. How can adverb clauses improve your writing?

ADVERB CLAUSES

An **ADVERB CLAUSE** gives details that modify the main event in a sentence, such as explaining:

- ★ **when** it happened
- ★ **why** it happened
- ★ **under what conditions** it happened.

An **ADVERB CLAUSE** meets three requirements:

1. It always contains a **subject** and a **verb**.
2. It contains **subordinate conjunctions**.

For example:

- ★ When: as, when, while, before, after, until, whenever
- ★ Why: because, as, since
- ★ Under what conditions: if, although, even though
3. It is a **dependent clause** and cannot stand on its own as a sentence because it relies on the main clause for meaning.

POSITION IN A SENTENCE

Adverb clauses can occur:

- ★ at the beginning of a sentence
- ★ in the middle – between a subject and a verb (s-v split)
- ★ at the end of a sentence.

PUNCTUATION

- ★ Beginning: one comma.
- ★ Middle (subject–verb split): bracketing commas.
- ★ End: usually none.

(Note: When the adverb clause comes at the end of the sentence, a comma is usually not required.)

FOR EXAMPLE

When her legs had started to cramp – adverb clause

She was forced to stop. – main clause

When her legs had started to cramp, she was forced to stop.

She was forced to stop when her legs had started to cramp.

EXAMPLES: WHEN, WHY, UNDER WHAT CONDITIONS

1. When it happened (while, as, when, before, after, until)

While she had been exploring the house, the sun had fallen like a sinking stone. (Reveals when the sun had fallen)

The sun, while she had been exploring the house, had fallen like a sinking stone.

The sun had fallen like a sinking stone while she had been exploring the house.

2. Why it happened (because, as, since)

He struggled to stay on his feet because the gusting wind shoved him from side to side.

Because the gusting wind shoved him from side to side, he struggled to stay on his feet.

3. Under what conditions it happened (if, although, even though, though)

It would be too late if she waited any longer.

If she waited any longer, it would be too late.

Although the wooden bridge was rickety and looked ready to collapse, it was their only way to get across the ravine.

She could hear the thud of their boots somewhere behind her even though she couldn't see them.

EXERCISE 1 – CHUNKING (LINKING READING AND WRITING)

1. **She had to keep going because there was nowhere to hide.**

i.   She had to keep going/ because there was nowhere to hide. √
ii. She had to/ keep going because/ there was nowhere to hide.

2. **If she had known what was waiting for her she would have run the other way.**

i.   If she had known what/ was waiting/ for her she/ would have run the/ other way.
ii. If she had known what was waiting for her/ she would have run the other way. √

3. **When he reached the end of the wall he peered cautiously round the corner.**

i.   When he reached the end of the wall/ he peered cautiously/ round the corner. √
ii. When he reached/ the end of/ the wall he peered/ cautiously round the corner.

4. **After sprinting for a few minutes Scarlett began to slow down.**

i.   After/ sprinting for a/ few minutes Scarlett began/ to slow down.
ii. After sprinting for a few minutes/ Scarlett began to slow down. √

5. **Although the building had been deserted for some time he thought he was being watched from one of the upper windows.**

i.   Although the building had been deserted for some time /he thought that he was being watched/ from one of the upper windows. √
ii. Although the building had been/ deserted for some/ time he thought that/ he was/ being watched from one/ of the upper windows.

EXERCISE 2 – CHUNKING INTO MEANINGFUL SENTENCE PARTS

1. Before he tried inserting the key into the lock/ he held it in the palm of his hand/ and stared at the strange interlocking symbols.
2. The puddles jumped to life/ as pellets of water drummed the surface.
3. It would be too dark/ if he waited any longer/ to find the trail.
4. When the sun sank below the horizon/ a black cloak was drawn across the sky.
5. While they had been struggling through the swamp/ the wolves had detected their scent.

EXERCISE 3 – IDENTIFYING THE FUNCTION, CONSTRUCTION, POSITION AND PUNCTUATION OF ADVERB CLAUSES

	Adverb clause	a. Position in sentence: Opening, middle (between subject and verb) or end b. Punctuation i. No commas ii. Bracketing commas iii. One comma separating the adverb clause (AC) from the main clause (MC)	What information does the adverb clause reveal?	Main clause
Model	*if they took any of the hairpin bends too quickly*	*a. beginning* *b. one comma (iii)*	*Under what conditions a sheer drop would await them.*	*A sickening sheer drop awaited them.*
1.	because he knew time was running out	a. end b. no commas	Why did Joe keep glancing at his watch.	Joe kept glancing at his watch.

2.	as she whirled round	a. opening b. one comma separating AC from MC	When her phone fell out of her pocket.	Her mobile phone fell out of her pocket.
3.	even though she was terrified	a. opening b. one comma separating AC from MC	Under what conditions she opened the door – she was terrified.	She was seized with a desperate need to open the door to check if there was anyone there.
4.	while she had been exploring the house	a. middle b. bracketing commas	When the sun had fallen.	The sun had fallen like a sinking stone.
5.	if they continued travelling south	a. end b.no commas	Under what conditions they would have to cross the river.	They would have to cross the river at some stage.
6.	after her eyes had adjusted to the dark	a. middle b. bracketing commas	When she started to pick out shapes.	She gradually started to pick out a few shapes scattered across the room.
7.	since she had no clue where she was	a. opening b. one comma separating AC from MC	Why she had to follow the main road.	Kitty had no choice but to follow the main road.
8.	until she was sure that the man wasn't coming back.	a. end b. no commas	Explains under what conditions she waited.	She waited silently in the shadows.
9.	before she could stagger to her feet	a. opening b. one comma separating AC from MC	When she heard the front door open.	She heard the front door creak open.
10.	whenever she looked up at the mountain	a. opening b. one comma separating AC from MC	When the images of the volcano erupting replayed in her mind.	The images of the day the volcano had erupted and destroyed her village replayed in her mind like a horror movie.

EXERCISE 3 – EXTENSION

	Adverb clause	Main clause	Punctuation a. No commas b. bracketing commas c. One comma separating the relative clause from the main clause	Does the adverb clause make sense without the main clause?
Model	*as the creature charged against the door*	*It rocked back and forth with each assault.*	*One comma*	*No – it does not tell the reader what happened when the creature charged against the door.*
1.	because he knew time was running out	Joe kept glancing at his watch.	No commas	No – it does not tell the reader what happened.
2.	as she whirled round	Her mobile phone fell out of her pocket.	One comma	No – it does not tell the reader what happened when she whirled round.
3.	even though she was terrified	She was seized with a desperate need to open the door to check if anyone was there.	One comma	No – it does not tell the reader what she did.
4.	while she had been exploring the house	The sun had fallen like a sinking stone.	Bracketing commas	No – it does not tell the reader what happened when she was in the house.

5.	if they continued travelling south	They would have to cross the river at some stage.	No comma	No – it does not tell the reader what would happen if they continued travelling south.
6.	after her eyes had adjusted to the dark	She gradually started to pick out a few shapes scattered across the room.	Bracketing commas	No – it does not tell the reader what happened when her eyes adjusted to the dark.
7.	since she had no clue where she was	Kitty had no choice but to follow the main road.	One comma	No – it does not tell the reader why Kitty had no choice.
8.	until she was sure that the man wasn't coming back.	She waited silently in the shadows.	No comma	No – it does not tell the reader what happened when she was sure that the man wasn't coming back.
9.	before she could stagger to her feet	She heard the front door creak open.	One comma	No – it does not tell the reader what happened.
10.	whenever she looked up at the mountain	The images of the day the volcano had erupted and destroyed her village replayed in her mind like a horror movie.	One comma	No – it does not tell the reader what happened when she looked up at the mountain.

EXERCISE 4 – IDENTIFYING ADVERB CLAUSES

1. The crater, <u>while</u> he was collecting fruit from the edge of the forest, had begun belching out a bubble of black smoke and gas.
2. <u>Because</u> the volcano continued to belch out huge clouds of black smoke, the town was covered in thick choking fumes.
3. She had to hold onto the rail to keep her balance <u>whenever the ground vibrated</u>.
4. <u>Before</u> he could warn the village, enormous fireballs had begun to rain from the volcano.
5. The fireballs, <u>as they struck the ground</u>, burst into clouds of sparks.
6. They made hurried preparations to evacuate the village <u>because the volcano was showing ominous signs of awakening</u>.
7. <u>When the truth had finally dawned on her</u>, she had been enveloped by a sense of horror.
8. The house, <u>although it was the middle of the day</u>, had become strangely dark.
9. <u>When the volcano erupted</u>, a hot mixture of rock, gas and ash was hurled from the vent.
10. <u>Although the river of lava was covered in a black crust</u>, there were still pockets of red.

EXERCISE 4 (continued)

	Adverb clause	Information supplied	Punctuation a. No commas b. Bracketing commas c. One comma separating the relative clause from the main clause	Main clause
	as the creature charged against the door	*Explains when the door rocked back and forth.. Beginning*	*c*	*It rocked back and forth with each assault.*
1.	while he was collecting fruit from the edge of the forest	Explains what he was doing when the crater belched out black smoke.	Bracketing commas	The crater had begun belching out a bubble of black smoke and gas.
2.	because the volcano continued to belch out huge clouds of black smoke	Explains why the town was covered in fumes	One comma	The town was covered in thick choking fumes.
3.	whenever the ground vibrated	Explains when she had to hold onto the rail.	No comma	She had to hold onto the rail to keep her balance.
4.	before he could warn the village	Explains when the fireballs rained from the volcano	One comma	Enormous fireballs had begun to rain from the volcano.

5.	**as** they struck the ground	Explains when the fireballs burst into clouds of sparks.	Bracketing commas	The fireballs burst into clouds of sparks.
6.	**because** the volcano was showing ominous signs of awakening	Explains why they prepared to evacuate the village.	No commas	They made hurried preparations to evacuate the village.
7.	**when** the truth had finally dawned on her	Explains when she had been enveloped by a sense of horror.	One comma	She had been enveloped by a sense of horror.
8.	**although** it was the middle of the day	Explains under what conditions it was strangely dark	Bracketing commas	The house had become strangely dark.
9.	**when** the volcano erupted	Explains when the hot mixture was hurled from the vent.	One comma	A hot mixture of rock, gases and ash was hurled from the vent.
10.	**although** the river of lava was covered in a black crust	Explains under what conditions there were pockets of red.	One comma	There were still pockets of red.

EXERCISE 5 – MATCHING ADVERB CLAUSES

Combined sentences
1.j. <u>While he was crossing the bridge</u>, a large chunk of rock had slammed into the rock-face above the bridge.
2.e. She prayed that the rickety wooden bridge over the rapids would hold her weight <u>because there was no other way to cross the rapids</u>.
3.a. <u>When the fog had descended</u>, it had cloaked the trees in wreaths of swirling grey.
4.b. She did not see the trip wire that wriggled across the ground <u>because its barbed spikes were hidden by layers of dead leaves</u>.
5.d. <u>Although it appeared dormant at the moment</u>, the volcano was boiling and bubbling deep underground.
6.g. <u>After a couple of minutes had passed</u>, she checked the corridor.
7.i. They were forced to retrace their steps to the iron gate <u>when they reached a dead end</u>.
8.c. <u>If they had chosen the right path</u>, they should be close to the entrance to the Inca city.
9.f. <u>Even though his legs felt like rubber</u>, he tried to keep moving.
10.h. Rob, <u>because he had heard footsteps on the stairs</u>, yanked Kitty back into the room.

EXERCISE 6 – UNSCRAMBLING SENTENCE PARTS

1.   Kitty prayed that she had taken the right path *because she was running out of time*.

Because she was running out of time, Kitty prayed that she had taken the right path.

Kitty, *because she was running out of time*, prayed that she had taken the right path.

2.   Rob opened the door and slipped through into the reception area *before stopping to think*.

Before stopping to think, Rob opened the door and slipped through into the reception area.

Rob, *before stopping to think*, opened the door and slipped through into the reception area.

3.   *After spring had thawed the frosty ground, green shoots started to appear in the woods.*

Green shoots started to appear in the *woods after spring had thawed the frosty ground*.

Green shoots, *after spring had thawed the frosty ground*, started to appear in the woods.

4.   *If he had never found that chest*, Rob would not have discovered his father's secret identity.

Rob would not have discovered his father's secret identity *if he had never found that chest*.

Rob, *if he had never found that chest*, would not have discovered his father's secret identity.

5.   *Although the main exit was blocked*, Kitty knew there was another way out of the building.

Kitty knew there was another way out of the building *although the main exit was blocked*.

Kitty, *although the main exit was blocked*, knew there was another way out of the building.

EXERCISE 7 – COMBINING SENTENCES

1.   When the trail became more difficult to follow, Rob had to use his staff to force a path through the undergrowth.

Rob had to use his staff to force a path through the undergrowth when the trail became more difficult to follow.

Rob, when the trail became more difficult to follow, had to use his staff to force a path through the undergrowth.

2.   Kitty knew he was standing in front of the bins because she could clearly smell the stench of his stale sweat.

Because she could clearly smell the stench of his stale sweat, Kitty knew he was standing in front of the bins.

Kitty, because she could clearly smell the stench of his stale sweat, knew he was standing in front of the bins.

3.   While she had been on the tube, night had fallen and blanketed the streets in darkness.

Night had fallen and blanketed the streets in darkness while she had been on the tube.

Night, while she had been on the tube, had fallen and blanketed the streets in darkness.

4.   Although she was in the middle of the city, the streets were deserted.

The streets were deserted although she was in the middle of the city.

The streets, although she was in the middle of the city, were deserted.

5.   Kitty waited silently in the shadows until she was sure that the man wasn't coming back.

Until she was sure that the man wasn't coming back, Kitty waited silently in the shadows.

Kitty, until she was sure that the man wasn't coming back, waited silently in the shadows.

CHALLENGE

6. <u>When the torch shone above her head</u>, every nerve in her body urged her not to move <u>even though pins and needles prickled painfully in her left leg</u>.

Every nerve in her body urged her not to move <u>when the torch shone above her head</u>, <u>even though pins and needles prickled painfully in her left leg</u>.

<u>Even though pins and needles prickled painfully in her left leg</u>, <u>when the torch shone above her head</u>, every nerve in her body urged her not to move.

EXERCISE 8 – CHOOSE THE APPROPRIATE CONJUNCTION (CUED EXERCISE)

1. *They would have been lost in the swirling blizzards <u>if they had not strung guide ropes between the buildings</u>.*

<u>If they had not strung guide ropes between the buildings</u>, they would have been lost in the swirling blizzards.

They, <u>if they had not strung guide ropes between the buildings</u>, would have been lost in the swirling blizzards.

2. *He needed to cross a narrow, knife-edged ridge <u>before he could reach the summit</u>.*

<u>Before he could reach the summit</u>, he needed to cross a narrow, knife-edged ridge.

He, *<u>before he could reach the summit</u>*, needed to cross a narrow, knife-edged ridge.

3. *<u>Because she was sprinting to get to the train</u> before the doors closed, she didn't have time to answer her phone.*

She didn't have time to answer her phone <u>because she was sprinting to get to the train before the doors closed</u>.

She, *<u>because she was sprinting to get to the train before the doors closed</u>*, didn't have time to answer her phone.

4. *An orange glow appeared on the horizon <u>while they watched the sun set</u>.*
    <u>While they watched the sun set</u>, an orange glow appeared on the horizon.

An orange glow, <u>while they watched the sun set</u>, appeared on the horizon.

5. *<u>Even though her hands were trembling</u>, she eventually managed to insert the key into the lock.*

She eventually managed to insert the key into the lock <u>even though her hands were trembling</u>.

She, *<u>even though her hands were trembling</u>,* eventually managed to insert the key into the lock.

EXERCISE 9 – COMBINING SENTENCES

1. *<u>Although they monitor Earth's movements</u>, scientists still can't predict exactly when a volcano will erupt.*

Scientists still can't predict exactly when a volcano will erupt <u>although they monitor Earth's movements</u>.

Scientists, <u>although they monitor Earth's movements</u>, still can't predict exactly when a volcano will erupt.

2. They had a nerve-wracking journey through dense, treacherous forests that were inhabited by outlaws <u>before they eventually reached their destination.</u>

<u>Before they eventually reached their destination</u>, they had a nerve-wracking journey through dense, treacherous forests that were inhabited by outlaws.

They, <u>before they eventually reached their destination</u>, had a nerve-wracking journey through dense, treacherous forests that were inhabited by outlaws.

3. *Someone had walked into his room when he was asleep.*

When he was asleep, someone had walked into his room.

Someone, when he was asleep, had walked into his room.

4. *Rob was on edge and kept checking his watch <u>while he waited for them to return</u>.*

<u>While he waited for them to return</u>, Rob was on edge and kept checking his watch.

Rob, <u>while he waited for them to return</u>, was on edge and kept checking his watch.

5. *Kitty couldn't see the man's eyes <u>because they were hidden behind a pair of silver-mirrored sunglasses</u>.*

<u>Because they were hidden behind a pair of silver-mirrored sunglasses</u>, Kitty couldn't see the man's eyes.

Kitty, <u>because they were hidden behind a pair of silver-mirrored sunglasses</u>, couldn't see the man's eyes.

EXERCISE 10 – COMBINING SENTENCES

1. *Rob paced backwards and forwards across the room <u>while he waited for the phone to ring</u>.*

Rob, <u>while he waited for the phone to ring</u>, paced backwards and forwards across the room.

<u>While he waited for the phone to ring</u>, Rob paced backwards and forwards across the room.

2. *Rob's pulse started to race <u>when he realised that he had run in the wrong direction</u>.*

<u>When he realised that he had run in the wrong direction</u>, Rob's pulse started to race.

Rob's pulse, <u>when he realised that he had run in the wrong direction</u>, started to race.

3. *His legs buckled under him <u>before he could get to the chair</u>,* and he fell to the floor.

<u>Before he could get to the chair</u>, his legs buckled under him, and he fell to the floor.

His legs, <u>before he could get to the chair,</u> buckled under him and he fell to the floor.

4. *<u>Even though he didn't want to leave the safety of his bedroom</u>, Rob knew he had no choice.*

Rob knew he had no choice <u>even though he didn't want to leave the safety of his bedroom</u>.

Rob, <u>even though he didn't want to leave the safety of his bedroom</u>, knew he had no choice.

5. *Rob couldn't see who was in the car <u>because the windows were tinted black</u>.*

<u>Because the windows were tinted black</u>, Rob couldn't see who was in the car.

Rob, <u>because the windows were tinted black</u>, couldn't see who was in the car.

7

Relative (adjective) clauses

EXERCISE 1 – CHUNKING (LINKING READING AND WRITING)

Punctuation has been removed for this exercise.

INSTRUCTIONS

1. In pairs, take turns to read each of the sentences aloud.
2. Decide which of the sentences is divided into meaningful sentence parts.
3. Discuss and explain your decisions.

EXERCISE

1. **She squeezed through the gap in the fence that led to the rear entrance.**

   i.   She squeezed through/ the gap in the fence that/ led to the rear entrance.
   ii. She squeezed/ through the gap in the fence/ that led to the rear entrance.

DOI: 10.4324/9781032662862-8

2. **John whose nerves were on edge saw potential dangers and traps behind every corner and every open door.**

i.   John whose nerves/ were on edge/ saw potential dangers/ and traps behind every corner/ and every open door.

ii.   John/ whose nerves were on edge/ saw potential dangers and traps/ behind every corner/ and every open door.

3. **The building that was at the top of the lane had been for sale for several years because it was rumoured to be haunted.**

i.   The building/ that was at the top/ of the lane/ had been for sale/ for several years/ because it was rumoured to be haunted.

ii.   The building that/ was at the top/ of the lane had/ been for sale for/ several years because/ it was rumoured to be haunted.

4. **The roaring rapids which poured out of the gorges plunged into the swirling mist below.**

i.   The roaring/ rapids which poured/ out of the gorges/ plunged into the swirling mist below.

ii.   The roaring rapids/ which poured out of the gorges/ plunged into the swirling mist below.

5. **James who was bubbling with anticipation shifted from one foot to the other.**

i.   James/ who was bubbling with anticipation/ shifted from one foot to the other.

ii.   James who was/ bubbling with anticipation/ shifted from one foot to the other.

EXERCISE 2 – CHUNKING INTO MEANINGFUL SENTENCE PARTS

Punctuation has been removed for this exercise.

INSTRUCTIONS

1. In pairs, read the sentences aloud.
2. Using a slash, chunk the sentences into meaningful parts.
3. Discuss and explain your decisions.

Note: The sentences can be chunked in a variety of ways. At this stage, the aim should be to guide students to chunking the relative clause as a sentence part.

EXAMPLE

The chilly air **which wrapped around Andrew like an icy blanket** froze his breath in clouds around him.

The chilly air/ which wrapped around Andrew/ like an icy blanket/ froze his breath/ in clouds around him.

The chilly air/ which wrapped around Andrew like an icy blanket/ froze his breath/ in clouds around him.

The chilly air/ which wrapped around Andrew like an icy blanket/ froze his breath in clouds around him.

EXERCISE

1. The beach which was a long arc of golden sand was sheltered by dunes and large umbrella pines.
2. The torch which was now directed at the bins sent a stream of light onto the ground inches from her left hand.
3. The man who had stopped to check they were okay had helped them to find their way back to the bus stop.
4. The hurricane which was roaring around the house rattled the windows pounded on the roof and hammered on the doors.
5. The gigantic mountains whose snowy peaks sparkled in the sunlight soared into the sky above the alpine village.

EXERCISE 3 – IDENTIFYING THE FUNCTION, CONSTRUCTION, POSITION AND PUNCTUATION OF RELATIVE (ADJECTIVE) CLAUSES

In the following sentences, the relative (adjective) clauses have been underlined.

INSTRUCTIONS

In the table provided:
1. Write out the relative clauses.
2. Highlight or circle the words (relative pronouns) at the start of each relative clause.
3. Identify what additional information is provided by the relative clause.
4. Make a note of where the relative clause is positioned in the sentence (middle or end).
5. Make a note of punctuation:
    ★ no commas
    ★ bracketing commas
    ★ one comma separating the relative clause from the main clause.

EXTENSION

Remove the relative clause from the sentence and identify whether the meaning of the sentence is still clear. See the Review section for additional guidance.

MODEL

The creature charged against the front door, <u>which rocked back and forth with each assault</u>.

Main clause:	The creature charged against the front door.
Relative clause:	which rocked back and forth with each assault.
Position:	end of the sentence
Punctuation:	one comma after the relative clause

What information is supplied?	*What happened to the door when the creature charged against it.*
Independent clause:	Adds detail but can be removed without affecting the meaning or clarity of the sentence.

EXERCISE

1. The dog <u>who was on a lead</u> barked viciously at any passer-by.
2. Kitty had been followed all morning by a girl <u>who was wearing a bright orange hoodie</u>.
3. Rob, <u>whose eyes were seething with fury</u>, slammed the door as he left the room.
4. She slipped and slid her way through the gooey slime, <u>which was now almost up to her calves</u>.
5. Making any progress was difficult through the boggy ground, <u>which was not only muddy but choked with dead branches and leaves</u>.
6. The only sign of life was a torn curtain <u>that hung askew on one of the upstairs windows</u>.
7. The narrow street <u>that branched off to the left of the high street</u> was dark and deserted and threatened danger from every shadowy corner and doorway.
8. Christopher Columbus, <u>who was an Italian explorer</u>, discovered America.
9. The location <u>that had been marked on the map</u> led him to a clearing in the forest and the ancient ruins of the Inca temple.
10. Nigel, <u>who had lathered large quantities of butter onto the warm croissant</u>, devoured it in two huge bites.

EXERCISE 3 (continued)

	Relative (adjective) clause	a. Position in sentence: Middle or end b. Punctuation i. No commas ii. Bracketing commas iii. One comma separating the relative clause from the main clause	What information does the relative clause reveal?	Main clause
	which rocked back and forth with each assault	*a. end* *b. iii*	*What happened to the door when the creature charged against it.*	*The creature charged against the front door.*
1.		a. b.		
2.		a. b.		
3.		a. b.		
4.		a. b.		
5.		a. b.		
6.		a. b.		
7.		a. b.		
8.		a. b.		
9.		a. b.		
10.		a. b.		

EXERCISE 3 – EXTENSION

	Relative (adjective) clause	Main clause	Punctuation a. No commas b. Bracketing commas c. One comma separating the relative clause from the main clause	Does the main clause make sense without the relative clause (RC)?
	which rocked back and forth with each assault	**The creature charged against the front door.**	**c. one comma**	**YES**
1.				
2.				
3.				
4.				
5.				
6.				
7.				
8.				
9.				
10.				

EXERCISE 4 – IDENTIFYING RELATIVE CLAUSES

INSTRUCTIONS

1.   Underline the relative clauses in the sentences below.

EXTENSION

This can be done orally as a discussion or by completing the table below.

2.   Identify where the relative clauses are positioned in the sentences.

i.   Middle (between the subject and verb)
ii. End (after the main clause)

3.   How are they punctuated?

i.   No commas
ii.   Bracketing commas
iii. One comma separating the relative clause from the main clause.

4.   What information does the relative clause provide?
5.   Is the relative clause essential to the meaning of the sentence or is it non-essential (the sentence will still make sense if the relative clause is removed)?

(At this stage, it is important to facilitate discussion as to whether the relative clause provides essential or non-essential information. Further guidance is provided in the Review section.)

EXERCISE

1. Carnivores are animals who eat mainly meat and hunt for their prey.
2. The mountain peaks, which were like gigantic arrowheads, rocketed above the alpine village.
3. There was a trumpet blast from the end of the lists, which brought a hush over the crowd.
4. The door that opened out onto the courtyard was blocked by a huge wooden chest wrapped in chains.
5. The elderly lady, whose face was ashen and twisted with pain, looked like a walking skeleton as she hobbled towards the bench.
6. Without thinking he took off down the street after the man who had grabbed his bag.
7. The pockets of corpse flowers, which are bright red blooms the size of dinner plates, emitted a rancid reek of rotting flesh.
8. The torrents of water that poured over the top of the cliffs created a raging, foaming waterfall.
9. Black fungi, which were like swollen dead fingers, poked out of the undergrowth.
10. Rob, whose arms were folded across his chest, clicked his tongue impatiently and rolled his eyes as he watched their childish antics.

EXERCISE 4 (continued)

	Relative (adjective) clause	What information does it reveal? Is it: a. Essential (E) b. Non-essential (N-E)	Punctuation a. No commas b. Bracketing commas c. One comma separating the relative clause from the main clause	Main clause
	Which rocked back and forth with each assault	*What happened to the door when the creature charged against it.* *Non-essential*	*C*	*The creature charged against the front door*
1.				
2.				
3.				
4.				
5.				
6.				
7.				
8.				
9.				
10.				

EXERCISE 5 – MATCHING RELATIVE CLAUSES

INSTRUCTIONS

1. Match the relative clauses with their respective main clauses.
2. Write out each sentence, inserting and underlining the correct relative clause, taking note of the punctuation indicated.

EXERCISE

Main clause	Relative clauses
1. She edged deeper into the tangled thicket ^.	a. which looked like crooked spires
2. A terrace of cottages, ^ , lined the streets leading to the harbour.	b. that would lead her to the Inca ruins
3. The tall, dark silhouette ^ had disappeared by the time she turned around.	c. which could be seen for miles
4. The volcano emitted a huge column of dense black smoke, ^	d. which exploded like bullets on the trees
5. The rain, ^, quickly flooded the path.	e. which had brightly coloured doors and shutters
6. Sophia Jex-Blake, ^, led a campaign for women to be allowed to attend university.	f. whose reflection she had seen in the mirror
7. Above their wooden cabin, icy mountain peaks, ^, burst out the trees.	g. who had answered the phone
8. Polar regions are permanently covered by an icecap, ^.	h. who was a doctor and a teacher
9. The woman ^ was rude and unhelpful.	i. [1]who was sure she had heard footsteps [2]that no one was following them
10. Kitty, ^, occasionally turned and walked backwards to check ^.	j. which is an enormous white dome of ice and snow

EXERCISE 6 – UNSCRAMBLING SENTENCE PARTS

INSTRUCTIONS

1. Unscramble the list of sentence parts and write out the sentence.
2. Underline the sentence parts that are relative clauses.
3. Use the same process as in previous exercises to decide whether the relative clause is essential or non-essential and punctuate the relative clause correctly.

Tip: The capitalized sentence parts begin the sentences.

Clue to punctuation: is the relative clause describing the noun or identifying it? Take out the relative clause and decide whether the sentence still makes sense. If it the meaning is no longer clear, it is an essential relative clause and there are no commas.

EXTENSION

4. Substitute your own relative clause into the main clause.
5. Use the sentence structure of each sentence to write your own imitation (including a relative clause)

EXAMPLE

a.   which was a swampy path of squelching rotten leaves
b. A narrow track
c. twisted between the trees

A narrow track, which was a swampy path of squelching rotten leaves, twisted between the trees.

EXAMPLE OF IMITATIONS

1. A narrow track, which was a tangled path of needle-sharp thorns, twisted between the trees.
2. A wide avenue, which was an uneven street of cobbled stones, ran between the ancient monuments.

EXERCISE

1a.   down the alley
1b.   that was opposite the coffee shop
1c.   She darted

_____
_____

_____

2a.   through a blazing, knee-high carpet of bluebells
2b.   They waded
2c.   whose fragrant scent lingered in the air

_____

_____

_____

3a.   who were lost
3b.   had little hope of rescue
3c.   The explorers
3d.   in an ice-bound wilderness
3e.   from the outside world

_____
_____

_____

4a.   which hung from the ceiling in the kitchen
4b.   The buzzing strip light
4c.   was covered in dead flies

_____
_____

_____

5a.   who was dragging an enormous suitcase
5b.   Kitty
5c.   struggled to get onto the train

_____
_____

_____

EXERCISE 7 – COMBINING SENTENCES (CUED EXERCISE)

Sentences are broken down into base sentences (called kernel sentences).

INSTRUCTIONS

1. Cross out any repeated or unnecessary words.
2. Using a relative clause, combine the two/three base sentences into one sentence.
3. Cues provided in brackets (,**WHO**…,) go at the beginning of the clause which is combined with the base sentence to complete the transformation (see example below).
4. The punctuation to be used is indicated.
5. The position of the relative clause is indicated by a ^.

EXAMPLE

a. The girl, ^, sat quietly in the window seat.
b. ~~She~~ had piercing bright blue eyes. (**WHO**)

The girl, who had piercing bright blue eyes, sat quietly in the window seat.

EXERCISE

1a. Kitty, ^, quickly covered her mouth.
1b. Kitty had blurted out a little squeak of delight. (**WHO**)
_____
_____

2a. The start of a river, ^ , can be found in upland areas.
2b. It is called the source. (**WHICH**)
_____
_____

3a. She forced herself to ignore the burning lactic acid ^.
3b. The lactic acid was creeping up her legs. (**THAT**)
_____
_____

4a. Kitty, ^ , took off her glasses, closed her eyes and slumped back in her chair.

4b. Kitty <u>vision was blurred with fatigue</u>. (**WHOSE**)

_____

_____

5a. The passage ^ was concealed behind a red curtain. ,^

5b. The passage <u>led into the main hall</u>. (**THAT**)

5c. The curtain <u>was embroidered with the family's coat of arms and a huge red lion</u>. (**WHICH**)

_____

_____

_____

_____

EXERCISE 8 – COMBINING SENTENCES (CUED EXERCISE)

The clause to be used to form a relative clause is underlined.

INSTRUCTIONS

1. Choose the appropriate relative pronoun to construct the relative clause: **which, who, whose, that**.

2. The position of the clause is marked with ^.

EXAMPLE

1a. Twilight was closing in. ,^

1b. It <u>made her feel uneasy</u>.

Relative clause: which made her feel uneasy.

Combined sentence: Twilight was closing in, <u>which made her feel uneasy</u>.

EXERCISE

1a. An enormous man, ^, blocked the doorway.

1b. The man had shoulders like granite boulders.

_____

_____

2a. Kitty, ^, stared intently at something in the distance.

2b. Her hands were pressed against her chin.

_____

_____

3a. A deafening boom, ^, echoed around the town.

3b. It sounded like the roar of a jet engine.

_____

_____

4a. The gigantic wave had formed into a raging wall of water. ^

4b. It was surging towards the beach.

_____

_____

5a. He had met a woman. ^ ^

5b. She knew where he could find the shop.

5c. The shop sold ancient maps.

_____

_____

EXERCISE 9 – COMBINING SENTENCES (CUED EXERCISES)

★ Relative pronouns to be used are indicated in brackets.
★ The position of the relative clause and the correct punctuation are not indicated.

Students need to know that relative clauses:
    a.   follow the noun (pronoun) to which they refer
    b.   can be positioned at the middle of the sentence (between the subject and verb) or at the end of the sentence
    c.   the punctuation depends on whether the relative clause is essential to the clarity of the sentence or not.

EXAMPLE

    a.   The mountain towered above them.
    b.   Its peaks pierced the clouds. (**WHOSE**)

INSTRUCTIONS

1.   Highlight the noun and use a ^ to indicate where the relative clause should be inserted.
    a.   The **mountain** ^ towered above them.
    b.   ~~Its~~ peaks pierced the clouds. (**WHOSE**)
2.   Cross out any repeated or unnecessary words.
3.   Write out the combined sentence.
    The mountain, **whose peaks pierced the clouds**, towered above them.

EXERCISE

1.1   A fiery red flare was visible above the burning mountain.

1.2   The flare was like a spectacular sunset. (**WHICH**)

_____

_____

2.1   A river of lava slid menacingly down the slopes.

2.2   Its red sludge oozed out of the cracks in the volcano. (**WHOSE**)

_____

_____

3.1   A volcano is located on the boundary of two tectonic plates.

3.2   It is a vent at the surface of the earth through which magma and other volcanic materials are ejected. (**WHICH**)

_____

_____

4.1   The candles were perfumed with pine needles and cinnamon.

4.2   They filled the room with the scents of Christmas. (**THAT**)

_____

_____

5.1   Maya cities usually had a ceremonial centre.

5.2   A Maya ceremonial centre contained great pyramids, temples and palaces. (**WHICH**)

_____

_____

_____

6.1   Scott, Shackleton and Amundsen set out on extremely hazardous expeditions to the Arctic and Antarctic.

6.2   They were famous explorers in the 20th century. (**WHO**)

_____

_____

_____

EXERCISE 10 – COMBINING SENTENCES (OPEN EXERCISE)

INSTRUCTIONS

Students must decide:

1. How to combine the two sentences.
2. On the appropriate relative pronoun to select.
3. Where to position the relative clause.
4. How to punctuate the clause correctly in the combined sentence.

TIPS

a. The relative clause follows the noun it describes or identifies. (insert a ∧ beside the noun).
b. Decide whether the noun is a person (who, whose) or an object, animal, idea, etc. (that, which, whose).
c. Delete any repeated or unnecessary words (as shown below).
d. Decide whether the additional information describes the noun (non-essential so comma(s) required) or identifies the noun (essential so no comma(s) required).

a. The loud chimes, ∧ , came from the ancient, grandfather clock in the main hall.
b. ~~The loud chimes~~ shattered the silence every night at midnight.

i. chimes – object (relative pronoun – that or which)
ii. Non-essential as the chimes have already been identified as coming from the grandfather clock in the main hall.

> The loud chimes, <u>which shattered the silence every night at midnight</u>, came from the ancient grandfather clock in the main hall.

EXAMPLE

She darted down the alley **that was opposite the coffee shop**.

1.   Is the relative clause '**that was opposite the coffee shop**' essential to the meaning of the sentence and therefore not separated from the main clause by a comma(s)?

   a.   *Essential*

She darted down the alley that was opposite the coffee shop.

This sentence tells the reader that there were other alleys, and she darted down the one opposite the coffee shop.

   b.   *Non-essential*

   She darted down the alley, that was opposite the coffee shop.

1.   This sentence tells the reader that there was only one alley, and it was opposite the coffee shop.

2.   Remove the relative clause

   She darted down the alley.

   Does the sentence still make sense?

a.   Yes – if there is only one alley.

b.   No – if there is more than one alley and it is necessary to identify which alley she darted down.

EXERCISE

1a.   There was no sign of the blood-spattered knight.

1b.   He had vanished into thin air at dawn.

_____

_____

2a.   From the top of the mountain, there was a dramatic view.

2b.   It took her breath away.

_____

_____

3a. The goblin was obviously the leader of the group.

3b. His white beard reached almost to his knees.

_____

_____

4a. The beam of light lit up an enormous dragon.

4b. It had been painted over the entrance to the cave.

_____

_____

5a. The smell of eucalyptus filled the room with its minty scent.

5b. It wafted in from the open window.

_____

_____

EXERCISE 11 – CREATING RELATIVE CLAUSES

INSTRUCTIONS

1. Use the relative clauses to write a main clause.
2. Insert the relative clause provided into main clause to complete the sentence.

MODEL

Relative clause: who had a mop of curly blonde hair

Main clause: i. The boy was the first to dive into the water.

ii. The woman was shouting at the waitress.

The boy who had a mop of curly blonde hair was the first to dive into the water.

The woman who had a mop of curly blonde hair was shouting at the waitress.

EXERCISE

1. who was wearing a red hoodie and faded jeans

    _____

    _____

2. whose voice was a high-pitched screech

    _____

    _____

3. whose eyes were scrunched shut

    _____

    _____

4. who was rude and unhelpful

    _____

    _____

5. who was kind and patient

    _____

    _____

6. whose face was a picture of determination

    _____

    _____

7. which dangled from the ceiling

    _____

    _____

8. that covered the walls

    _____

    _____

9. which wafted in from the open window

    _____

    _____

10. that echoed around the building

_____

_____

Note:

It is important to connect reading and writing by highlighting and collecting relative clauses found in class texts to add to students' writing toolkit. The exercises above can be used as a template to investigate relative clauses found in a class text.

SECTION 2 – REVIEW

1. What information do relative (adjective) clauses reveal? What questions do they answer?
2. Which words usually begin relative clauses?
3. Where can relative clauses be positioned in a sentence?
4.a. When is one comma used for a relative clause?
   b. When are two commas used for a relative clause?
   c. When are no commas used?
6. How can relative clauses improve your writing?

WHAT ARE RELATIVE (ADJECTIVE) CLAUSES?

A relative clause (also called an adjective clause) is a sentence part (grammar tool) that:

a. Makes a statement about a **NOUN** (person, place, object, idea, process etc.) in a sentence.

b. Functions as **an adjective** and answer the questions:
   ★ **Who** or **what** is the **NOUN**? OR **what** did the **NOUN do**? (**who, which, that**)
   ★ What did the **NOUN** have? (**whose**)

1.   Begins with a **relative pronoun:**
WHO, WHICH, THAT, WHOSE

a.   who (refers to people)
b.   that, which (refers to things, animals and ideas)
c.   whose (refers to people, things, animals, ideas etc.)

2.   It contains a **SUBJECT** and a **VERB.**
Therefore, it is a **CLAUSE** not a **PHRASE**.

POSITION IN A SENTENCE

Relative (adjective) clauses occur:

★   immediately after the <u>noun (pronoun)</u> they refer to.

FOR EXAMPLE

The <u>girl</u>, **who had short pink hair**,
The <u>house</u>, **whose door was painted bright red**,
The <u>thunder</u>, **which had been rumbling in the distance**,
The <u>door</u> **that led to the basement**

They can be positioned:

a.   in the middle of the sentence
b.   at the end of a sentence.

THE POSITION OF THE RELATIVE CLAUSE IS IMPORTANT.

For example:

Main clause: The creature charged against the front door.
Relative clause: which rocked back and forth with each assault

In the above example, there are two nouns – **creature** and **front door**.

    a.   The creature, **which rocked back and forth with each assault**, charged against the front door.

    b.   The creature charged against the front door, **which rocked back and forth with each assault**.

The position of the relative clause is important because (as shown in examples (a) and (b) above) it changes the meaning of the sentence.

In (a) the creature rocked back and forth with each assault.

In (b) the door rocked back and forth with each assault.

TWO TYPES OF RELATIVE CLAUSES

1. ESSENTIAL (DEFINING) CLAUSES

    ★   Identify the **specific** noun or pronoun being described.

FOR EXAMPLE

a.   *Alison is staying with her sister **who lives by the sea**.*

Relative clause:	**who** lives by the sea
Position in the sentence:	at the **end** of the sentence after **the noun it is identifying**, 'her sister'
Information supplied:	identifies which sister Alison is living with – the one who lives 'by the sea'
How is it punctuated?	*no commas – therefore, it is essential to identifying the noun*

Remove the relative clause: Alison is staying with her sister.

Is the relative clause <u>essential</u> to the meaning or clarity of the sentence?

If Alison has **more than one sister**: YES, otherwise the reader doesn't know **which sister** Alison is staying with.

---

2. NON-ESSENTIAL (NON-DEFINING) CLAUSES

★ Describe a noun or pronoun whose meaning has already been clearly defined.

EXAMPLE 1

2a.   *Alison is staying with her sister, **who lives by the sea**.*

Relative clause:	**who** lives by the sea
Position in the sentence:	at the **end** of the sentence after **the noun it is describing**, 'Alison's sister'
Information supplied:	describes where Alison's sister lives – 'by the sea'
How is it punctuated?	*one comma separating the relative clause from the main clause, which indicates the relative clause can be removed without affecting the meaning of the sentence.*
Remove the relative clause:	Alison is staying with her sister.

If Alison only has one sister, the main clause will still make sense without the relative clause.

2b.   *Alison is staying with her sister, Trish, who lives by the sea.*

Position in the sentence:	at the **end** of the sentence after **the noun it is describing,** 'Trish'
Information supplied:	describes where Trish lives – 'by the sea'
How is it punctuated?	*one comma separating the relative clause from the main clause, which indicates the relative clause can be removed without affecting the meaning of the sentence.*
Remove the relative clause:	Alison is staying with her sister, Trish.

Alison's sister is identified as Trish, so the main clause still makes sense.

EXAMPLE 2

*An old tramp, **who was frail and hunched**, shuffled across the road.*

Relative clause:	**who** was frail and hunched
Position:	middle of the sentence (between the **subject** and **verb**) – bracketing commas
Information supplied:	what the old tramp man was like – **frail and hunched**
Remove the relative clause:	An old tramp shuffled across the road.

Is the relative clause <u>essential</u>: **NO**

Does the main clause give sufficient information about the tramp? **YES**

How is the relative clause punctuated?

Bracketing commas because it is a **non-essential clause** (describes the tramp) and can be removed without affecting the meaning or clarity of the sentence.

NOTE:

That should only be used to introduce an **essential relative clause,** i.e. if the clause is removed, the sentence does not make sense and the reader would not know which **NOUN** is being referred to.

For example:

* ★ The clumps of dark wiry hair **that hung from his nostrils** waggled when he talked.
* ★ The key **that opens the back door** has gone missing.

Every aspect of writing instruction should make use of authentic texts (books or articles being read by a class or an individual student) to collect examples of where an author has used the grammar tool under investigation.

PUNCTUATION

1. Essential (defining)

no commas

2. Non-essential (non-defining)

i. middle of the sentence:	bracketing commas
ii. end of the sentence:	single comma separating the relative clause from the main clause

TIPS: DECIDING WHETHER RELATIVE CLAUSE IS ESSENTIAL OR NON-ESSENTIAL

The explorers **who were lost in an ice-bound wilderness** had little hope of any rescue from the outside world.

Is the relative clause '**who were lost in an ice-bound wilderness**' essential to the meaning of the sentence and therefore not separated from the main clause by a comma(s)?

a. Essential

The explorers **who were lost in an ice-bound wilderness** had little hope of any rescue from the outside world.

This sentence tells the reader that there were other explorers who weren't lost in the ice-bound wilderness.

b. Non-essential

The explorers, **who were lost in an ice-bound wilderness**, had little hope of any rescue from the outside world.

This tells the reader that all the explorers were lost in an ice-bound wilderness.

EXERCISE 1 – CHUNKING (LINKING READING AND WRITING)

1. **She squeezed through the gap in the fence that led to the rear entrance.**

   i. She squeezed through/ the gap in the fence that/ led to the rear entrance.

   ii. She squeezed/ through the gap in the fence/ that led to the rear entrance. √

2. **John whose nerves were on edge saw potential dangers and traps behind every corner and every open door.**

   i. John whose nerves/ were on edge/ saw potential dangers/ and traps behind every corner/ and every open door.

   ii. John/ whose nerves were on edge/ saw potential dangers and traps/ behind every corner/ and every open door. √

3. **The building that was at the top of the lane had been for sale for several years because it was rumoured to be haunted.**

   i. The building/ that was at the top/ of the lane/ had been for sale/ for several years/ because it was rumoured to be haunted. √

   ii. The building that/ was at the top/ of the lane had/ been for sale for/ several years because/ it was rumoured to be haunted.

4. **The roaring rapids which poured out of the gorges plunged into the swirling mist below.**

   The roaring/ rapids which poured/ out of the gorges/ plunged into the swirling mist below.

   The roaring rapids/ which poured out of the gorges/ plunged into the swirling mist below. √

5. **James who was bubbling with anticipation shifted from one foot to the other.**

   James/ who was bubbling with anticipation/ shifted from one foot to the other. √

   James who was/ bubbling with anticipation/ shifted from one foot to the other.

EXERCISE 2 – CHUNKING INTO MEANINGFUL SENTENCE PARTS

1. The beach/ <u>which was a long arc of golden sand</u>/ was sheltered by dunes and large umbrella pines.
2. The torch/ <u>which was now directed at the bins</u>/ sent a stream of light/ onto the ground inches from her left hand.
3. The man/ <u>who had stopped to check they were okay</u>/ had helped them to find their way/ back to the bus stop.
4. The hurricane/ <u>which was roaring around the house</u>/ rattled the windows/ pounded on the roof/ and hammered on the doors.
5. The gigantic mountains/ <u>whose snowy peaks sparkled in the sunlight</u>/ soared into the sky/ above the alpine village.

EXERCISE 3 – IDENTIFYING THE FUNCTION, CONSTRUCTION, POSITION AND PUNCTUATION OF RELATIVE (ADJECTIVE) CLAUSES

	Relative clause	Position in sentence: Middle or end Punctuation	What information does it reveal? Is it: a. Essential (E) b. Non-essential (N-E)	Main clause
	which rocked back and forth with each assault	*a. End*	*What happened to the door (N-E)*	*The creature charged against the front door*
1.	who was on a lead	middle no commas	Identifies which dog was barking viciously (E)	The dog barked viciously at any passer-by.
2.	who was wearing a bright orange hoodie	end no commas	Identifies which girl had been following Kitty (E)	Kitty had been followed all morning by a girl.
3.	whose eyes were seething with fury	middle bracketing commas	Describes Rob's eyes (NE)	Rob slammed the door as he left the room.
4.	which was now almost up to her calves	end one comma	Describes the depth of the gooey slime (N-E)	She slipped and slid her way through the gooey slime.
5.	which was not only muddy but choked with dead branches and leaves	end one comma	Describes the boggy ground (N-E)	Making any progress was difficult through the boggy ground.

6.	that hung askew on one of the upstairs windows	end no commas	Identifies which curtain (E)	The only sign of life was a torn curtain.
7.	that branched off to the left of the high street	middle no commas	Identifies which narrow street (E)	The narrow street was dark and deserted and threatened danger from every shadowy corner and doorway.
8.	who was an Italian explorer	middle bracketing commas	Describes what Columbus did (N-E)	Christopher Columbus discovered America.
9.	that had been marked on the map	middle no commas	Identifies the location (E)	The location led him to a clearing in the forest and the ancient ruins of the Inca temple.
10.	who had lathered great quantities of butter onto the warm croissant	middle bracketing commas	Describes what Nigel did to the croissant. (N-E)	Nigel devoured it in two huge bites.

EXERCISE 4 – IDENTIFYING RELATIVE CLAUSES

1. Carnivores are animals <u>who eat mainly meat and hunt for their prey</u>.
2. The mountain peaks, <u>which were like gigantic arrowheads</u>, rocketed above the alpine village.
3. There was a trumpet blast from the end of the lists, <u>which brought a hush over the crowd</u>.
4. The door <u>that opened out onto the courtyard</u> was blocked by a huge wooden chest wrapped in chains.
5. The elderly lady, <u>whose face was ashen and twisted with pain</u>, looked like a walking skeleton as she hobbled towards the bench.
6. Without thinking he took off down the street after the man <u>who had grabbed his bag</u>.
7. The pockets of corpse flowers, <u>which are bright red blooms the size of dinner plates</u>, emitted a rancid reek of rotting flesh.
8. The torrents of water <u>that poured over the top of the cliffs</u> created a raging, foaming waterfall.
9. Black fungi, <u>which were like swollen dead fingers</u>, poked out of the undergrowth.
10. Rob, <u>whose arms were folded across his chest</u>, clicked his tongue impatiently and rolled his eyes as he watched their childish antics.

EXERCISE 4 (continued)

	Relative (adjective) clause	What information does it reveal? Is it: a. Essential (E) b. Non-essential (N-E)	Punctuation a. No commas b. Bracketing commas c. One comma separating the relative clause from the main clause	Main clause
	which rocked back and forth with each assault	*What happened to the door when the creature charged against it.* *Non-essential*	*C*	*The creature charged against the front door.*
1.	who eat mainly meat and hunt for their prey	Identifies what carnivores are. Essential	No commas	Carnivores are animals.
2.	which were like gigantic arrowheads	Describes the peaks. Non-essential	Bracketing commas	The mountain peaks rocketed above the alpine village.
3.	which brought a hush over the crowd	Describes the effect of the trumpet blast. Non-essential	One comma separating relative clause and the main clause.	There was a trumpet blast from the end of the lists.
4.	that opened out onto the courtyard	Identifies which door. Essential	No commas	The door was blocked by a huge wooden chest wrapped in chains.

5.	whose face was ashen and twisted with pain	Describes the elderly lady Non-essential	Bracketing commas	The elderly lady looked like a walking skeleton as she hobbled towards the bench.
6.	who had grabbed his bag	Identifies which man. Essential	No commas	Without thinking, he took off down the street after the man.
7.	which are bright red blooms the size of dinner plates	Describes the corpse flowers. Non-essential	Bracketing commas	The pockets of corpse flowers emitted a rancid reek of rotting flesh.
8.	that poured over the top of the cliffs	Identifies which torrents of water. Essential	No commas	The torrents of water created a raging, foaming waterfall.
9.	which were like swollen dead fingers	Describes the black fungi. Non-essential	Bracketing commas	Black fungi poked out of the undergrowth.
10.	whose arms were folded across his chest	Describes Rob's body language. Non-essential	Bracketing commas	Rob clicked his tongue impatiently and rolled his eyes as he watched their childish antics.

EXERCISE 5 – MATCHING RELATIVE CLAUSES

Combined sentences
1.b. She edged deeper into the tangled thicket **that would lead her to the Inca ruins**.
2.e. A terrace of cottages, **which had brightly coloured doors and shutters**, lined the streets leading to the harbour.
3.f. The tall, dark silhouette **whose reflection she had seen in the mirror** had disappeared by the time she turned around.
4.c. The volcano emitted a huge column of dense black smoke, **which could be seen for miles.**
5.d. The rain, **which exploded like bullets on the trees**, quickly flooded the path.
6.h. Sophia Jex-Blake, **who was a doctor and teacher,** led a campaign for women to be allowed to attend university.
7.a. Above their wooden cabin, icy mountain peaks, **which looked like crooked spires**, burst out of the trees.
8.j. Polar regions are permanently covered by an icecap, **which is an enormous white dome of ice and snow**.
9.g. The woman **who had answered the phone** was rude and unhelpful.
10.i. Kitty, **who was sure she had heard footsteps**, occasionally turned and walked backwards to check **that no one was following them**.

EXERCISE 6 – UNSCRAMBLING SENTENCE PARTS

1. She darted down the alley that was opposite the coffee shop.
2. They waded through a blazing, knee-high carpet of bluebells, whose fragrant scent lingered in the air.
3. The explorers, who were lost in an ice-bound wilderness, had little hope of rescue from the outside world.
4. The buzzing strip light which hung from the ceiling in the kitchen was covered in dead flies.
5. Kitty, who was dragging an enormous suitcase, struggled to get onto the train.

EXERCISE 7 –COMBINING SENTENCES (CUED EXERCISE)

1. Kitty, <u>who had blurted out a little squeak of delight</u>, quickly covered her mouth.
2. The start of a river, <u>which is called the source</u>, can be found in upland areas.
3. She forced herself to ignore the burning lactic acid <u>that was creeping up her legs</u>.
4. Kitty, <u>whose vision was blurred with fatigue</u>, took off her glasses, closed her eyes and slumped back in her chair.
5. The passage <u>that led into the main hall</u> was concealed behind a red curtain, <u>which was embroidered with the family's coat of arms and a huge red lion</u>.

EXERCISE 8 –COMBINING SENTENCES (CUED EXERCISE)

1. An enormous man, <u>who had shoulders like granite boulders</u>, blocked the doorway.
2. Kitty, <u>whose hands were pressed against her chin</u>, stared intently at something in the distance.
3. A deafening boom, <u>which sounded like the roar of a jet engine</u>, echoed around the town.
4. The gigantic wave had formed into a raging wall of water <u>that was surging towards the beach</u>.
5. He had met a woman <u>who knew where he could find the shop that sold antique maps</u>.

EXERCISE 9 –COMBINING SENTENCES (CUED EXERCISE)

1. A fiery red flare, which was like a spectacular sunset, was visible above the mountain.
2. A river of lava, whose red sludge oozed out of the cracks of the volcano, slid menacingly down the slopes.
3. A volcano, which is a vent at the surface of the earth through which magma and other volcanic materials are ejected, is located on the boundary of two tectonic plates.
4. The candles were perfumed with pine needles and cinnamon that filled the room with the scents of Christmas.
5. Maya cities usually had a ceremonial centre, which contained great pyramids, temples and palaces.
6. Scott, Shackleton and Amundsen, who were famous explorers in the 20th century, set out on extremely hazardous expeditions to the Arctic and Antarctic.

EXERCISE 10 – COMBINING SENTENCES (OPEN EXERCISE)

1. There was no sign of the blood-splattered knight, <u>who had vanished into thin air at dawn</u>.
2. From the top of the mountain, there was a dramatic view <u>that took her breath away</u>.
3. The goblin <u>whose white beard reached almost to his knees</u> was obviously the leader of the group.
4. The beam of light lit up an enormous dragon <u>that had been painted over the entrance to the cave</u>.
5. The smell of eucalyptus, <u>which wafted in from the open window</u>, filled the room with its minty scent.

8

Participipial phrases

What is a present participle?

A participle is a word that is:

a. formed from adding **-ING** to a root verb.

Root verb	Participle
flicker	flickering

b. used as an adjective or a noun. (For this exercise, the focus will be on participles used as adjectives.)

Noun		Verb
moonlight		flickered
Participle/adjective		**Noun**
flickering		moonlight

c. a useful tool to combine two coordinated clauses into one main clause.

DOI: 10.4324/9781032662862-9

FOR EXAMPLE

The moonlight **flickered**, and it **painted** the garden with streaks of silver.

In this sentence the moonlight does two things at the same time:

flickered, painted

This **coordinated sentence** can be combined into **one main clause** by:

a. converting the verb **flickered** into a participle (**using -ING verb ending**).

b. using the participle as an adjective.

Transformed sentence:

The **flickering** moonlight **painted** the garden with streaks of silver.

SECTION 1 – INVESTIGATING

EXERCISE 1 – PARTICIPLES

INSTRUCTIONS

1. Convert the verb in the first clause into a participle by adding -ING to the root verb.
2. Use the participle as an adjective to create a noun phrase.
3. Combine the noun phrase with the second main clause.

MODEL

The branches swayed, and they rattled in the wind.

a. Participle: swayed – sway**ing**

b. Noun phrase: The swaying branches

c. Transformed sentence: The swaying branches rattled in the wind.

EXERCISE

1. **The bluebells blazed and carpeted the wood.**

a. Participle: _____

b. Noun phrase: _____

c. Transformed sentence: _____

2. **The mist slithered and spread through the forest.**

a. Participle: _____

b. Noun phrase: _____

c. Transformed sentence: _____

3. **The owl screeched and soared above the barn.**

a. Participle: _____

b. Noun phrase: _____

c. Transformed sentence: _____

4. **The wind whistled and bent the tops of the trees.**

a. Participle: _____

b. Noun phrase: _____

c. Transformed sentence: _____

5. **The snow shimmered and blanketed the paths.**

a. Participle: _____

b. Noun phrase: _____

c. Transformed sentence: _____

PARTICIPIAL PHRASES

Participial phrases are formed by adding words or phrases to participles.

> **FOR EXAMPLE**
>
> **Flickering** through the trees
> **Belching** from the volcano

> **EXERCISE 2 – CHUNKING (LINKING READING AND WRITING)**
>
> *Punctuation has been removed for this exercise.*
>
> **INSTRUCTIONS**
>
> 1. In pairs, take turns to read each of the sentences aloud.
> 2. Decide which of the sentences is divided into meaningful sentence parts.
> 3. Discuss and explain your decisions.
>
> **EXERCISE**
>
> 1. **Using its front flippers and belly the seal flopped in a worm-like motion across the ice.**
>
> i. Using its/ front flippers and belly the seal/ flopped in a worm-like motion/ across the ice.
>
> ii. Using its front flippers and belly/ the seal flopped in a worm-like motion/ across the ice.

2. **The polar bear's large broad feet crunching across the snow created a trail of prints the size of dinner plates.**

   i.   The polar bear's large broad feet/ crunching across the snow/ created
        a trail of prints the size of dinner plates.
   ii. The polar bear's/ large broad feet crunching across/ the snow created
        a trail/ of prints the size of dinner plates.

3. **Yapping furiously the dog launched itself at the gate.**
   Yapping furiously/ the dog launched itself at the gate.
   Yapping/ furiously the dog launched/ itself at the gate.

4. **Alfie stared at the bacon rasher watching every bite Kitty took and
   licking his lips in anticipation.**
   Alfie stared at the bacon rasher/ watching every bite Kitty took/ and
   licking his lips in anticipation.
   Alfie stared/ at the bacon rasher watching/ every bite Kitty/ took and
   licking/ his lips in anticipation.

5. **Balancing on his hind legs and gripping the top of the iron gate
   Monty let out an excited yelp.**
   Balancing on his hind/ legs and gripping the/ top of the iron/ gate
   Monty/ let out an excited yelp.
   Balancing on his hind legs/ and gripping the top of the iron gate/
   Monty let out an excited yelp.

EXERCISE 3 – CHUNKING INTO MEANINGFUL SENTENCE PARTS

Punctuation has been removed for this exercise.

INSTRUCTIONS

1.   In pairs, read the sentences aloud.
2.   Using a slash, chunk the sentence into meaningful sentence parts.
3.   Discuss and explain your decisions.

Note: Some students with more experience of reading may divide the sentences into larger chunks. The focus should be on dividing into 'meaningful chunks'.

EXERCISE

1.   Suddenly the dolphin leapt out of the water announcing its arrival with a series of clicks whistles and squeaks.
2.   The dolphin cackling and whistling with excitement frolicked alongside the boat.
3.   Moving its tail up and down and arching its back the dolphin propelled itself through the water.
4.   The tumbling breakers crashed onto the rocks spraying them with an icy mist.
5.   Plunging over the top of the cliffs the torrent of water sent huge clouds of spray into the air.

EXERCISE 4 – IDENTIFYING THE FUNCTION, CONSTRUCTION, POSITION AND PUNCTUATION OF PARTICIPIAL PHRASES

The participial phrase is underlined in each of the sentences.

INSTRUCTIONS

1. In pairs, take turns to read each sentence aloud.
2. Write each participial phrase into the table.
3. Make a note of where it is positioned in the sentence: opening, middle (between the subject and the verb) or at the end.
4. Make a note of the punctuation:
   - ☆ bracketing commas
   - ☆ one comma separating the participial phrase from the main clause.
5. Highlight the words at the start of each participial phrase, paying particular attention to the verb ending.

EXERCISE

1. He writhed on the floor, <u>clutching his leg</u>.
2. <u>Muttering under his breath</u>, he stomped out of the room and slammed the door behind him.
3. He muttered under his breath and stomped out of the room, <u>slamming the door behind him</u>.
4. <u>Shrieking with joy</u>, she darted across the room and threw her arms around his neck.
5. Kitty, <u>pumping the air with her fist</u>, raced down the pitch towards her teammates.
6. She stared at the notification on her phone, <u>trying to decide whether to open the message or delete it</u>.

7. His eyes, <u>darting wildly from side to side</u>, strained to pierce the darkness.
8. <u>Leaning back in his chair,</u> he exhaled deeply.
9. Shoved and tugged by the ferocious wind, <u>struggling to stay on his feet</u>, Tom staggered back and forth.
10. Kitty, <u>feeling a blush creep up her neck to her cheeks</u>, lowered her head and looked intently at her feet.

EXERCISE 4 (continued)

	Participial phrase(s)	Position in sentence: opening, middle or end Punctuation: one comma or bracketing comma	Main clause
1.			
2.			
3.			
4.			
5.			
6.			
7.			
8.			
9.			
10.			

EXERCISE 5 – IDENTIFYING PARTICIPIAL PHRASES

INSTRUCTIONS

1.   Underline the participial phrases in the following sentences.

EXTENSION

In the table:

2.   Identify where the participial phrases are positioned in the sentences:

i.   Beginning
ii.   Middle
iii.   End.

3.   How are they punctuated?

i.   One comma
ii.   Bracketing commas.

4.   What would be the impact on the sentence if the participial phrase was moved to a different position in the sentence?

EXERCISE

1.   The hurricane roared round the house, rattling the windows, pounding on the roof and hammering at the door.
2.   Rob, leaping from one stepping-stone to another, crossed to the other side of the river.
3.   Suddenly, everyone moved, reaching for their rucksacks and running to their bikes.
4.   Ignoring the stones scraping her knees and elbows, Rachel crawled as fast as she could towards the hedge.
5.   A cold clammy breeze wafted against his face, bringing with it a smell of rotting fish.
6.   Kitty, clutching her phone in her right hand, watched and waited.
7.   Drawing her knees up against her chest, Rachel huddled beneath the stairs, praying she wouldn't be seen.

8.   Rob, seeing a door ahead, darted up the stairs and raced towards it.
9.   Pressing her lips tightly together, Kitty tried to smother the giggles that were bubbling in the back of her throat.
10. Throwing his arms out in front of him and waving them from side to side, James felt his way gingerly down the dark passage.

EXERCISE 5 (continued)

	Participial phrase(s)	Position in sentence: opening, middle or end Punctuation: one comma or bracketing comma	Main clause
1.			
2.			
3.			
4.			
5.			
6.			
7.			
8.			
9.			
10.			

EXERCISE 6 – MATCHING PARTICIPIAL PHRASES

INSTRUCTIONS

1. Match the participial phrases with their respective main clauses.
2. Write out each sentence, inserting and underlining the correct participial phrase.

DIFFERENTIATION

For those students for whom this exercise could prove to be difficult, the table can be photocopied and cut into individual boxes to enable those students to physically add each participial phrase to individual sentences to work out which is the correct combination.

EXERCISE

Main clause	Participial phrases
1. The killer whale swam around the ship. ,^	a. floating above the grass outside the window
2. The turbulent sea battered the boat. ,^	b. sliding on the loose stones
3. ^, She peered through the hedge that screened the hotel.	c. whirling round
4. ^, He searched for the source of the mysterious sound.	d. tossing it from side to side and burying its decks in a deluge of water.
5. ^, He stumbled down the slope.	e. jutting out of the river like fangs
6. ^, Kitty covered her head with her hands.	f. hoovering up mouthfuls of crabs, lobsters and shrimps in its gargantuan mouth
7. Huge jagged rocks, ^, churned it into boiling rapids.	g. raising her head cautiously
8. ^, She took a deep breath.	h. clutching his hands to stop them shaking
9. A billowing grey mist, ^, had appeared out of nowhere.	i. shivering violently and curling herself into a ball
10. James, ^ , stepped up onto the stage.	j. sucking in her cheeks

EXERCISE 7 – UNSCRAMBLING SENTENCE PARTS

INSTRUCTIONS

1. Unscramble the list of sentence parts and write out the sentence.
2. Underline the participial phrases.
3. The capitalized sentence parts begin the sentence.

EXERCISE

1c. to stop them chattering
1b. against each other
1a. he gnashed his teeth
1d. Clenching his jaw

_____

_____

2a. she folded her arms
2b. Chewing nervously on her tongue
2c. across her chest
2d. and stared at the floor

_____

_____

3a. forced her to grope her way
3b. enveloping her like a blanket
3c. The dark
3d. blindly down the stairs

_____

_____

4a. The fog crept up on the house
4b. to fill the room
4c. and squeezing through any gaps
4d. sliding along the windows
4e. slithering up the walls

_____

_____

_____

5a.   and lashing them from side to side
5b.   The wind wound
5c.   bending their tops
5d.   around the trunks of the ancient yew trees

_____

_____

EXERCISE 8 – COMBINING SENTENCES (CUED EXERCISE)

The sentences are broken down into base sentences (called kernel sentences).

INSTRUCTIONS

1.   Cross out repeated or unnecessary words.
2.   Using a participial phrase, combine the two/three base sentences into one sentence.
3.   Cues provided in brackets (-ING…) at the end of a base sentence indicate that the verb ending in that sentence should be changed to an **-ING** ending. For example, mov~~ed~~ – mov**ing**.
4.   The position of the participial phrase is indicated by a ^.
5.   The punctuation to be used is indicated.

EXTENSION

6.   What would be the impact on the sentence if the participial phrase was moved to a different position in the sentence?

EXAMPLE

a.1   ^, She took a deep breath.
a.2   ~~She~~ sucked in her cheeks. (**-ING**)
      Sucking in her cheeks, she took a deep breath.

EXERCISE

1.1 ∧, Kitty hurried towards the exit without any explanation or a goodbye.
1.2 ~~She~~ **rose** up from the table suddenly. (**-ING**)
  (Clue: rise is the root verb of rose)

_____

_____

2.1 Rob's eyes, ∧, scanned the street for any movement.
2.2 Rob's eyes **darted** left and right. (**-ING**)

_____

_____

3.1 Kitty listened to her voicemail several times. , ∧
3.2 She **tried** to figure out the identity of the mystery caller. (**-ING**)

_____

_____

4.1 ∧, Kitty left the room.
4.2 She **muttered** under her breath. (**-ING**)

_____

_____

5.1 Rob, ∧, motioned for them to get back behind the stables.
5.2 Rob **turned** round suddenly (**-ING**)

_____

_____

EXERCISE 9 – OPEN EXERCISES

INSTRUCTIONS

★ Use a participial phrase(s) to combine the sentences.
★ Punctuate the clause correctly in the combined sentence.
★ Where there are two or more participial phrases in a row, it is often better to use **AND** to join the last two participial phrases.

For example: … slithering across the streets, crawling up the walls **and** covering the building in a swirling mist.

The benefit of an open exercise is that individual students will combine the sentences in a variety of ways. Comparing the combined sentences and discussing what options are preferred (or are confusing) is a vital part of learning about language and grammar as a communication tool. (Suggestions are included in the Answers section.)

★ Note: Present participial phrases (-ING) often describe events that are happening at the same time (as in the example above) and in this case the order of the participial phrases is flexible. However, when they describe events that happen in a sequence or as result of an action, the order of the participial phrases is important.

EXAMPLE 1

a.   Blowing out her candle, the draft of icy air plunged her into darkness.
b.   The draft of icy air plunged her into darkness, blowing out her candle.

Explanation

She was plunged into darkness because the draft of icy air blew out her candle, so the blowing out of the candle does not make sense at the end of the sentence.

EXAMPLE 2

a. Rising from the table suddenly, Kitty hurried towards the exit without any explanation or a goodbye.

b. Kitty hurried towards the exit without any explanation or a goodbye, rising from the table suddenly.

(b) does not make sense as the sentence describes a sequence of events and Kitty rose from the table before hurrying towards the exit.

EXTENSION

What would be the impact on the sentence if the participial phrase was moved to a different position in the sentence?

Discussion of effective sentence structures and preferences is an important part of learning about language and supports students to be able to spot and comment on the techniques and structure used in a class text or in their independent reading. It is also an important part of recognising circumstances where the position of a participial phrase is important to the meaning and clarity of the sentence.

For example:

Hiding what might lay in wait behind them, the trees stood silent and dark.

Participial phrase: hiding what might lay in wait behind them

Position: beginning of the sentence

Punctuation: one comma after the participial phrase to separate it from the main clause.

What information does the participial phrase provide?

The trees hid what could be lying in wait. It adds suspense to the description of the trees which are standing silent and dark.

Change the position of the participial phrase

Hiding what might lay in wait behind them, the trees stood silent and dark.

The trees stood silent and dark, **hiding what might lay in wait behind them**.

CONNECTING GRAMMAR TOOLS

When to do this is at the discretion of each teacher based on the experience, confidence and understanding of their class or students.

Convert the sentence into two main clauses.

1.1   The trees stood silent and dark.

1.2   The trees hid what might lay in wait behind them.

★   In what other ways could these two sentences be combined?

a.   Co-ordination

The trees stood silent and dark, and they hid what might lay in wait behind them.

b.   Relative (adjective) clauses

The trees, which stood silent and dark, hid what might lay in wait behind them.

★   Students could then compare the options and discuss which they prefer and why.

This exercise serves two purposes:

i.   Revising the use of other grammar tools, such as coordination and relative clauses.

ii.   Engaging in a process that forms the basis of the revision process – evaluating the effectiveness of a sentence construction and considering alternatives.

EXERCISE

1.1   The wolf let out a mournful howl.

1.2   It threw back its head.

_____

_____

2.1 The skunk waved its tail in the air.

2.2 The skunk stomped its feet.

2.3 The skunk growled.

2.4 The skunk warned the puma not to come any closer.

_____

_____

3.1 The snake spat out a stream of venom at his feet.

3.2 The snake whipped its head around.

_____

_____

4.1 Rob bent over.

4.2 Rob tried to get his breath.

_____

_____

5.1 Kitty sat in the shadows.

5.2 She watched.

5.3 She waited.

5.4 She clutched her phone in her right hand.

_____

_____

6.1 The night wind swept through the garden.

6.2 It whispered through the trees.

6.3 It rattled the branches.

_____

_____

7.1 He launched himself at the lower branch.

7.2 He grasped it with both hands.

7.3 He hauled himself up.

_____

_____

8.1 The wind grew stronger with each passing minute.

8.2 It whirled up in strange clouds.

8.3 It flurried and swirled.

8.4 It lashed their legs and faces with dirt and gravel.

_____

_____

9.1 Rob dived headfirst through the gaping doorway.

9.2 Rob struck the ground in a tuck.

9.3 He rolled to his feet.

_____

_____

10.1 Rob moved his torch.

10.2 He moved it from side to side.

10.3 He searched for the light switch.

_____

_____

EXERCISE 10 – CREATING PARTICIPIAL PHRASES

INSTRUCTIONS

1. Convert the clauses provided into participial phrases.

2. Complete the sentence with your own main clause. Make sure that it links with the information provided by the participial phrase.

EXAMPLE

[2]She [1]shrieked (-ING) with joy.

a. **Participial phrase:** [1]Shrieking with joy, [2]she …

b. **Sentence:** Shrieking with joy, she jumped up and down on the spot.

EXERCISE

1. She pumped the air with her fist.

a. _____

b. _____

2. She felt a blush creeping up her neck and cheeks.

a. _____
b. _____

3. He bent over.

a. _____
b. _____

4. She swatted the air.

a. _____
b. _____

5. He quivered with excitement.

a. _____
b. _____

6. She muttered under her breath.

a. _____
b. _____

7. He winked at Kitty.

a. _____
b. _____

8. He chewed his tongue nervously.

a. _____
b. _____

9.   She dodged and weaved through the crowds.

a.   _____

b.   _____

10. She paused at the end of the street.

a.   _____

b.   _____

SECTION 2 – REVIEW

1.   What questions do present participial phrases answer?
2.   Which words begin present participial phrases?
3.   What do those words end in?
4.   Where can participial phrases be placed in a sentence?
5.   When is the order of participial phrases in a sentence important?
6.   When is one comma used for a participial phrase? When are two bracketing commas used for a participial phrase?
7.   What other grammar tools could be used instead of a participial phrase?
8.   How can participial phrases improve your writing?

A PARTICIPIAL PHRASE

FUNCTION

★ Describes the subject of the sentence (noun or pronoun) or what s(he) or it is doing.

★ Adds detail or movement to a sentence to produce a more vivid image.

★ Adds variety to sentences.

★ Uses fewer words than relative (adjective) clauses and creates a different emphasis and rhythm.

★ Adds suspense.

★ Makes things more exciting for the reader.

★ Can combine short, choppy sentences to improve the flow of the text.

POSITION

Can be positioned at the:

★ beginning of the sentence
★ middle of the sentence
★ end of the sentence.

PUNCTUATION

★ Beginning – one comma (separating participial phrase from main clause).
★ Middle – bracketing commas.
★ End – one comma (separating participial phrase from main clause).

PRESENT PARTICIPLES AND PARTICIPIAL PHRASES ACTING AS ADJECTIVES

What is a present participle?

★ Formed by adding -ING to a root verb (gust – gusting).
★ Used as an adjective.

Examples:

1. *The moonlight **flickered** and cast eerie shadows through the trees.*
    The **flickering** moonlight cast eerie shadows through the trees.
    Flickering (participle of the root verb **flicker**) used an adjective to describe the moonlight.
2. *Kitty **trembled** and opened the box.*
    Trembling, Kitty opened the box.
    Trembling (participle of the root verb **tremble**) used as an adjective to describe the subject, Kitty.

Participial phrases are formed by adding words to these participles.

FOR EXAMPLE

1b. **Flickering through the trees**, the moonlight cast eerie shadows.
2b. **Trembling with anticipation**, she opened the box.

WHY IS IT A PHRASE NOT A CLAUSE?

FOR EXAMPLE

Flickering through the trees, the moonlight cast eerie shadows.

1. A clause requires a **subject** and **verb** unit.

Participial phrase: **flickering through the trees**

Subject: moonlight is the subject of the main clause but is not included in the participial phrase, '**flickering through the trees**'.

Verb: in this context, flickering is a participle not a verb. To be the main verb in a sentence it would need to be accompanied by an auxiliary (helping) verb, for example, **is** or **was** (**is flickering** through the trees).

Participial phrases

★ Add more information about the subject of the main clause: reasons, results or other actions that occur simultaneously with the main verb.

EXERCISE 1 – PARTICIPLES

1a. blazing
 b. the blazing bluebells
 c. The blazing bluebells carpeted the wood.

2a. slithering
 b. the slithering mist
 c. The slithering mist spread through the forest.

3a. screeching
 b. the screeching owl
 c. The screeching owl soared above the barn.

4a. whistling
 b. the whistling wind
 c. The whistling wind bent the tops of the trees.

5a. shimmering
 b. the shimmering snow
 c. The shimmering snow blanketed the paths.

EXERCISE 2 – CHUNKING (LINKING READING AND WRITING)

1. **Using its front flippers and belly the seal flopped in a worm-like motion across the ice.**

   i.   Using its/ front flippers and belly the seal/ flopped in a worm-like motion/ across the ice.

   ii. Using its front flippers and belly/ the seal flopped in a worm-like motion/ across the ice. √

2. **The polar bear's large broad feet crunching across the snow created a trail of prints the size of dinner plates.**

   i.   The polar bear's large broad feet/ crunching across the snow/ created a trail of prints the size of dinner plates. √

   ii. The polar bear's/ large broad feet crunching across/ the snow created a trail/ of prints the size of dinner plates.

3. **Yapping furiously the dog launched itself at the gate.**
   Yapping furiously/ the dog launched itself at the gate. √
   Yapping/ furiously the dog launched/ itself at the gate.

4. **Alfie stared at the bacon rasher watching every bite Kitty took and licking his lips in anticipation.**
   Alfie stared at the bacon rasher/ watching every bite Kitty took/ and licking his lips in anticipation. √
   Alfie stared/ at the bacon rasher watching/ every bite Kitty/ took and licking/ his lips in anticipation.

5. **Balancing on his hind legs and gripping the top of the iron gate Monty let out an excited yelp.**
   Balancing on his hind/ legs and gripping the/ top of the iron/ gate Monty/ let out an excited yelp.
   Balancing on his hind legs/ and gripping the top of the iron gate/ Monty let out an excited yelp. √

EXERCISE 3 – CHUNKING INTO MEANINGFUL SENTENCE PARTS

1. Suddenly/ the dolphin leapt out of the water/ <u>announcing its arrival with a series of clicks whistles and squeaks</u>.
2. The dolphin/ <u>cackling and whistling with excitement</u>/ frolicked along-side the boat.
3. <u>Moving its tail up and down</u>/ and <u>arching its back</u>/the dolphin pro-pelled itself through the water.
4. The tumbling breakers crashed onto the rocks/ <u>spraying them with an icy mist</u>.
5. <u>Plunging over the top of the cliffs</u>/ the torrent of water sent huge clouds of spray into the air.

EXERCISE 4 – IDENTIFYING THE FUNCTION, CONSTRUCTION, POSITION AND PUNCTUATION OF PARTICIPIAL PHRASES

	Participial phrase(s)	Position in sentence: opening, middle or end Punctuation: one comma or bracketing comma	Main clause
1.	clutching his leg	a. end b. one comma	He writhed on the floor.
2.	muttering under his breath	a. opening b. one comma	He stomped out of the room and slammed the door shut behind him.
3.	slamming the door behind him	a. end b. one comma	He muttered under his breath and stomped out of the room.

4.	shrieking with joy	a. opening b. one comma	She darted across the room and threw her arms around his neck.
5.	pumping the air with her fist	a. middle b. bracketing commas	Kitty raced down the pitch towards her teammates.
6.	trying to decide whether to open the message or delete it	a. end b. one comma	She stared at the notification on her phone.
7.	darting wildly from side to side	a. middle b. bracketing commas	His eyes strained to pierce the darkness.
8.	leaning back in his chair	a. opening b. one comma	He exhaled deeply.
9.	struggling to stay on his feet	a. middle b. bracketing commas (series of phrases before main clause)	Shoved and tugged by the ferocious wind, Tom staggered back and forth.
10.	feeling a blush creep up her neck to her cheeks	a. middle b. bracketing commas	Kitty lowered her head and looked intently at her feet.

EXERCISE 5 – IDENTIFYING PARTICIPIAL PHRASES

1. The hurricane roared round the house, <u>rattling the windows</u>, <u>pounding on the roof</u> and <u>hammering at the door</u>.

2. Rob, <u>leaping from one stepping-stone to another</u>, crossed to the other side of the river.

3. Suddenly, everyone moved, <u>reaching for their rucksacks</u> and <u>running to their bikes</u>.

4. <u>Ignoring the stones scraping her knees and elbows</u>, Rachel crawled as fast as she could towards the hedge.

5. A cold clammy breeze wafted against his face, <u>bringing with it a smell of rotting fish</u>.

6. Kitty, <u>clutching her phone in her right hand</u>, watched and waited.

7. <u>Drawing her knees up against her chest</u>, Rachel huddled beneath the stairs, <u>praying she wouldn't be seen</u>.

8. Rob, <u>seeing a door ahead</u>, darted up the stairs and raced towards it.

9. <u>Pressing her lips tightly together</u>, Kitty tried to smother the giggles that were bubbling in the back of her throat.

10. <u>Throwing his arms out in front of him</u> and <u>waving them from side to side</u>, James felt his way gingerly down the dark passage.

EXERCISE 5 (continued)

	Participial phrase(s)	Position in sentence: opening, middle or end Punctuation: one comma or bracketing comma	Main clause
1.	rattling the windows pounding on the roof hammering at the door	end one comma	The hurricane roared round the house.
2.	leaping from one stepping-stone to another	middle bracketing commas	Rob crossed to the other side of the river.
3.	reaching for their rucksacks running to their bikes	end one comma	Suddenly, everyone moved.
4.	ignoring the stones scraping her knees and elbows	beginning one comma	Rachel crawled as fast as she could towards the hedge.
5.	bringing with it a smell of rotting fish	end one comma	A cold clammy breeze wafted against his face.
6.	clutching her phone in her right hand	middle bracketing commas	Kitty watched and waited.
7.	[1]drawing her knees up against her chest [2]praying she wouldn't be seen	beginning one comma end one comma	Rachel huddled beneath the stairs.
8.	seeing a door ahead	middle bracketing commas	Rob darted up the stairs and raced towards it.
9.	pressing her lips tightly together	beginning one comma	Kitty tried to smother the giggles that were bubbling in the back of her throat.
10.	throwing his arms out in front of him waving them from side to side	beginning one comma	James felt his way gingerly down the dark passage.

EXERCISE 6 – MATCHING PARTICIPIAL PHRASES

Combined sentence
1.f. The killer whale swam around the ship, <u>hoovering up mouthfuls of crabs, lobsters and shrimps in its gargantuan mouth</u>.
2.d. The turbulent sea battered the boat, <u>tossing it from side to side</u> and <u>burying its decks in a deluge of water</u>.
3.g. <u>Raising her head cautiously</u>, she peered through the hedge that screened the hotel.
4.c. <u>Whirling round</u>, he searched for the source of the mysterious sound.
5.b. <u>Sliding on the loose stones</u>, he stumbled down the slope.
6.i. <u>Shivering violently and curling herself into a ball</u>, Kitty covered her head with her hands.
7.e. Huge jagged rocks, <u>jutting out of the river like fangs</u>, churned it into boiling rapids.
8.j. <u>Sucking in her cheeks</u>, she took a deep breath.
9.a. A billowing grey mist, <u>floating above the grass outside the window</u>, had appeared out of nowhere.
10.h. James, <u>clutching his hands to stop them shaking</u>, stepped up onto the stage.

EXERCISE 7 – UNSCRAMBLING SENTENCE PARTS

1. <u>Clenching his jaw</u>, he gnashed his teeth against each other to stop them chattering.
2. <u>Chewing nervously on her tongue</u>, she folded her arms across her chest and stared at the floor.
3. The dark, <u>enveloping her like a blanket</u>, forced her to grope her way blindly down the stairs.
4. The fog crept up on the house, <u>slithering up the walls</u>, <u>sliding along the windows</u> and <u>squeezing through any gaps to fill the room</u>.
5. The wind wound around the trunks of the ancient yew trees, <u>bending their tops</u> and <u>lashing them from side to side</u>.

EXERCISE 8 – COMBINING SENTENCES (CUED)

1. **Rising from the table suddenly**, Kitty hurried towards the exit without any explanation or a goodbye.
   Kitty, **rising from the table suddenly**, hurried towards the exit without any explanation or a goodbye.

2. Rob's eyes, **darting left and right**, scanned the street for any movement.
   Darting left and right, Rob's eyes scanned the street for any movement.

3. Kitty listened to her voicemail several times, **trying to figure out the identity of the mystery caller**.
   Kitty, **trying to figure out the identity of the mystery caller**, listened to her voicemail several times.
   Trying to figure out the identity of the mystery caller, Kitty listened to her voicemail several times.

4. **Muttering under her breath**, Kitty left the room.
   Kitty, **muttering under her breath**, left the room.
   Kitty left the room, **muttering under her breath**.

5. Rob, **turning round suddenly**, motioned for them to get back behind the stables.
   Turning round suddenly, Rob motioned for them to get back behind the stables.

EXERCISE 9 – COMBINING SENTENCES (OPEN)

1. **Throwing back its head**, the wolf let out a mournful howl.
   The wolf, **throwing back its head**, let out a mournful howl.
   Coordinating conjunction (CC): The wolf threw back its head **and** let out a mournful howl.
   Relative clause (RC): The wolf, **which threw back its head**, let out a mournful howl.

   _____

2. **Waving its tail in the air**, the skunk stomped its feet and growled, **warning the puma not to come any closer**.
   The skunk waved its tail in the air, stomped its feet and growled, **warning the puma not to come any closer**.
   Stomping its feet and growling, the skunk waved its tail in the air, **warning the puma not to come any closer**.
   Stomping its feet and growling, the skunk waved its tail in the air and warned the puma not to come any closer.
   Waving its tail in the air, **stomping its feet and growling**, the skunk warned the puma not to come any closer.
   The skunk waved its tail in the air and, **stomping its feet and growling**, warned the puma not to come any closer.
   CC: The skunk waved its tail in the air, **and** it stomped its feet **and** it growled, **and** it warned the puma not to come any closer.
   RC: The skunk, **who was waving its tail in the air**, stomped its feet and growled, **warning the puma not to come any closer**.

   _____

3. **Whipping its head around**, the snake spat out a stream of venom at his feet.
   The snake whipped its head around, **spitting out a stream of venom at his feet**.
   The snake, **whipping its head around**, spat out a stream of venom at his feet.
   CC: The snake whipped its head around **and** spat out a stream of venom at his feet.
   RC: The snake, **which had whipped its head around**, spat out a stream of venom at his feet.

   _____

4. **Bending over**, Rob tried to get his breath.
    Rob bent over, **trying to get his breath**.
    Rob, **bending over**, tried to get his breath.
    CC: Rob bent over **and** tried to get his breath.
    RC: Rob, who was bent over, tried to get his breath.

---

5. Kitty sat in the shadows, **watching, waiting** and **clutching her phone in her right hand**.
    Watching and waiting, Kitty sat in the shadows, **clutching her phone in her right hand**.
    Clutching her phone in her right hand, Kitty sat in the shadows, **watching and waiting**.
    Sitting in the shadows, clutching her phone in her right hand, Kitty watched and waited.
    Sitting in the shadows, watching and waiting, Kitty clutched her phone in her right hand.
    CC: Kitty sat in the shadows, **and** she watched and waited, **and** she clutched her phone in her right hand.
    RC: Kitty, **who was sat in the shadows**, watched and waited, clutching her phone in her right hand.

---

6. The night wind swept through the garden, **whispering through the trees** and **rattling** the branches.
    Sweeping through the garden, the night wind whispered through the trees and rattled the branches.
    CC: The night wind swept through the garden, **and** it whispered through the trees, **and** it rattled the branches.
    RC: The night wind, **which swept through the garden**, whispered through the trees and rattled the branches.

---

7. **Launching himself at the lower branch**, Rob grasped it with both hands and hauled himself up.

   Rob launched himself at the lower branch, **grasping it with both hands** and **hauling himself up**.

   Launching himself at the lower branch and **grasping it with both hands**, Rob hauled himself up.

   CC: Rob launched himself at the lower branch, **and** he grasped it with both hands, **and** he hauled himself up.

   RC: Rob, **who had launched himself at the lower branch**, grasped it with both hands and hauled himself up.

---

8. The wind grew stronger with each passing minute, **whirling up in strange clouds, flurrying and swirling**, and **lashing their legs and faces with dirt and gravel**.

   Growing stronger with each passing minute, the wind whirled up in strange clouds, flurried and swirled, and lashed their legs and faces with dirt and gravel.

   The wind, which grew stronger with each passing minute, whirled up in strange clouds, **flurrying and swirling, and lashing their legs and faces with dirt and gravel**.

   CC: **The wind grew stronger with each passing minute**, and it whirled up in strange clouds, and it flurried and swirled, and it lashed their legs and faces with dirt and gravel.

   RC: The wind, **which grew stronger with each passing minute**, whirled up in strange clouds, flurried and swirled, and lashed their legs with dirt and gravel.

---

9.   Rob dived headfirst through the gaping doorway, **striking the ground in a tuck**, then **rolling to his feet**.
Diving headfirst through the gaping doorway, Rob struck the ground in a tuck, then rolled to his feet.
Rob, **diving headfirst through the gaping doorway**, struck the ground in a tuck, then rolled to his feet.
CC: Rob dived headfirst through the gaping doorway, **and** he struck the ground in a tuck, then rolled to his feet.
RC: Rob, **who had dived headfirst through the gaping door**, struck the ground in a tuck, then rolled to his feet.

10.   **Moving his torch from side to side**, Rob searched for the light switch.
Searching for the light switch, Rob moved his torch from side to side.
Rob, **moving his torch from side to side**, searched for the light switch.
Rob, **searching for the light switch**, moved his torch from side to side.
CC: Rob moved his torch from side to side **and** searched for the light switch.
RC: Rob, **who was searching for the light switch**, moved his torch from side to side.

EXERCISE 10

1.   Pumping the air with her fist, she …
2.   Feeling a blush creeping up her neck and cheeks, she …
3.   Bending over, he …
4.   Swatting the air, she …
5.   Quivering with excitement, he …
6.   Muttering under her breath, she …
7.   Winking at Kitty, he …
8.   Chewing his tongue nervously, he …
9.   Dodging and weaving through the crowds, she …
10.   Pausing at the end of the street, she …

Part 2

Imitating

9
Sentence imitation method

As with learning to talk, imitation is part of the process of learning to write. Whereas avid readers and skilled writers have an almost subconscious understanding of sentence construction, basic writers spend a disproportionate amount of time thinking about constructing a sentence rather than its content. This results in an inability to adequately communicate their knowledge, ideas and thoughts and, ultimately, under-performance in all subjects. For these students, imitation provides a scaffold to learning how to craft sentences and develop well-structured paragraphs and aids an automaticity in this process. It means that students do not have to invent a new structure every time they try to express an idea or construct an argument.

> Writing is learned by imitation. If anyone asked me how I learned to write, I'd say I learned by reading the men and women who were doing the kind of writing I wanted to do and trying to figure out how they did it.
> *– William Zinsser,* On Writing Well *(1988)*

Imitation is a powerful learning tool to:

★ model the wealth of words, phrases and clauses that are part of a writer's toolkit

DOI: 10.4324/9781032662862-11

* scaffold students' knowledge, understanding and usage of increasingly more complex constructions until they develop automaticity in sentence construction and manipulation
* gain control over the way they communicate in writing their thoughts, ideas and knowledge and make conscious choices from the alternatives at their disposal.

Chunking the sentences to be imitated into meaningful sentence parts breaks this process down into a step-by-step method: changing the subject and content of the sentence and its component parts but using the same sentence structure as in the model.

Imitation guides students to an awareness of what structures work by discussing their main stylistic and syntactic features.

> Whenever we read a sentence and like it, we unconsciously store it away in our model-chamber; and it goes with the myriad of its fellows, to the building, brick by brick, of the eventual edifice which we call our style.
>
> *– Mark Twain, Letter to George Bainton (15 October 1888)*

Using Mark Twain's analogy that a text is built one sentence at a time, as is the quality of the text (just like the quality and originality of the building is determined by the quality of the bricks used and how they are arranged), a text is determined by the quality of the sentences. This encompasses the quality of the words, phrases and clauses used, as well as how they are arranged – how they fit together to create the desired effect and how they link to the preceding and succeeding sentences to make a coherent whole.

Each section of this handbook provides numerous opportunities to imitate different sentence structures, and each chapter of *Descriptosaurus* and the website also include a wide range of sentence models to provide an easy reference guide for teachers, students and parents. However, there is no substitute for using texts that are being studied or read to collect effective models and keep them as a resource bank or as part of a student's writing toolkit. It is particularly empowering for students to highlight and collect sentence structures that appeal to them and mirror a style they would like to imitate.

THE 5W SENTENCE

To scaffold the process of work on sentence expansion and sentence imitation, start with basic 5W sentences to ensure that students are first confident and adept at substituting word classes (nouns, verbs, prepositions, adjectives and adverbs) to imitate a simple single-clause sentence structure.

   Work on substituting words will build a solid foundation for working on the revision stage of the writing process – examining the effect and impact of word choice, for example:

*   **Use of nouns:**
    Can a general noun be replaced by a more specific noun to give a more vivid image and thus replace some of the adjectives?
*   **Use of adverbs:**
    Do they add anything to the meaning of the sentence, or can they be deleted?
    Can they be substituted for a stronger alternative?
    Can the adverb be removed and replaced by a stronger verb?

STEP 1: CONSTRUCTING A BASIC 5W SENTENCE

MODEL

Step 1: **Noun:**	What is your sentence about? (**snake**)
Step 2: **Adjective:**	What does it look like? (**enormous, green**).
Step 3: **Verb:**	What did it do? (**slithered**)
Step 4: **Adverb:**	How did it do it? (**slowly**)
Step 5: **Preposition:**	Where or when (**through the tangled undergrowth**)
Step 6:	Construct a complete sentence.

The enormous green snake slithered slowly through the tangled undergrowth.

Step 1	**Noun**	What is your sentence about?
Step 2	**Adjective(s)**	What does it* look like? (*He, she, you, they)
Step 3	**Verb**	What did it do?
Step 4	**Adverb**	How did it do it?
Step 5	**Prepositional phrase**	Where or when did it do it?
Step 6	**Sentence:**	

STEP 2: IMITATING A BASIC 5W SENTENCE USING A DIFFERENT SUBJECT

A. TEACHER MODELLING

Teachers model the process using the structure and table shown below (including talking aloud as they consider the options available).

1. Choose a different subject.
2. Substitute each word class one at a time.
3. Discuss how word choices affect the meaning of a sentence.
4. List four synonyms for either adjectives, verbs or adverbs and experiment with the different word choices, discussing which is most effective and why.

B. GUIDED PRACTICE

1. With input from the class, guide the students through the process as outlined above.

C. INDEPENDENT PRACTICE

2. Either individually or in pairs, using their own subject and the same method as outlined above, students practise constructing a simple, single-clause sentence.

METHOD

1. Change the noun

a. The enormous green **snake** slithered slowly through the tangled undergrowth.

b. The enormous green **lizard** slithered slowly through the tangled undergrowth.

2. Change the adjective

a. The **enormous green** lizard slithered slowly through the tangled undergrowth.

b. The **huge grey** lizard slithered slowly through the tangled undergrowth.

3. Change the verb

The huge grey lizard **slithered** slowly through the tangled undergrowth.

The huge grey lizard **waited** slowly through the tangled undergrowth.

4. Change the adverb

The huge grey lizard waited **slowly** through the tangled undergrowth.

The huge grey lizard waited **patiently** through the tangled undergrowth.

5. Change the prepositional phrase

The huge grey lizard waited patiently **through the tangled undergrowth**.

The huge grey lizard waited patiently **in the bushes**.

	Example 1 (teacher)	Guided	Independent	Example 4
Noun	snake	lizard	wind	
Adjective	enormous green	huge grey	fierce, icy	
Verb	slithered	waited	hammered	
Adverb	slowly	patiently	relentlessly	
Preposition	through the tangled undergrowth	in the bushes	against the windows	

Sentence(s):

1. The enormous green snake/ slithered slowly/ through the tangled undergrowth.
2. The huge grey lizard/ waited patiently/ in the bushes.
3. The fierce, icy wind/ hammered relentlessly/ against the windows.
4.

ADVANCED: USING PHRASES AND CLAUSES

	Example 1	Example 2	Example 3	Example 4
Noun phrase	an enormous snake	a colossal lizard	a high wind	
Appositive phrase	a green and yellow cobra	a grey armour-plated Komodo dragon	a ferocious swirling gale	
Relative clause	whose black forked tongue flicked from side to side	whose long neck peered over the bushes	whose icy gusts slithered through gaps in the rotting frames	

	Example 1	**Example 2**	**Example 3**	**Example 4**
Predicate	slithered slowly through the tangled undergrowth of the dense rainforest	waited patiently in the long grass beside the trail	hammered relentlessly against the windows of her bedroom	
Participial phrase	tasting the air for any threats	searching the mud wallow for any sign of the wild boar	slamming the shutters against the walls	

Sentence(s)

1. An enormous snake, a venomous green and yellow cobra, whose black forked tongue flicked from side to side, slithered slowly through the tangled undergrowth of the dense rainforest, tasting the air for any threats.

2. A colossal lizard, a grey armour-plated Komodo dragon, whose long neck peered over the bushes, waited patiently in the long grass beside the trail, searching the mud wallow for any sign of the wild boar.

3. A wind, a fierce swirling gale, whose icy gusts hammered against the windows of her bedroom, tore viciously through gaps in the rotting frames, slamming the shutters against the walls.

4.

STEP 3: EXPERIMENTING WITH WORD CHOICE

★ Are there any words that can be improved?

a. Nouns

★ Is there a more specific noun?
★ What type of lizard is it? **A Komodo dragon.**

b. Adjectives

* ★ Can another adjective be substituted for huge?
* ★ Collect synonyms and experiment by substituting each word into the sentence. Discuss which adjective is preferred and why.

For example: colossal, gigantic, hulking, massive

c. Verbs

* ★ Is there a stronger verb than **waited**?
* ★ Collect synonyms and experiment by substituting each alternative into the sentence. Discuss which verb is preferred and why.

For example: loitered, lurked, skulked

d. Adverbs

* ★ Is there a stronger adverb than **patiently**?
* ★ Collect synonyms and experiment by substituting each alternative into the sentence. Discuss which adverb is preferred and why.

For example: tirelessly, perseveringly, doggedly, tirelessly, watchfully
    Remind students that sometimes the first choice is the most effective.

APPLY THE PROCESS TO STUDENTS' OWN SENTENCES

Students use the same process to experiment with different words in their own sentence. The aim is for students to be able to replicate these steps when revising their own texts.

> STEP 4: EXPERIMENTING WITH WORD ORDER

A. TEACHER MODELLING

Use the model sentences to experiment with different ways of arranging the words in a sentence, talking through the process and decisions to make it visible for the students. Chunking the sentence into meaningful sentence parts will assist in this process.

> **FOR EXAMPLE**
>
> 1a. <u>The enormous green cobra</u>/ **slithered slowly**/ *through the tangled undergrowth.*
>
> 2. *Through the tangled undergrowth,*/ <u>the enormous green cobra</u> **slithered slowly**.
>
> 3. <u>The cobra,</u>/ <u>enormous and green,</u>/ **slithered slowly**/ *through the tangled undergrowth.*
>
> 4. **Slowly**,/ <u>the enormous green cobra</u>/ **slithered**/ *through the tangled undergrowth.*
>
> 5. **Slithering slowly**/ *through the tangled undergrowth*/ **was**/ <u>the enormous green cobra.</u>
>
> 6. <u>The cobra</u>/ **slithering slowly**/ *through the tangled undergrowth*/ **was**/ <u>enormous and green.</u>
>
> 7. <u>The cobra</u>/ **was**/ <u>enormous and green</u> and **slithering slowly**/ *through the tangled undergrowth.*

Read each alternative aloud and discuss which option is the most effective and why.

B. GUIDED ACTIVITY

With the students offering suggestions, imitate the above process and models to construct several different sentence arrangements.

1. The huge grey Komodo dragon/ waited patiently/ in the bushes.
2. In the bushes/, the huge grey Komodo dragon/ waited patiently.
3. The Komodo dragon/ waiting patiently/ in the bushes/ was huge and grey.
4. The Komodo dragon,/ huge and grey,/ waited patiently/ in the bushes.

5. Patiently,/ the huge grey Komodo dragon/ waited in the bushes.
6. Waiting patiently/ in the bushes/ was/ a huge grey Komodo dragon.

Read each alternative aloud and discuss which option is the most effective and why.

C. INDEPENDENT PRACTICE

Students:

☆ use their own sentence (constructed in Step 2) to experiment with different word orders and openers to construct a variety of sentences
☆ can use the same process when revising their own texts and then consider each alternative structure in the context of their paragraph as a whole (how it links with the preceding and subsequent sentences).

10

Expanded noun phrases

1. Give more detail, description or information about a **NOUN**.
2. Use adjectives and prepositional phrases to describe a **NOUN**.

	Determiner +	adjective(s) +	Noun +	prepositional phrase(s)
Level 1	the	soaring	summits	
Level 2	a	soaring snow-capped	summit	
Level 3	several	icy	peaks	like arrowheads
Level 4	several	icy, jagged	peaks	like arrowheads above the village

DOI: 10.4324/9781032662862-12

INSTRUCTIONS

1. The tables below model how to construct an expanded noun phrase.
2. Use the model provided (and vocabulary collected from *Descriptosaurus*) to create your own expanded noun phrases.

Determiner	Adjective(s)	Noun	Prepositional phrase(s)
A	huge snow-covered	mountain	
	majestic, snow-capped	mountains	above the picturesque alpine village
	huge ice-capped	summits	with peaks like granite spires
The	soaring shadowy	summit	at dusk
The	soaring black	peak	like a granite spire
The	soaring shadowy	summit	at dusk with peaks like granite spires
The	perilous, icy	slopes	during the winter
The	snow-capped	summit	at dawn

Determiner	Adjective(s)	Noun	Prepositional phrase(s)
The	majestic	mountains	with snow-capped peaks
The	majestic	mountains	with snow-capped peaks in winter
The	peach-tinted	summit	at sunrise
The	snow-capped, peach-tinted	summit	at sunrise
The	sheer, deadly	slopes	of ice

Determiner	Adjectives	Noun	Prepositional phrase/ Simile and metaphor
A	beautiful, sunny	wood	
A	magnificent, sun-dappled	forest	of towering trees
The	magnificent, sun-dappled	forest	of towering trees with column-like trunks
An	autumnal	cloak	of scarlet and golden leaves
A	huge green	canopy	like a crowd of vivid umbrellas
A	huge vivid-green	canopy	of enormous bowl-shaped leaves
A	huge vivid-green	canopy	of enormous bowl-shaped leaves like a crowd of umbrellas
A	huge vivid-green	canopy	of enormous bowl-shaped leaves like a crowd of umbrellas over the forest floor

A	bright yellow	layer of lichen	like gold dust
Numerous	black, blister-like	fungi	like swollen dead fingers
Numerous	black, blister-like	fungi	like swollen dead fingers in the undergrowth

Determiner	Adjectives	Noun	Prepositional phrase/ Simile and metaphor
A	quaint	village	with narrow cobbled streets
A	small enchanting	haven	away from the polluted city
A	small enchanting	haven	of picturesque, whitewashed cottages with brightly coloured doors and shutters
A	derelict ghost	town	of crumbling houses
A	derelict ghost	town	of crumbling houses like stone skeletons

Determiner	Adjectives	Noun	Prepositional phrase/ Simile and metaphor
A	dramatic	horizon	of blazing bright orange streaks of light
The	first	fingers	of daylight
A	hazy, golden	light	over the mountains
A	grey, ghostly	blanket	of swirling mist
The	smoky	scent	of barbecued food
A	terrifying winged	creature	with an enormous, serpentine body

Determiner	Adjectives	Noun	Prepositional phrase/ Simile and metaphor
A	short, squat	body	with huge muscular shoulders
Two	stumpy little	legs	like a scrawny chicken
	small buggy	eyes	as black as coal
	wispy auburn	strands	of greasy hair over his egg-shaped skull

11

Opening and delayed adjectives

Opening and delayed adjectives
The **vivid colourful** banners fluttered from the windows.
EXAMPLE: A. Move the highlighted adjectives to the beginning of the sentence and combine using **and**.
Vivid and colourful, the banners fluttered from the windows.
B. Move the highlighted adjectives after the noun/noun phrase.
The banners, **vivid and colourful**, fluttered from the windows.

DOI: 10.4324/9781032662862-13

EXERCISE

1A. Move the highlighted adjectives to the beginning of the sentence.

The **ancient, moss-covered** steps led deep beneath the city**.**

1B. Move the highlighted adjectives after the noun/noun phrase.

2A. Move the highlighted adjectives to the beginning of the sentence.

The **dark winding** tunnels were as cold as a crypt.

2B. Move the highlighted adjectives after the noun/noun phrase.

3A. Move the highlighted adjectives to the beginning of the sentence.

The **round rusty** ring poked between the floorboards.

3B. Move the highlighted adjectives after the noun/noun phrase.

4A. Move the highlighted adjectives to the beginning of the sentence.

The **sharp pointed** quill could pierce a man's skin.

4B. Move the highlighted adjectives after the noun/noun phrase.

5A. In this example, there are three adjectives before the noun. Move the highlighted adjectives to the beginning of the sentence.

The **golden**, **curved**, **serrated** sickle was attached to the side of the urn.

5B. Move the highlighted adjectives after the noun/noun phrase.

5C. A more effective way of using these adjectives is to split them up as shown below. Experiment with different combinations and positions of the adjectives.

The **golden, curved and serrated** sickle was attached to the side of the urn.

The **golden** sickle, **curved and serrated**, was attached to the side of the urn.

Opening and delayed adjectives

EXAMPLE:

A. Instead of using a coordinating conjunction, combine the two sentences by moving the highlighted adjectives to the beginning of the sentence.

Scarlett was **slim and athletic** and ran with a natural rhythm.

Slim and athletic, Scarlett ran with a natural rhythm.

B. Move the highlighted adjectives after the noun/noun phrase.

Scarlett, **slim and athletic**, ran with a natural rhythm.

EXERCISE

6A. Combine the two sentences by moving the highlighted adjectives to the beginning of the sentence.
The old tramp was **frail, crumpled and hunched like a question mark** and shuffled painfully across the road.
6B. Move the highlighted adjectives after the noun/noun phrase.

7A. Combine the two sentences by moving the highlighted adjectives to the beginning of the sentence.
Her eyes were **yellow and unblinking like a hawk** and took in every detail, every move.
7B. Move the highlighted adjectives after the noun/noun phrase.

8A. Combine the two sentences by moving the highlighted adjectives to the beginning of the sentence.
The stairs were **narrow and spiralling** and descended steeply to the tunnel below.
8B. Move the highlighted adjectives after the noun/noun phrase.

12

Opening and delayed adverbs

Opening and delayed adverbs

Adverbs can go in four positions:
 	
   i.   at the beginning
   ii. at the end
   iii. after auxiliary verbs (is, was, can, may, will etc.)
   iv. before all other verbs.
 	
EXAMPLE:
 	
A. Rewrite the sentence to include the adverb:
 	
   i.   **at the beginning of the sentence**
   ii. **at the end of the sentence**
   iii. **after the auxiliary verb.**

Adverb: instantly	**Main clause**: The ground was painted with flickering shadows.

i.   **Instantly**, the ground was painted with flickering shadows. ii. The ground was painted with flickering shadows **instantly**. iii. The ground was **instantly** painted with flickering shadows.
B. Write your own sentences using the adverb instantly, varying its position as indicated above.
i.   **Instantly**, the room was plunged into darkness. ii. The room was plunged into darkness **instantly**. iii. The room was **instantly** plunged into darkness.

DOI: 10.4324/9781032662862-14

EXERCISE

1A. Rewrite the sentence to include the adverb:

i.   **at the beginning of the sentence**
ii. **at the end of the sentence**
iii. **before the verb.**

Adverb: boldly	**Main clause**: The gigantic warrior staggered forward.

i.

ii.

iii.

1B. Write your own sentences using the adverb **boldly**, varying its position as indicated above.

i.

ii.

iii.

2A. Rewrite the sentence to include the adverb:

i.   **at the beginning of the sentence**
ii. **after the auxiliary verb**
iii. **at the end of the sentence.**

Adverb: soon	**Main clause**: They would reach the watering-hole.

i.

ii.

iii.

2B. Write your own sentences using the adverb **soon**, varying its position as indicated above.

i.

ii.

iii.

3A. Rewrite the sentence to include the adverb:

i.   **at the beginning of the sentence**
ii. **after the verb**
iii. **at the end of the sentence.**

Adverb: endlessly	**Main clause**: The ice-bound wilderness stretched ahead of them.
i. ii. iii.	

3B. Write your own sentences using the adverb **endlessly**, varying its position as indicated above.

i.
ii.
iii.

4A. Rewrite the sentence to include the adverb:

i.   **at the beginning of the sentence**
ii. **after the verb**
iii. **at the end of the sentence.**

Adverb: mercilessly	**Main clause**: The sun beat down on their heads.
i. ii. iii.	

4B. Write your own sentences using the adverb **mercilessly**, varying its position as indicated above.

i.
ii.
iii.

5A. Rewrite the sentence to include the adverb:

i. **at the beginning of the sentence**
ii. **before the conjunction 'so'**
iii. **before the verb 'leaned'.**

Adverb: cautiously	**Main clause**: Scarlett leaned forward so that she could see around the pillar.
i. ii. iii.	

5B. Write your own sentences using the adverb **cautiously**, varying its position as indicated above.

i.
ii.
iii.

6A. Rewrite the sentence to include the adverb:

i. **at the beginning of the sentence**
ii. **after the verb.**

Adverb: desperately	**Main clause**: She clawed at the ground to stop herself falling into the chasm.
i. ii.	

6B. Write your own sentences using the adverb **desperately**, varying its position as indicated above.

i.
ii.

13

Compound verbs

Compound verbs

EXAMPLE:

A.   Imitate the sentence structure below to write your own sentence using three verbs to describe the wind.

    i.   The shadows flickered, swayed and danced in the dim light.
    ii.   The leaves fluttered, skipped and danced in the gusting breeze.

EXERCISE

1A.   Write your own sentence using three verbs to describe lightning.

1B.   Imitate the sentence structure below to write your own sentence to describe the effect of bright sunshine.

    i.   The trees overhead shut out the light, covering the alley in shadows and painting darting shapes on the walls.
    ii.

2A.   Imitate the sentence structure below to write your own sentence to describe waves gently lapping onto the shore.

    i.   The waves soared high into the air, crashing onto the shore and covering the rocks in swirling white foam.
    ii.

DOI: 10.4324/9781032662862-15

2B. Using the structure below and personification, write your own sentence to describe the heat from the sun.

    i.   The savage cold stung his eyes, blistered his skin and gnawed at his toes and fingers.

    ii.

2C. Using the structure below and personification, write your own sentence to describe a flooding river.

    i.   The fog crept up on the house like a ghostly serpent, slid along the window, flicked its tongue into the corners of the house, waited a moment, and slipped back along the path.

    ii.

3A. Using the structure below, write your own sentence to describe a character celebrating a victory with another team-mate.

    i.   She slid a comforting arm around Scarlett's shoulders, gave her a gentle squeeze and whispered in her ear.

    ii.

4A. Using the structure below, write your own sentence to describe creeping through the shadows.

    i.   She ran, swerved to the right, crashing through the boxes, shoving the bins out of the way and stumbled into the next alley.

    ii.

4B. Using the structure below, write your own sentence to describe being captured by a mythical creature.

    i.   It hovered above them, then plunged out of the night sky, hooking him with its talons.

    ii.

14

Imitating examples from literature

1. *SKELLIG* BY DAVID ALMOND

He was lying in there in the darkness behind the tea chests in the dust and dirt.

Original

STEP 1 – CHUNK INTO MEANINGFUL SENTENCE PARTS

He was lying in there in the darkness behind the tea chests in the dust and dirt.

STEP 2 – CHANGE THE LOCATION AND DESCRIPTION

For example: *a cellar, swamp, mountain, desert, museum*
Make a list of what could be found in that location.

STEP 3 – SUBSTITUTE THE VOCABULARY INTO THE SENTENCE STRUCTURE

He was lying in there in the darkness behind the tea chests in the dust and dirt.

DOI: 10.4324/9781032662862-16

2. *CHARLOTTE'S WEB* BY E. B. WHITE

Original

The next day was rainy and dark.

STEP 1 – CHUNK INTO MEANINGFUL SENTENCE PARTS

The next day was rainy and dark.

STEP 2 – CHANGE

1. The time of day or time period.
   For example: *the following morning, the next few hours*
2. The adjectives to describe the weather or feelings.
   For example: *surprising, unexpected, exciting, terrifying*

STEP 3 – SUBSTITUTE THE VOCABULARY INTO THE SENTENCE STRUCTURE

The next day was rainy and dark.

3. *THE LAST BEAR* BY HANNAH GOLD (PAGE 60)

Original

STEP 1 – CHUNK INTO MEANINGFUL SENTENCE PARTS

The fog was already starting to creep in, slithering along the ground.

STEP 2 – CHANGE

1. The weather
      For example: *the moon, sun, wind, thunder, lightning, rain*
2. The verbs (think of movement, sound and light)
      For example: *racing, darting, tearing, skipping, dancing, leaping, thudding, pounding, hammering, flickering, shimmering, blinding*

STEP 3 – SUBSTITUTE THE VOCABULARY INTO THE SENTENCE STRUCTURE

The fog was already starting to creep in, slithering along the ground.

CHALLENGE

4. *HOW TO BUILD A FIRE* BY JACK LONDON

Day had broken cold and grey, exceedingly cold and grey, when the man turned aside from the main Yukon trail and climbed the high earth-bank, where a dim and little-travelled trail led eastward through the fat spruce timberland.

Original

STEP 1 – CHUNK INTO MEANINGFUL SENTENCE PARTS

Day had broken cold and grey, exceedingly cold and grey, when the man turned aside from the main Yukon trail and climbed the high earth-bank, where a dim and little-travelled trail led eastward through the fat spruce timberland.

STEP 2 – CHANGE

The time of day, temperature, location
   For example: *night, damp and dark, sea*

STEP 3 – SUBSTITUTE THE VOCABULARY INTO THE SENTENCE STRUCTURE

_____

_____

SECTION B – IMITATING A PARAGRAPH

1. *CHARLOTTE'S WEB* BY E. B. WHITE

- ★ Take one sentence at a time.
- ★ Chunk it into meaningful sentence parts.
- ★ Change the subject.
- ★ Imitate each of the sentence parts.
- ★ Combine the sentences into a paragraph.

Original paragraph:

[1]The next day was rainy and dark. [2]Rain fell on the roof of the barn and dripped steadily from the eaves. [3]Rain fell in the barnyard and ran in crooked courses down into the lane where thistles and pigweed grew. [4]Rain spattered against Mrs Zuckerman's kitchen window and came gushing out of the downspouts. [5]Rain fell on the backs of the sheep as they grazed in the meadow.

Follow Steps 1–3 in Section A to imitate each sentence (chunking, changing the subject of the sentence, collecting adjectives and verbs, etc.).

1. **The next day was rainy and dark.**

   _____

2. **Rain** fell on the roof of the barn and dripped steadily from the eaves.

   _____

3. **Rain** fell in the barnyard and ran in crooked courses down into the lane where thistles and pigweed grew.

    _____

4. **Rain** spattered against Mrs Zuckerman's kitchen windows and came gushing out of the downspouts.

    _____

5. **Rain** fell on the backs of the sheep as they grazed in the meadow.

    _____

2. *HOUND OF THE BASKERVILLES* BY CONAN DOYLE

[1]I found myself weary and yet wakeful, tossing restlessly from side to side, seeking for the sleep which would not come. [2]Far away a chiming clock struck out the quarters of the hours, but otherwise a deathly silence lay upon the old house. [3]And then suddenly, in the very dead of the night, there came a sound, clear and resonant, and unmistakeable. [4]It was the sob of a woman.

Original paragraph:
Follow Steps 1–3 in Section A to imitate each sentence (chunking, changing the subject of the sentence, collecting adjectives and verbs, etc.).

1. I found myself weary and yet wakeful, tossing restlessly from side to side, seeking for the sleep which would not come.

    _____

2. Far away a chiming clock struck out the quarters of the hours, but otherwise a deathly silence lay upon the old house.

    _____

3. And then suddenly, in the very dead of the night, there came a sound, clear and resonant, and unmistakeable.

    _____

4. It was the sob of a woman.

    _____

SUGGESTIONS

SECTION A – IMITATING SENTENCES

SKELLIG BY DAVID ALMOND

1. He was lying/ in there/ in the darkness/ behind the tea chests,/ in the dust and dirt.
2. A cellar, swamp, mountain

   a. **Cellar**: shadows, cobwebs, boxes and chests
   b. **Swamp**: mud, moss hanging from the branches, duckweed on the surface, bogbean and spearwort
   c. **Mountain**: slope, scree and boulders, ice, snow, mist

3. He was lying in there in the darkness behind the tea chests in the dust and dirt.

   a. He was hiding/ in the shadows/ in the cellar,/ behind the boxes and chests.
   b. He was hiking/ through the mud/ in the swamp,/ through the spearwort and bogbean.
   c. He was scrambling/ up the slope/ of the mountain,/ over the boulders and scree.

CHARLOTTE'S WEB BY E. B. WHITE

1. The next day/ was/ rainy and dark.
2a. last night, the following morning, the next day, the following hours
   b. hot and humid, snowy and cold, exciting and unexpected, endless and nerve-wracking
3. Last night/ <u>was</u>/ hot and humid.

   <u>The</u> following morning/ <u>was</u>/ snowy and cold.
   <u>The</u> next day/ <u>was</u>/ exciting and unexpected.
   <u>The</u> following hours/ <u>were</u>/ endless and nerve-wracking.

THE LAST BEAR BY HANNAH GOLD

1. The fog/ was already <u>starting to creep in,</u>/ slithering along the ground.
2a. moon, wind
   b. beam, slant, brush, rise, gust, swirling, racing
3. The moon/ was already starting to beam down,/ brushing over the rooftops.
4. The wind/ was already starting to get up,/ swirling through the trees.

HOW TO BUILD A FIRE BY JACK LONDON

1. Day had broken/ cold and grey,/ exceedingly cold and grey,/ when the man turned aside/ from the main Yukon trail/ and climbed the high earth-bank,/ where a dim and little-travelled trail/ led eastward/ through the fat spruce timberland.
2a. Day, night, evening, dusk
   b. warm and bright, damp and dark
   c. tent, desert, sun, skies, rays, shimmering, dazzling, sizzling, arid, merciless

Day had dawned warm and bright, exceptionally warm and bright, when she emerged from her tent and searched the shimmering skies, where the dazzling and sizzling rays blasted westward across the arid merciless desert.

SECTION B – IMITATING A PARAGRAPH

CHARLOTTE'S WEB BY E. B. WHITE

1. **The next day was rainy and dark.**
   <u>The</u> following morning/ <u>was</u>/ snowy and cold.
   <u>The</u> following hours/ were endless/ and nerve-wracking.
2. **Rain/** fell on the roof/ of the barn/ and/ dripped steadily/ from the eaves.
   Snow/ fell on the trees/ in the wood/ and/ clung steadfastly/ to their branches.
   Wind/ blew against the tiles/ of the roof/ and/ thudded relentlessly/ at the windows.

3. **Rain/** fell in the barnyard/ and/ ran in crooked courses/ down into the lane/ where thistles and pigweed grew.
   Snow/ spilled out of the sky/ and/ bunched in lofty drifts/ against the trees/ where the dead branches and leaves collected.
   Wind/ blew against the house/ and/ pounded in fierce gusts/ onto the roof/ where the tiles and gutters rattled.
4. **Rain/** spattered/ against Mrs Zuckerman's kitchen windows/ and/ came gushing out of the downspouts.
   Snow/ slithered/ down Joe's bedroom windows/ and/ bunched on the windowsills.
   Wind/ roared/ down the chimney/ and/ swirled around the room.
5. Rain/ fell on the backs of the sheep/ as they grazed in the meadow.
   Snow/ fell on the roofs of the houses/ as they shivered in the storm.
   Wind spiralled around the house as it tore at its foundations.

Imitation 1 – Snow

The following morning was snowy and cold. Snow fell on the trees in the wood and clung steadfastly to their branches. Snow spilled out of the sky and bunched in lofty drifts against the trees where the dead branches and leaves collected. Snow slithered down Joe's bedroom window and bunched on the windowsill. Snow fell on the roofs of the houses as they shivered in the storm.

Imitation 2 – Wind

The following hours were endless and nerve-wracking. Wind whirled around the house and thudded relentlessly at the windows. Wind hammered against the doors and pounded in fierce gusts onto the roof where the tiles and gutters rattled. Wind roared down the chimney and swirled into the room. Wind spiralled around the house as it tore at its foundations.

HOUND OF THE BASKERVILLES BY CONAN DOYLE

1. I found myself weary/ and yet wakeful,/ tossing restlessly/ from side to side,/ seeking for the sleep/ which would not come.
   She discovered herself warm/ and yet shivery,/ wrapped up tightly/ from top to toe,/ searching for the warmth/ which did not arrive.

2.   Far away/ a chiming clock/ struck out the quarters of the hours,/ but otherwise/ a deathly silence/ lay upon the old house.
      From the churchyard,/ the ancient clock/ chimed the hours,/ but elsewhere/ a throbbing silence/ blanketed the house.
4.   And then suddenly,/ in the very dead of the night,/ there came a sound,/ clear and resonant,/and unmistakeable.
      And then unexpectedly,/ in the grey hours of dawn,/ there came a noise,/ faint and fleeting,/ yet distinct.
5.   It was the sob/ of a woman.
      It was the creak/ of the front door.

Imitation:

She discovered herself warm and yet shivery, wrapped up tightly from top to toe, searching for the warmth which did not arrive. From the churchyard the ancient clock chimed the hours, but elsewhere a throbbing silence blanketed the house. And then unexpectedly, in the grey hours of dawn, there came a noise, faint and fleeting, yet distinct. It was the creak of the front door.

Part 3

Sentence combining

15

Sentence combining method

Sentence combining is a method of developing writing skills through **structured language workout exercises** that can be easily incorporated into a classroom writing task. It builds on students' prior knowledge and it aims, through collaboration and experimentation, to increase students' ability to create and revise written sentences. It can be used to teach the style and structure appropriate to any academic discipline. These exercises also provide an invaluable insight into any problem areas for individual students, groups or a class that require additional attention or consolidation.

Its goal is to teach students how:

* to construct good sentences
* to be able to evaluate and make considered choices in their own writing.

It does not require:

* any special materials, the source for the exercises being class texts (fiction, non-fiction poetry and all curriculum subjects) and students' own writing
* lengthy lessons (short, sharp bursts are most effective)
* any specialist knowledge on the part of the teacher to incorporate into a lesson.

Since sentence combining was first developed in the 1960s, there have been over 80 studies which have produced overwhelming evidence that this method is effective for helping students to:

DOI: 10.4324/9781032662862-18

⋆   develop automaticity in sentence construction
⋆   craft accurate and syntactically mature sentences
⋆   make considered choices as to the effectiveness of each sentence in producing a cohesive text.

Sentence combining is a controlled, purposeful language exercise that expands students' knowledge of the syntactic options available to them and provides direct and targeted practise in combining, manipulating and rewriting basic phrases, clauses and sentences to produce more concise, varied and mature constructions. It is a valuable exercise for writers at all levels because it represents a structured composition exercise that directly parallels the tasks routinely undertaken by writers. Sentence combining is particularly effective in respect of the revision stage of the writing process, which involves taking a set of sentences composed in a first draft and rearranging, deleting, expanding, manipulating and transforming them to improve their construction and the cohesion, clarity and precision of the text. Very often, the crucial revision stage of the writing process is neglected or given minimal attention. Students, having committed significant time and effort to a first draft, are so invested in that draft that they are reluctant to make changes. It is, therefore, important to encourage students to take on more active, self-assessing roles rather than relying on teachers to point out their mistakes and instruct them how to 'fix' their writing.

⋆   What are the effects of one choice versus another?
⋆   How will communication to the reader best be served?

Sentence combining exercises give students ample practice at selecting effective sentences, experimenting with different structures and arrangements, and this better equips them to revisit their texts and revise for clarity and effect. They are more willing to experiment and take risks as errors are viewed as part of the learning process. When students make usage errors, this provides an opportunity for immediate feedback and discussion, resolving any misunderstandings and problems; therefore, this speeds up learning and transfer to their own writing. Through participation in sentence combining exercises, students begin to understand that sentences require drafting and persistent revision, patience and commitment. With an increased awareness of the grammar tools at their disposal and competence in using them, students will consider alternative options and make more thoughtful choices in the context of their own texts.

Students enjoy sentence combining exercises as there are lots of right answers, which reduces any anxiety and encourages risk-taking and experimentation. It provides a context for students to teach and support one another in discovering different language patterns. As each student gives and receives immediate feedback on whether the sentence makes sense, sentence combining serves as a skill-building supplement to any language curriculum.

CONTEXTUALISED, PURPOSEFUL LANGUAGE EXERCISES

Reading and writing skills are inextricably linked; reading skills support and develop writing skills and writing supports reading skills. When we provide models from authentic texts and encourage students to pay attention to patterns and how a text is crafted, as well as observing what is good and how writers achieve it, language becomes the teacher.

Student writers, particularly those who have more limited reading experience, do not have a visual image of what a sentence looks like or what options (craft tools) are available to them when constructing a sentence. The aim of any purposeful language exercise should be to get students to pay attention to language by noticing syntax in their reading texts and exploring how it was achieved by the author.

Sentence combining makes use of students' in-built linguistic competence, their intuition about how sentences are supposed to sound. By comparing the options created by the class, group or a peer (and the original professional sentence), most students immediately recognise that certain constructions are clearer and easier to understand than others. By providing a practical way of paying attention to language and patterns in texts and experimenting with language, sentence combining trains students to 'read like a writer'.

GRAMMAR AND PUNCTUATION AS A SET OF CRAFT TOOLS

A skilled writer depends mainly on their ability to craft sentences, not to label parts of speech or recite rules. The foundation of sentence combining exercises is developing an awareness of syntactic options, and learning grammar and punctuation not as a set of rules but as tools of a writer's craft. Technical knowledge of grammar without application will not improve students' ability to communicate in writing with precision and clarity.

While the aim of sentence combining is to explore the options available for constructing sentences, this process will also naturally increase students' working knowledge of punctuation, grammar terms and syntax functions. When students have more experience of sentence combining exercises, they become more confident with combining and moving modifiers, and automatically develop a knowledge of grammar terms: a common language they can use when discussing the sentence options available.

DISCUSSION AND COLLABORATION

An essential part of the process is using discussion and collaboration to get students to consider the effectiveness of the different variations of a sentence or sentences. This process of making repeated judgements about how sentences sound, including in the larger context of a paragraph, is one of the fundamentals of writing instruction. However, for sentence combining exercises to be effective, it is essential to create an environment that facilitates collaborative endeavour and exploration, with discussion and experimentation at the heart of the process, where everyone writes, where every voice is heard, and where every student has a stake in the improvement of the collective.

TEACHING SEQUENCE

1. TEACHERS MODELLING AND THINKING ALOUD

Teachers model how to combine the kernel sentences, reading the kernel sentences aloud and explaining what they are doing and why. For example, deleting unnecessary words, adding a conjunction to form a subordinate clause, changing word endings etc. Where possible, explore more than one combination (at least two transformations in each category), read them aloud and then discuss which transformation is preferred and why.

2. GUIDED PRACTICE

Scaffolded practice in which teachers guide students to develop multiple solutions to a problem, gradually reducing their own input and increasing the amount of discussion and quality judgements by the students.

3. INDEPENDENT PRACTICE (GROUP, PEER AND INDIVIDUAL)

Independent practice during which the students create several transformations for each cluster and discuss and evaluate the effectiveness of each transformation. These transformations should then be discussed as a whole class, evaluated (with an understanding that mistakes are an opportunity for learning), and the best sentences chosen and recorded. By comparing options, students begin to understand that some sentences are clearer and sound better.

Group work (three or four students)

Each student:

1. Works on a separate sheet of paper.
2. Focuses on the same cluster.
3. After each cluster has been completed, swaps papers.
4. Moves on to the next cluster.
5. Repeats the process until all the clusters have been combined.

Discuss and evaluate each paragraph, sentence by sentence and vote on which combination is preferred.

As a whole class, discuss which of the paragraphs presented by the groups is preferred, and make a note of the techniques used. Finally, compare the best transformation with the original. Students also need to understand that, on occasions, sentences may be more effective uncombined, as short sentences can create emphasis, improve clarity, and create suspense and tension where required.

METHOD

1. **Base (kernel) sentences**
   Sentences are broken down into **base sentences** (called kernel sentences).
2. **Modifying clauses**
   The **base clause** comes first and is followed by **one or more modifying clauses**.

For example: Cluster 1

1.1   There was a mist. (Base clause)
1.2   The mist was strange. (Modifying clause)
1.3   The mist was swirling. (Modifying clause)
1.4   The mist shrouded the house. (Modifying clause)
1.5   The house was old. (Modifying clause)

3. **Combined sentences including modifying clauses**
   The challenge is to combine the kernel clauses by incorporating the information contained in the modifying sentences into the base clause, and to experiment with different combinations of the words and phrases and then choose the most effective.

Transformations:

a.   There was a strange, swirling mist. It shrouded the old house.
b.   There was a strange, swirling mist, and it shrouded the old house.
c.   A strange, swirling mist shrouded the old house.
d.   The old house was shrouded by a strange, swirling mist.
e.   Shrouding the old house was a strange, swirling mist.
f.   A mist, strange and swirling, shrouded the old house.
g.   Strange and swirling, a mist shrouded the old house.

4. **Clusters**
   Groups of connected sentences (the base sentence and its modifiers) are arranged in **clusters**.

Each cluster represents a potential new sentence. As students gain in experience and knowledge, a number of clusters can be included that can then be combined into a paragraph.

Combining the sentences could involve:

- ☆ deleting any unnecessary (repeated) words
- ☆ rearranging words
- ☆ adding co-ordinating conjunctions to combine clauses
- ☆ adding subordinating conjunctions to form a dependent clause
- ☆ moving words around
- ☆ changing word endings (for example, changing a verb ending to -ing or -ed to construct a participial phrase, or adding -ly to change an adjective to an adverb).

The exercises can be:

1A. cued

1B. open

2A. oral

2B. written.

1A. CUED EXERCISES

There are several cues that can scaffold the exercise:

1. Words to be combined are underlined.
2. A ^ is used to indicate the position of the cued underlined word or phrase.
3. The punctuation to be used can be indicated.
4. A key word(s) is placed in brackets at the end of the modifying clause(s) that guides students to combine the kernels in a particular way, for example, [,WHO…,]. The **key word** is placed at the **beginning of the modifying clause** to be combined with the base clause to complete the transformation.

EXAMPLE 1

    a.   The girl, ^, sat quietly in the window seat. (**KERNEL SENTENCE**)

    b.   ~~She~~ had piercing bright blue eyes. (WHO) (**MODIFIYING SENTENCE**)

           The girl, <u>who had piercing bright blue eyes</u>, sat quietly in the window seat.

EXAMPLE 2

    1.1 She ran towards the door.

    1.2 ~~She~~ fumbled ^ for the lock. (AND)

    1.3 ~~She was~~ frantic (-LY).[1]

[1](-LY) prompts the student to change the adjective **frantic** to the adverb **frantically**.

She ran towards the door and fumbled frantically for the lock.

EXAMPLE 3

    1.1 ^ , She raced to the door.^

    1.2 <u>She heard the car pull up outside</u>. (WHEN)

    1.3 She <u>fumbled ^ for the lock</u>. (-ING)[2]

    1.4 She was **frantic**. (-LY)

[2](-ING) is a clue to change the verb ending to -ING to construct a participial phrase (fumbled to fumbling).

    a.   When she heard the car pull up outside, she raced to the door, **fumbling** frantically for the lock.

    b.   When she heard the car pull up outside, she raced to the door and fumbled frantically for the lock.

    c.   She raced to the door when she heard the car pull up outside and fumbled frantically for the lock.

EXAMPLE 4

1.1 ∧, The sun had fallen.
1.2 She had been exploring the house. (WHILE…,)
1.3 It was <u>like a sinking stone.</u>
1.4 ∧ There was <u>a mist</u>. (AND)
1.5 It was <u>strange and swirling</u>.
1.6 It <u>shrouded the house</u>.

a. While she had been exploring the house, the sun had fallen like a sinking stone, and a strange, swirling mist shrouded the house.
b. The sun had fallen like a sinking stone while she had been exploring the house, and a strange, swirling mist shrouded the house.

EXAMPLE 5

1.1 ∧, She waited a few more minutes.
1.2 She was sure no one was following her. (ALTHOUGH)
1.3 She approached the house. (BEFORE)

a. Although she was sure no one was following her, she waited a few more minutes before she approached the house.
b. She waited a few more minutes before she approached the house, although she was sure no one was following her.

When discussing the above two options, discuss what should be emphasised, the fact that:

a. she waited before approaching the house, or
b. she was sure no one was following her.

Gradually move away from basic problems that offer only a limited number of possible solutions to longer problems that can be combined in many ways.

1B. OPEN

Once students are confident with these exercises, the next step is to eliminate the clues and transfer the responsibility to the students to decide what material is important to include in the base sentence, what connectors to use and experiment with combining them in a variety of ways. Eventually, the challenge is increased to combining clusters of sentences into a paragraph.

The teacher can give oral prompts, such as begin with a subordinate clause, open with a participial phrase.

EXAMPLE 6

1.1 He stopped.
1.2 He took a closer look.
1.3 His stomach lurched.

When he stopped and took a closer look, his stomach lurched.

EXAMPLE 7

1.1 It was a snake.
1.2 It was enormous and venomous.
1.3 It was a green and yellow cobra.
1.4 It slithered slowly through the tangled undergrowth.

An enormous and venomous, green and yellow cobra slithered slowly through the tangled undergrowth.

COMBINING CLUSTERS INTO A PARAGRAPH

1.1 The torch swept back and forth.
1.2 The torch swept up and down.
1.3 The torch spread a strip of light over the ground.
1.4 It spread across the bins.
1.5 It spread up the wall.

2.1 The edges of the metal stabbed.

2.2 The edges were sharp.

2.3 The edges were chipped.

2.4 The edges were like needles.

2.5 They stabbed into her side.

2.6 Scarlett pressed her head and side against the bin.

3.1 Five minutes came.

3.2 Five minutes went.

4.1 Her heart was now pounding.

4.2 It was so fast it was hammering against her ribs.

5.1 He could decide to move the bins.

5.2 It could happen any moment.

5.3 She would be trapped.

The torch swept back and forth, up and down, spreading a strip of light over the ground, across the bins and up the wall. Even though the sharp, chipped edges of the metal stabbed like needles into her side, Scarlett pressed against the bin. Five minutes came and went. Her heart was pounding so fast it was hammering against her ribs; any moment, he could decide to move the bins and she would be trapped.

Sentence combining exercises can be oral or written.

2A. ORAL

When combining sentences, it is important for students to hear the alternatives to enable them to choose the sentence that sounds best, so begin each session with oral practice. Oral rehearsal gives students an opportunity to rely on their intrinsic linguistic knowledge developed over years of listening and reading to decide on the correctness and sound quality of their combinations and to test them out in a safe, no-risk environment, with each student serving as an audience for the others as they share and compare their solutions.

2B. WRITTEN

These exercises are most effective when students write out their transformations as complete sentences rather than merely filling in the blanks.

16

Expanded noun phrases

EXAMPLE 1

1.1 The mountains soared into the sky.
1.2 ~~The mountains were~~ huge.
1.3 ~~The mountains were~~ hostile.

A. Combine the kernel sentences.

a. The huge hostile mountains soared into the sky.

B. Combine the kernel sentences in at least two other ways and decide which is preferred and why.

b. Huge and hostile, the mountains soared into the sky.
c. The mountains, huge and hostile, soared into the sky.
d. Soaring into the sky were huge hostile mountains.
e. Into the sky soared the huge hostile mountains.
f. Into the sky soared the mountains, huge and hostile.
g. Into the sky, huge and hostile, soared the mountains.

DOI: 10.4324/9781032662862-19

C. Imitate the model sentence using your own adjectives, verbs and prepositional phrases.

The bleak, treacherous mountains loomed over the village.

1. Bleak and treacherous, the mountains loomed over the village.
2. The mountains, bleak and treacherous, loomed over the village.
3. Looming over the village, the mountains were bleak and treacherous.
4. Over the village, loomed the bleak, treacherous mountains.
5. Over the village, loomed the mountains, bleak and treacherous.
6. Over the village, bleak and treacherous, loomed the mountains.

EXERCISE

1.1 Torrents of ash and rock rained.

1.2 The ash and rock were sizzling.

1.3 The ash and rock were smouldering.

1.4 They rained down from the sky.

_____

Variation:

_____

_____

Imitation:

_____

2.1 A man waited in the entrance.

2.2 The man was short.

2.3 The man was burly.

_____

Variation:

_____

_____

Imitation:

_____

3.1 Mountains of cloud glided.

3.2 The mountains of cloud were dense.

3.3 The mountains of cloud were grey.

3.4 They glided like a mist.

3.5 They glided over the hills.

Variation:

Imitation:

4.1 His arms were like a gorilla.

4.2 His arms were long.

4.3 His arms were hairy.

4.4 His arms were muscular.

Variation:

Imitation:

5.1 SOMETHING scuttled towards them. **(-ING)**

5.2 It was a moth.

5.3 The moth was hideous.

5.4 The moth was black.

Variation:

_____

_____

Imitation:

_____

6.1 Ropes of drool hung from its mouth.

6.2 The drool was slimy.

6.3 The drool was yellow.

6.3 Its mouth was gaping.

Variation:

_____

_____

Imitation:

_____

7.1 A stench hung in the air.

7.2 The stench was foul and putrid.

7.3 The stench was of rotten eggs.

7.4 The air was smoky.

Variation:

_____

_____

Imitation:

_____

8.1 The frost glittered.
8.2 It was like a crystal necklace.
8.3 The frost was on the spider's web.

_____

Variation:

_____

_____

Imitation:

_____

9.1 The branches grasped at her ankles.
9.2 The branches were dead.
9.3 The branches were like fingers.
9.4 The fingers were gnarled.
9.5 The fingers were bony.

_____

Variation:

_____

_____

Imitation:

_____

10.1 A sensation gripped the back of his neck.
10.2 The sensation was cold.
10.3 The sensation was spider-like.

_____

Variation:

_____

_____

Imitation:

_____

11.1 The ocean was a picture postcard of paradise.

11.2 The ocean was turquoise.

11.3 The ocean was crystal clear.

11.4 The ocean was as smooth as silk.

_____

Variation:

_____

_____

Imitation:

_____

12.1 The air was pounding on his head.

12.2 The air was hot.

12.3 The air was humid.

12.4 The air was like an invisible hammer.

_____

Variation:

_____

_____

Imitation:

_____

13.1 Snow tumbled from the sky.

13.2 The snow was like tiny pieces of lace.

13.3 The lace was delicate.

13.4 The snow sprinkled the ground. (**AND/-ING**)

13.5 It sprinkled it with patches of white dust.

_____

Variation:

_____

_____

Imitation:

_____

14.1 Its teeth were like arrowheads.

14.2 Its teeth were huge.

14.3 The arrowheads were steel.

14.4 Its teeth could tear a shark in two. (**AND/THAT**)

_____

Variation:

_____

_____

Imitation:

_____

15.1 Two figures had been tracking them through the city.

15.2 The figures were furtive.

15.3 The figures were like bloodhounds.

15.4 The tracking had been for days.

_____

Variation:

_____

_____

Imitation:

_____

16.1 A sensation gripped the back of her neck.

16.2 The sensation was strange.

16.3 The sensation was prickling.

16.4 The sensation was like a hand.

16.5 The hand was cold.

16.6 The hand was skeletal.

_____

Variation:

_____

_____

Imitation:

_____

17.1 Beams of sunlight penetrated the canopy.

17.2 The sunlight was bright.

17.3 The sunlight was like a shower of golden mist.

17.4 The canopy was dense.

17.5 The canopy was tangled.

_____

Variation:

_____
_____

Imitation:

_____

18.1 Layers of clouds spiralled down the hill.

18.2 The clouds were heavy.

18.3 The clouds were black.

18.4 The clouds blanketed the city. (**AND/TO**)

_____

Variation:

_____
_____

Imitation:

_____

19.1 Fingers of swirling mist slithered down the hill.

19.2 The mist was grey and icy.

19.3 The mist spread across the ground.

19.4 The mist curled around the trees.

19.5 The mist shrouded the forest. (**AND**)

_____

Variation:

_____
_____

Imitation:

_____

20.1 A guillotine blade of lightning streaked.

20.2 The lightning was immense.

20.3 The lightning was dazzling.

20.4 It streaked across the night sky.

_____

Variation:

_____

_____

Imitation:

_____

21.1 A wind blew.

21.2 The wind was cold.

21.3 The wind was shivering.

21.4 It blew on the back of their necks.

Variation:

_____

_____

Imitation:

_____

22.1 The embers of the fire flickered.

22.2 The embers were glowing.

22.3 The embers were red.

22.4 The embers then died.

_____

Variation:

_____

_____

Imitation:

_____

23.1 She held a mirror.

23.2 She held it in her hand.

23.3 The mirror was small.

23.4 The mirror was gilt-edged.

_____

Variation:

_____

_____

Imitation:

_____

24.1 A beam of light shone.

24.2 The beam was intense.

24.3 The light was blinding and white.

24.4 It was like a spotlight.

24.5 It shone on the stone.

_____

Variation:

_____

_____

Imitation:

_____

25.1 Pinpricks of light flickered.

25.2 The light was purple.

25.3 The light was vibrant.

25.4 It flickered in waves.

25.5 It flickered against the doors.

_____

Variation:

_____

_____

Imitation:

_____

26.1 A column of smoke whirled.
26.2 The column was huge.
26.3 The smoke was dense and black.
26.4 It whirled at tremendous speed.
26.5 It was like a tornado.
26.6 It whirled towards the town.

_____

Variation:

_____

_____

Imitation:

_____

27.1 The peaks glinted.
27.2 The peaks were sheer and jagged.
27.3 They glinted in the sun.

_____

Variation:

_____

_____

Imitation:

_____

28.1 The surface of the sea glittered.
28.2 The surface was glassy and emerald.
28.3 They glittered with a million crystals.
28.4 The crystals were of sunlight.

_____

Variation:

_____

_____

Imitation:

_____

29.1 A thick blanket surrounded them.
29.2 The blanket was black.
29.3 The blanket was of sea and sky.
29.4 The sea was swirling.
29.5 The sky was stormy.

Variation:

Imitation:

30.1 The plume of vapour was a reminder.
30.2 The vapour was white and belching.
30.3 The plume of vapour was above the volcano.
30.4 The reminder was silent.
30.5 The reminder was menacing.
30.6 The reminder was of its awesome power.

Variation:

Imitation:

In this next section substitute **with** for **had** and, where necessary, add the appropriate possessive pronoun: *his, her, its, our, their.* Clues have been included for the first few combinations.

EXAMPLE 2

1.1 The mountains loomed above the village.

1.2 ~~The mountains were~~ hostile.

1.3 ~~The mountains~~ had jagged peaks. (*substitute* **with** *for* **had**)
   with their jagged peaks

1.5 The peaks were like arrowheads.

1.4 ~~The mountains loomed~~ menacingly.

   The hostile mountains, with their jagged peaks like arrowheads, loomed menacingly above the village.

B. Combine the kernel sentences in at least two different ways and decide which is preferred and why.

With their jagged peaks like arrowheads, the hostile mountains loomed menacingly above the village.

Looming menacingly above the village were the hostile mountains with their jagged peaks like arrowheads.

Menacingly, above the village loomed the hostile mountains with their jagged peaks like arrowheads.

Menacingly, above the village, with their jagged peaks like arrowheads, loomed the hostile mountains.

C. Imitate the model sentence using your own
adjectives, verbs and prepositional phrase.

The savage summits with their dagger-like peaks soared ominously over their heads.

With their dagger-like peaks, the savage summits soared ominously over their heads.

Soaring ominously over their heads were the savage summits with their dagger-like peaks.

Ominously, over their heads soared the savage summits with their dagger-like peaks.

Ominously, over their heads, with their dagger-like peaks soared the savage summits.

EXERCISE

31.1 It was a town.
31.2 The town was quaint and medieval.
31.3 The town had narrow streets. (**WITH**)
31.4 The streets were cobbled.

_____

Variation:

_____

_____

Imitation:

_____

32.1 She was a tall woman.

32.2 She was scrawny.

32.3 She had a face like a weasel. (**WITH**)

32.4 She had bony hands. (**AND**)

32.5 Her hands had long clawed fingers. (**WITH**)

_____

Variation:

_____

_____

Imitation:

_____

33.1 He was a brute.

33.2 He was towering and muscular.

33.3 He had a mop of hair. (**WITH**)

33.4 His hair was flaming.

33.5 His hair was red.

_____

Variation:

_____

_____

Imitation:

_____

34.1 Her face had a haunted look.

34.2 Her face was pale.

34.3 Her face was sickly.

34.4 Her face had sunken eyes. (**WITH**)

34.5 Her eyes were as black as coal.

_____

Variation:

_____

_____

Imitation:

_____

35.1 The man looked like a hawk.

35.2 The man had slit-like eyes. (**WITH HIS)**

35.3 The man had a long, pointed nose. (**AND)**

_____

Variation:

_____

_____

Imitation:

_____

36.1 His face was lit up by a huge smile.

36.2 His face was ruddy.

36.3 He had bright eyes.

36.4 His eyes were twinkling.

36. 5 His eyes were grey.

_____

Variation:

_____

_____

Imitation:

_____

37.1 Her eyes shone.

37.4 Her eyes <u>had</u> a strange power.

37.2 Her eyes were piercing.

37.3 Her eyes were violet.

_____

Variation:

_____

_____

Imitation:

_____

38.1 The river, ^ , was a dangerous place to swim.

38.4 The river had swirling currents. **(WITH ITS)**

38.2 ~~It had~~ brown water. **(AND)**

38.3 ~~It had~~ murky water.

_____

Variation:

_____

_____

Imitation:

_____

39.1 The island was guarded by a sea-monster.

39.2 The sea-monster was fierce.

39.3 It <u>had</u> an enormous body.

39.4 The body was humped.

39.5 The body was serpentine.

_____

Variation:

_____

_____

Imitation:

_____

40.1 In front of him was a book.

40.2 The book was huge.

40.3 The book was leather-bound.

40.4 The book <u>had</u> mystical symbols and sigils.

40.5 The symbols and sigils were etched into the cover.

40.6 Its cover was gilt-edged.

_____

Variation:

_____

_____

Imitation:

_____

COLLECTION OF EXPANDED NOUN PHRASES

_____
_____
_____
_____
_____
_____
_____
_____
_____
_____
_____
_____
_____
_____
_____
_____
_____
_____
_____

ANSWERS

SECTION A

1. *Torrents of sizzling, smouldering ash and rock rained down from the sky.*

Variations:

a. Torrents of ash and rock, sizzling and smouldering, rained down from the sky.
b. Sizzling and smouldering, torrents of ash and rock rained down from the sky.
c. Raining down from the sky were torrents of sizzling, smouldering ash and rock.
d. Raining down from the sky, sizzling and smouldering, were torrents of ash and rock.
e. Down from the sky, sizzling and smouldering, rained torrents of ash and rock.

2. *A short, burly man waited in the entrance.*

Variations:

a. Waiting in the entrance was a short, burly man.
b. In the entrance waited a short, burly man.

3. *Dense grey mountains of cloud glided like a mist over the hills.*

Variations:

a. Mountains of cloud, dense and grey, glided like a mist over the hills.
b. Dense and grey, mountains of cloud glided like a mist over the hills.
c. Like a mist, dense grey mountains of cloud glided over the hills.
d. Gliding like a mist over the hills were dense grey mountains of cloud.

4. His arms were long, hairy and muscular like a gorilla.

Variations:

a. Long and hairy, his arms were muscular like a gorilla.

b. His arms, long, hairy and muscular, were like a gorilla.

c. Like a gorilla, his arms were long, hairy and muscular.

5. Scuttling towards him was a hideous black moth.

Variations:

a. A hideous black moth scuttled towards him.

b. Hideous and black, a moth scuttled towards him.

c. A moth, hideous and black, scuttled towards him.

6. Ropes of slimy yellow drool hung from its gaping mouth.

Variations:

a. Slimy and yellow, ropes of drool hung from its gaping mouth.

b. Ropes of drool, slimy and yellow, hung from its gaping mouth,

c. Hanging from its gaping mouth were ropes of slimy yellow drool.

7. A foul, putrid stench of rotten eggs hung in the smoky air.

Variations:

a. Foul and putrid, a stench of rotten eggs hung in the smoky air.

b. A stench of rotten eggs, foul and putrid, hung in the smoky air.

c. Hanging in the smoky air was a foul, putrid stench of rotten eggs.

d. Hanging in the smoky air, foul and putrid, was a stench of rotten eggs.

e. Hanging in the smoky air was a stench of rotten eggs, foul and putrid.

8. The frost glittered like a crystal necklace on the spider's web.

Variations:

a. Like a crystal necklace, the frost glittered on the spider's web.

b. On the spider's web, frost glittered like a crystal necklace.

c. The frost, like a crystal necklace, glittered on the spider's web.

9. *Dead branches grasped at her ankles like gnarled bony fingers.*

Variations:

a. Like gnarled bony fingers, the dead branches grasped at her ankles.
b. Grasping at her ankles like gnarled bony fingers were dead branches.
c. Grasping at her ankles were dead branches like gnarled bony fingers.

10. *A cold, spider-like sensation gripped the back of his neck.*

Variations:

a. Cold and spider-like, a sensation gripped the back of his neck.
b. A sensation, cold and spider-like, gripped the back of his neck.
c. Gripping the back of his neck was a cold, spider-like sensation.

11. *Crystal clear and as smooth as silk, the turquoise ocean was a picture post-card of paradise.*

Variations:

a. The turquoise ocean, crystal clear and as smooth as silk, was a picture postcard of paradise.
b. A picture postcard of paradise, the turquoise ocean was crystal clear and as smooth as silk.

12. *The hot humid air was like an invisible hammer pounding on his head.*

Variations:

a. Hot and humid, the air was like an invisible hammer pounding on his head.
b. The air, hot and humid, was like an invisible hammer pounding on his head.
c. Like an invisible hammer, the hot humid air pounded on his head.
d. Like an invisible hammer, the air, hot and humid, pounded on his head.
e. Pounding on his head, hot and humid, the air was like an invisible hammer.

13. *Snow tumbled from the sky like tiny pieces of delicate lace and sprinkled the ground with patches of white dust.*

Variations:

a. Snow, like tiny pieces of delicate lace, tumbled from the sky and sprinkled the ground with patches of white dust.

b. Like pieces of delicate lace, snow tumbled from the sky, sprinkling the ground with patches of white dust.

c. Tumbling from the sky like pieces of delicate lace, the snow sprinkled the ground with patches of white dust.

d. Snow, tumbling from the sky like pieces of delicate lace, sprinkled the ground with patches of white dust.

14. *Its huge teeth were like steel arrowheads and could tear a shark in two.*

Variations:

a. Its huge teeth like steel arrowheads could tear a shark in two.

b. Like steel arrowheads, its huge teeth could tear a shark in two.

c. Its huge teeth were like steel arrowheads that could tear a shark in two.

15. *Two furtive figures like bloodhounds had been tracking them for days through the city.*

Variations:

a. For days, two furtive figures had been tracking them like bloodhounds through the city.

b. Like bloodhounds, two furtive figures had been tracking them for days through the city.

16. *A strange prickling sensation gripped the back of her neck like a cold skeletal hand.*

Variations:

a. A sensation, strange and prickling, gripped the back of her neck like a cold skeletal hand.
b. Strange and prickling, a sensation gripped the back of her neck like a cold skeletal hand.
c. Like a cold skeletal hand, a sensation, strange and prickling, gripped the back of her neck.
d. Like a cold skeletal hand, a strange prickling sensation gripped the back of her neck.
e. Gripping the back of her neck was a strange prickling sensation like a cold skeletal hand.
f. Gripping the back of her neck like a cold skeletal hand was a sensation, strange and prickling.

17. *Beams of bright sunlight, like a shower of golden mist, penetrated the dense tangled canopy.*

Variations:

a. Like a shower of golden mist, beams of bright sunlight penetrated the dense tangled canopy.
b. Penetrating the dense tangled canopy like a shower of golden mist were beams of bright sunlight.
c. Penetrating the dense tangled canopy were beams of bright sunlight like a shower of golden mist.
d. Beams of bright sunlight penetrated the dense tangled canopy like a shower of golden mist.

18. *Layers of heavy black cloud spiralled down from the hill and blanketed the city.*

Variations:

a. Heavy and black, layers of cloud spiralled down from the hill to blanket the city.
b. Layers of cloud, heavy and black, spiralled down from the hill to blanket the city.
c. Spiralling down from the hill, layers of heavy black cloud blanketed the city.

19. *Fingers of swirling, grey, icy mist slithered down the hill, spread across the ground, curled around the trees and shrouded the forest.*

a. Swirling fingers of mist, grey and icy, slithered down the hill, spread across the ground and curled around the trees to shroud the forest.
b. Grey and icy, swirling fingers of mist slithered down the hill, spreading across the ground and curling around the trees to shroud the forest.
c. Slithering down the hill, swirling fingers of mist, grey and icy, spread across the ground, curled around the trees and shrouded the forest.

20. *An immense, dazzling guillotine blade of lightning streaked across the night sky.*

Variations:

a. Immense and dazzling, a guillotine blade of lightning streaked across the night sky.
b. A guillotine blade of lightning, immense and dazzling, streaked across the night sky.
c. Streaking across the night was an immense guillotine blade of dazzling lightning.
d. Streaking across the night sky, immense and dazzling, was a guillotine blade of lightning.
e. Across the night sky streaked an immense guillotine blade of dazzling lightning.

21. *A cold shivering wind blew on the back of their necks.*

Variations:

a.   A wind, cold and shivering, blew on the back of their necks.
b.   Blowing on the back of their necks was a cold shivering wind.
c.   Blowing on the back of their necks was a wind, cold and shivering.
d.   On the back of their necks blew a wind, cold and shivering.
e.   On the back of their necks blew a cold shivering wind.

22. *The glowing red embers of the fire flickered then died.*

Variations:

a.   The embers, glowing and red, flickered then died.
b.   Glowing and red, the embers flickered then died.

23. *In her hand she held a small gilt-edged mirror.*

Variations:

a.   She held a small gilt-edged mirror in her hand.
b.   A small gilt-edged mirror was held in her hand.

24. *An intense beam of blinding white light like a spotlight shone on the stone.*

Variations:

a.   Blinding and white, an intense beam of light shone like a spotlight on the stone.
b.   An intense beam of light, blinding and white, shone like a spotlight on the stone.
c.   Shining like a spotlight on the stone was an intense beam of blinding white light.
d.   Shining like a spotlight on the stone was an intense beam of light, blinding and white.
e.   Like a spotlight, an intense beam of light, blinding and white, shone on the stone.

25. *Pinpricks of vibrant purple light flickered in waves against the doors.*

Variations:

a. Purple and vibrant, pinpricks of light flickered in waves against the doors.
b. Pinpricks of light, purple and vibrant, flickered in waves against the doors.
c. Flickering against the doors, purple and vibrant, were pinpricks of light.
d. Against the doors flickered pinpricks of purple vibrant light.

26. *A huge column of dense black smoke like a tornado whirled at tremendous speed towards the town.*

Variations:

a. Dense and black, a huge column of smoke swirled at tremendous speed like a tornado towards the town.
b. A huge column of smoke, dense and black, swirled at tremendous speed like a tornado towards the town.
c. Like a tornado, a huge column of dense black smoke swirled at tremendous speed towards the town.
d. Swirling at tremendous speed like a tornado towards the town was a huge column of dense black smoke.
e. Swirling at tremendous speed towards the town was a huge dense column of black smoke like a tornado.

27. *The sheer, jagged peaks glinted in the sun.*

Variations:

a. Sheer and jagged, the peaks glinted in the sun.
b. The peaks, sheer and jagged, glinted in the sun.

28. *The glassy, emerald surface of the sea glittered with a million crystals of sunlight.*

Variations:

a. Glassy and emerald, the surface of the sea glittered with a million crystals of sunlight.
b. The surface of the sea, glassy and emerald, glittered with a million crystals of sunlight.
c. Glittering with a million crystals of sunlight, the surface of the sea was glassy and emerald.

29. *A thick black blanket of swirling sea and stormy sky surrounded them.*

Variations:

a. Thick and black, a blanket of swirling sea and stormy sky surrounded them.
b. A blanket of swirling sea and stormy sky, thick and black, surrounded them.
c. They were surrounded by a thick black blanket of swirling sea and stormy sky.
d. Surrounding them was a thick black blanket of swirling sea and stormy sky.
e. Surrounding them, thick and black, was a blanket of swirling sea and stormy sky.

30. *The plume of white belching vapour above the volcano was a silent, menacing reminder of its awesome power.*

Variations:

a. The plume of belching vapour above the volcano, silent and menacing, was a reminder of its awesome power.
b. Silent and menacing, the plume of belching vapour above the volcano was a reminder of its awesome power.

SECTION B

31. It was a quaint medieval town with narrow cobbled streets.

Variations:

a. With narrow cobbled streets, the town was quaint and medieval.
b. The town, quaint and medieval, had narrow cobbled streets.
c. Quaint and medieval, the town had narrow cobbled streets.

32. She was a tall, scrawny woman with a face like a weasel and bony hands with long clawed fingers.

Variations:

a. Tall and scrawny, with a face like a weasel, the woman had bony hands with long clawed fingers.
b. The woman, tall and scrawny, had a face like a weasel and bony hands with long clawed fingers.

33. He was a towering, muscular brute with a mop of flaming red hair.

Variations:

a. Towering and muscular, he was a brute with a mop of flaming red hair.
b. He was a brute, towering and muscular, with a mop of flaming red hair.

34. Her pale sickly face, with sunken eyes as black as coal, had a haunted look.

Variations:

a. Her face, pale and sickly with sunken eyes as black as coal, had a haunted look.

35. The man, with his slit-like eyes and long pointed nose, looked like a hawk.

Variations:

a. With his slit-like eyes and long pointed nose, the man looked like a hawk.
b. The man looked like a hawk with his slit-like eyes and long pointed nose.

36. *His ruddy face with bright twinkling grey eyes was lit up by a huge smile.*

Variations:

a.   His face, ruddy with bright twinkling grey eyes, was lit up by a huge smile.

37. *Her piercing violet eyes shone with a strange power.*

Variations:

a.   Piercing and violet, her eyes shone with a strange power.
b.   Her eyes, piercing and violet, shone with a strange power.

38. *The river, with its brown murky water and swirling currents, was a dangerous place to swim.*

Variations:

a.   Brown and murky, the river with its swirling currents was a dangerous place to swim.
b.   The river, brown and murky with swirling currents, was a dangerous place to swim.
c.   With its swirling currents and brown murky water, the river was a dangerous place to swim.

39. *The island was guarded by a fierce sea-monster with an enormous, humped, serpentine body.*

Variations:

a.   A fierce sea-monster, with an enormous body, humped and serpentine, guarded the island.
b.   A sea-monster, fierce and enormous, with a humped and serpentine body, guarded the island.
c.   Guarding the island was a sea-monster, fierce and enormous, with a humped, serpentine body.

40. *In front of him was a huge leather-bound book with mystical symbols and sigils etched into its gilt-edged cover.*

Variations:

a. Huge and leather-bound, the book in front of him had mystical symbols and sigils etched into its gilt-edged cover.
b. The book in front of him, huge and leather-bound, had mystical symbols and sigils etched into its gilt-edged cover.
c. In front of him, the book, huge and leather-bound, had mystical symbols and sigils etched into its gilt-edged cover.

17

Adverb clauses

Adverb clauses are sentence parts that usually begin with *when, as, since, while, although, even though, if, before, after* etc.

They tell us when, where, why and how something mentioned in the sentence happened.

FOR EXAMPLE

A. Combine the kernel sentences.

1.1 He took a step forward. (**WHEN**)
1.2 He could feel the oozing mud of the swamp squelching beneath his feet.
1. **When he took a step forward**, he could feel the oozing mud of the swamp squelching beneath his feet.

B. Experiment with the position of the adverb clause.
Decide which position is preferred and why.

a. He could feel the oozing mud of the swamp squelching beneath his feet **when he took a step forward**.

C. Imitate the model sentence using your own adverb clause.

a. **As he moved deeper into the forest**, he could feel the oozing mud of the swamp squelching beneath his feet.

DOI: 10.4324/9781032662862-20

EXERCISE

1.1 She would have run the other way.

1.2 She had known what was waiting for her. (**IF**)

_____

_____

Variation:

_____

_____

Imitation:

_____

_____

2.1 He heard a scuttling of its clawed feet.

2.2 He saw the creature. (**BEFORE**)

_____

_____

Variation:

_____

_____

Imitation:

_____

_____

3.1 The house fell silent.
3.2 The clock struck midnight. (**AFTER**)

_____

_____

Variation:

_____

_____

Imitation:

_____

_____

4.1 She stopped.
4.2 She reached the narrow track. (**WHEN**)

_____

_____

Variation:

_____

_____

Imitation:

_____

_____

5.1 He arrived at the campsite.
5.2 The sun had set. (**BEFORE)**

_____

_____

Variation:

_____

_____

Imitation:

_____

_____

6.1 It would have been all over for him.
6.2 He had been caught. (**IF**)

_____

_____

Variation:

_____

_____

Imitation:

_____

_____

7.1 It never seemed to get any nearer.
7.2 She had been trudging towards the summit for hours. (**ALTHOUGH**)

_____

_____

Variation:

_____

_____

Imitation:

_____

_____

8.1 She saw the mountains stretching above her.
8.2 The mist cleared. (**AS**)

_____

_____

Variation:

_____

_____

Imitation:

_____

_____

9.1 His frozen fingers scrabbled for a grip on the rocks.

9.2 His body swung perilously over the drop. (**AS**)

_____

_____

Variation:

_____

_____

Imitation:

_____

_____

10.1 It would be fatal to breathe in the freezing water.

10.2 He went under the water for even a moment. (**IF**)

_____

_____

Variation:

_____

_____

Imitation:

_____

_____

11.1 His skin became covered in a coat of goosebumps.

11.2 The cold and shock struck. (**WHEN**)

_____

_____

Variation:

_____

_____

Imitation:

_____

_____

12.1 It took a few minutes.
12.2 Scarlett began to slow down. (**AFTER**)

_____

_____

Variation:

_____

_____

Imitation:

_____

_____

13.2 Scarlett spun round.
13.1 She sensed that someone had entered the room. (**BECAUSE**)

_____

_____

Variation:

_____

_____

Imitation:

_____

_____

14.1 It was daylight.
14.2 She woke up. (**WHEN**)

_____

_____

Variation:

_____

_____

Imitation:

_____

_____

15.1 The sun had fallen like a sinking stone.
15.2 She had been exploring the house. (**WHILE**)

_____

_____

Variation:

_____

_____

Imitation:

_____

_____

16.1 She was intrigued to find his grave.
16.2 She was nervous of entering the graveyard at night. (**EVEN THOUGH**)

_____

_____

Variation:

_____

_____

Imitation:

_____

_____

17.1 He had the distinct feeling that they were being watched from one of the upper windows.

17.2 He knew that the building had been deserted for some time. (**ALTHOUGH**)

_____

_____

Variation:

_____

_____

Imitation:

_____

_____

18.1 Someone had walked into her room.

18.2 She was asleep. (**WHILE**)

_____

_____

Variation:

_____

_____

Imitation:

_____

_____

19.1 She thought she had caught sight of a reflection in the mirror behind her.
19.2 The cloud of mist had descended over the hall. (**BEFORE**)

_____

_____

Variation:

_____

_____

Imitation:

_____

_____

20.1 She paused for a moment to listen for any sounds from down the passage.
20.2 She opened the door. (**BEFORE**)

_____

_____

Variation:

_____

_____

Imitation:

_____

_____

21.1 She had to tug on the handle a couple of times.
21.2 She was convinced that the door was locked. (**BEFORE**)

_____

_____

Variation:

_____

_____

Imitation:

_____

_____

22.1 The water turned into wild white, flying foam.

22.2 It rampaged down the rocks. (**AS**)

_____

_____

Variation:

_____

_____

Imitation:

_____

_____

23.1 The roar of the wave was deafening.

23.2 It thundered into sight. (**AS**)

_____

_____

Variation:

_____

_____

Imitation:

_____

_____

24.1 They were faced by a low, ancient-looking door.

24.2 The door was studded with ancient symbols.

24.3 The path ended. (**WHERE**)

_____

_____

Variation:

_____

_____

Imitation:

_____

_____

25.1 There was a deafening boom.

25.2 The ground trembled and shook.

25.3 The volcano erupted. (**AS**)

_____

_____

Variation:

_____

_____

Imitation:

_____

_____

26.1 There was only silence thudding in his ears.
26.2 The echoes died away. (**WHEN**)

_____

_____

Variation:

_____

_____

Imitation:

_____

_____

27.1 He shivered.
27.2 He looked up at the human pyramid towering above him. (**AS**)

_____

_____

Variation:

_____

_____

Imitation:

_____

_____

28.1 She would have heard the scampering of tiny feet behind her.
28.2 She had stopped and listened. (**IF**)

_____

_____

Variation:

_____

_____

Imitation:

_____

_____

29.1 It would be too dark to find the trail.
29.2 She waited any longer. (**IF**)

_____

_____

Variation:

_____

_____

Imitation:

_____

_____

30.1 A black cloak was drawn across the sky.
30.2 Night came. (**WHEN**)

_____

_____

Variation:

_____

_____

Imitation:

_____

_____

31.1 It was like looking in a mirror at her reflection.
31.2 She looked into the crystal-clear water. (**WHEN**)

_____

_____

Variation:

_____

_____

Imitation:

_____

_____

32.1 There was a sudden thud on the floorboards upstairs.
32.2 She could take a step. (**BEFORE**)

_____

_____

Variation:

_____

_____

Imitation:

_____

_____

33.1 They started along the trail once again.
33.2 They had a brief rest. (**AFTER**)

_____

_____

Variation:

_____

_____

Imitation:

_____

_____

34.1 The wolves had detected their scent.
34.2 They had been thrashing through the swamp. (**WHILE**)

_____

_____

Variation:

_____

_____

Imitation:

_____

_____

35.1 The wood was filled with the sound of birds singing and insects humming.

35.2 It was early in the morning. (**EVEN THOUGH**)

_____

_____

Variation:

_____

_____

Imitation:

_____

_____

36.1 They were faced with an impenetrable maze of tangled thorns.

36.2 The path ended. (**WHERE**)

_____

_____

Variation:

_____

_____

Imitation:

_____

_____

37.1 Her face froze in horror.

37.2 She listened to the news. (**AS**)

_____

_____

Variation:

_____

_____

Imitation:

_____

_____

38.1 Her head was thrown back.

38.2 Her eyes rolled in their sockets.

38.3 She struck the wall. (**AS**)

_____

_____

Variation:

_____

_____

Imitation:

_____

_____

39.1 She had no choice but to scale the wall.

39.2 Time was running out. (**BECAUSE**)

_____

_____

Variation:

_____

_____

Imitation:

_____

_____

40.1 The streets were deserted.

40.2 She was in the middle of the city. (**ALTHOUGH**)

_____

_____

Variation:

_____

_____

Imitation:

_____

_____

41.1 She waited silently in the shadows.

41.2 She was sure that the man wasn't coming back. (**UNTIL**)

_____

_____

Variation:

_____

_____

Imitation:

_____

_____

42.1 She did not see the chain.

42.2 It wriggled across the floor.

42.3 It was hidden by layers of dust and dirt. (**BECAUSE**)

_____

_____

Variation:

_____

_____

Imitation:

_____

_____

43.1 She kept looking over her shoulder.

43.2 In her mind every shadow in the gloom had grown eyes and arms. (**BECAUSE**)

_____

Variation:

_____

_____

Imitation:

_____

_____

44.1 She had been enveloped by a sense of horror and dread.

44.2 The truth had finally dawned on her. (**WHEN**)

_____

_____

Variation:

_____

_____

Imitation:

_____

_____

45.1 She was sure she had heard footsteps outside the door.

45.2 She had turned down the television. (**AFTER**)

_____

_____

Variation:

_____

_____

Imitation:

_____

_____

46.1 A padlocked metal gate blocked the entrance.

46.2 The corridor ended. (**WHERE**)

_____

_____

Variation:

_____

_____

Imitation:

_____

_____

47.1 Her flailing hand sent the suit of armour clattering to the floor.

47.2 She tripped over the chain. (**AS**)

_____

_____

Variation:

_____

_____

Imitation:

_____

_____

48.1 The hours seemed endless.

48.2 He waited for the phone to ring. (**WHILE**)

_____

_____

Variation:

_____

_____

Imitation:

_____

_____

49.1 Everything he had been through would have been for nothing.

49.2 He arrived too late. (**IF**)

_____

_____

Variation:

_____

_____

_____

Imitation:

_____

_____

_____

50.1 It would be dangerous to attempt to cross at night.

50.2 The ground was covered with potholes the size of bomb craters. (**BECAUSE**)

_____

_____

Variation:

_____

_____

Imitation:

_____

_____

ANSWERS

1. *If she had known what was waiting for her,* she would have run the other way.
   She would have run the other way <u>if she had known what was waiting for her</u>.
   She, <u>if she had know what was waiting for her,</u> would have run the other way.

2. *Before he saw the creature,* he heard the scuttling of its clawed feet.
   He heard the scuttling of its clawed feet <u>before he saw the creature</u>.
   He, <u>before he saw the creature,</u> heard the scuttling of its clawed feet.

3. *After the clock struck midnight,* the house fell silent.
   The house fell silent <u>after the clock struck midnight</u>.
   The house, <u>after the clock struck midnight,</u> fell silent.

4. *She stopped when she reached the narrow track.*
   When she reached the narrow track, she stopped dead in her tracks.
   She, <u>when she reached the narrow track,</u> stopped dead in her tracks.

5. *Before the sun had set* he arrived at the campsite.
   He arrived at the campsite <u>before the sun had set</u>.
   He had, <u>before the sun had set,</u> arrived at the campsite.

6. *If he had been caught,* it would have been all over for him.
   It would have been all over for him if he had been caught.
   It, <u>if he had been caught,</u> would have been all over for him,

7. *Even though she had been trudging towards the summit for hours,* it never seemed to get any nearer.
   It never seemed to get any nearer <u>even though she had been trudging towards the summit for hours</u>.
   It, <u>even though she had been trudging towards the summit for hours,</u> never seemed to get any nearer.

8. *When the mist cleared,* she saw the mountains stretching above her.
   She saw the mountain stretching above her <u>when the mist cleared</u>.
   She, <u>when the mist cleared,</u> saw the mountain stretching above her.

9. *As his frozen fingers scrabbled for a grip on the rocks, his body swung perilously over the drop.*

    His body swung perilously over the drop <u>as his frozen fingers scrabbled for a grip on the rocks</u>.

    His body, <u>as his frozen fingers scrabbled for a grip on the rocks</u>, swung perilously over the drop.

10. *If he went under even for a moment, it would be fatal to breathe in the freezing water.*

    It would be fatal to breathe in the freezing water <u>if he went under even for a moment</u>.

    It, <u>if he went under even for a moment</u>, would be fatal to breathe in the freezing water.

11. *As the cold and shock struck, his skin became covered in a coat of goosebumps.*

    His skin became covered in a coat of goosebumps <u>as the cold and shock struck</u>.

    His skin, <u>as the cold and shock struck</u>, became covered in a coat of goosebumps.

12. *After a few minutes, Scarlett began to slow down.*

    Scarlett began to slow down <u>after a few minutes</u>.

    Scarlett, <u>after a few minutes</u>, began to slow down.

13. *Scarlett spun round because she sensed that someone had entered the room.*

    <u>Because she sensed that someone had entered the room</u>, Scarlett spun round.

    She, <u>because she sensed that someone had entered the room,</u> spun round.

14. *When she woke up, it was daylight.*

    It was daylight when she woke up.

    It, <u>when she woke up,</u> was daylight.

15. <u>*While she had been exploring the house*</u>, *the sun had fallen like a sinking stone.*

    The sun had fallen like a sinking stone <u>while she had been exploring the house</u>.

    The sun, <u>while she had been exploring the house</u>, had fallen like a sinking stone.

16. <u>*Even though she was nervous of entering the graveyard at night*</u>, *she was intrigued to find his grave.*

    She was intrigued to find his grave <u>even though she was nervous of entering the graveyard at night</u>.

    She, <u>even though she was nervous of entering the graveyard at night</u>, was intrigued to find his grave.

17. <u>*Although he knew that the building had been deserted for some time*</u>, *he had the distinct feeling that they were being watched from one of the upper windows.*

    He had the distinct feeling that they were being watched from one of the upper windows <u>even though he knew that the building had been deserted for some time</u>.

    He, <u>even though he knew that the building had been deserted for some time,</u> had the distinct feeling that they were being watched from one of the upper windows.

18. *Someone had walked into her room* <u>*while she was asleep*</u>.

    <u>While she was asleep</u>, someone had walked into her room.

    Someone, <u>while she was asleep</u>, had walked into her room.

19. <u>*Before the cloud of mist had descended over the hall*</u>, *she thought she had caught sight of a reflection in the mirror behind her.*

    She thought she had caught sight of a reflection in the mirror behind her <u>before the cloud of mist had descended over the hall</u>.

    She, <u>before the cloud of mist had descended over the hall</u>, thought she had caught sight of a reflection in the mirror behind her.

20. *Before she opened the door, she paused for a moment to listen for any sounds from down the passage.*

    She paused for a moment to listen for any sounds from down the passage <u>before she opened the door</u>.

    She, <u>before she opened the door</u>, paused for a moment to listen for any sounds from down the passage.

21. *She had to tug on the handle a couple of times <u>before she was convinced that the door was locked</u>.*

    <u>Before she was convinced that the door was locked</u>, she had to tug on the handle a couple of times.

    She, <u>before she was convinced that the door was locked,</u> had to tug on the handle a couple of times.

22. *<u>As it rampaged down the rocks</u>, the water turned into wild white, flying foam.*

    The water turned into wild white flying foam <u>as it rampaged down the rocks.</u>

    The water, <u>as it rampaged down the rocks,</u> turned into wild, white, flying foam.

23. *The roar of the wave was deafening <u>as it thundered into sight</u>.*

    <u>As it thundered into sight</u>, the roar of the wave was deafening.

    The roar of the wave, <u>as it thundered into sight</u>, was deafening.

24. *<u>Where the path ended</u>, they were faced by a low, ancient-looking door, studded with ancient symbols.*

    They were faced by a low, ancient-looking door, studded with ancient symbols <u>where the path ended</u>.

25. *<u>As the volcano erupted</u>, there was a deafening boom and the ground trembled and shook.*

    There was a deafening boom and the ground trembled and shook <u>as the volcano erupted</u>.

26. *<u>When the echoes died away</u>, there was only silence thudding in his ears.*

    There was only silence thudding in his ears <u>when the echoes died away</u>.

27. *He shivered <u>as he looked up at the human pyramid towering above him.</u>*

    <u>As he looked up at the human pyramid towering above him</u>, he shivered.

28. <u>*If she had stopped and listened,*</u> *she would have heard the scampering of tiny feet behind her.*

    She would have heard the scampering of tiny feet behind her <u>if she had stopped and listened</u>.

    She, <u>if she had stopped and listened,</u> would have heard the scampering of tiny feet behind her.

29. <u>*If she waited any longer,*</u> *it would be too dark to find the trail.*

    It would be too dark to find the trail <u>if she waited any longer</u>.

30. <u>*When night came,*</u> *a black cloak was drawn across the sky.*

    A black cloak was drawn across the sky <u>when night came</u>.

    A black cloak, <u>when night came</u>, was drawn across the sky.

31. <u>*When she looked into the crystal-clear water,*</u> *it was like looking in a mirror at her reflection.*

    It was like looking in a mirror at her reflection <u>when she looked into the crystal-clear water</u>.

32. <u>*Before she could take a step,*</u> *there was a sudden thud on the floorboards upstairs.*

    There was a sudden thud on the floorboards upstairs <u>before she could take a step.</u>

33. <u>*After a brief rest,*</u> *they started along the trail once again.*

    They started along the trail once again <u>after a brief rest</u>.

    They, <u>after a brief rest</u>, started along the trail once again.

34. <u>*While they had been thrashing through the swamp,*</u> *the wolves had detected their scent.*

    The wolves had detected their scent <u>while they had been thrashing through the swamp</u>.

35. <u>*Even though it was early in the morning,*</u> *the wood was filled with the sound of birds singing and insects humming.*

    The wood was filled with the sound of birds singing and insects humming <u>even though it was early in the morning</u>.

    The wood, <u>even though it was early</u> in the morning, was filled with the sound of birds singing and insects humming.

36. <u>*Where the path ended*</u>*, they were faced with an impenetrable maze of tangled thorns.*

    They were faced with an impenetrable maze of tangled thorns <u>where the path ended</u>.

37. *<u>As she listened to the news</u>, her face froze in horror.*

    Her face froze in horror <u>as she listened to the news</u>.

    Her face, <u>as she listened to the news,</u> froze in horror.

38. As she struck the wall, *her head was thrown back, and her eyes rolled in their sockets.*

    Her head was thrown back and her eyes rolled in their sockets <u>as she struck the wall</u>.

39. *She had no choice but to scale the wall <u>because time was running out</u>.*

    <u>Because time was running out</u>, she had no choice but to scale the wall.

    She, <u>because time was running out</u>, had no choice but to scale the wall.

40. <u>*Although she was in the middle of the city*</u>*, the streets were deserted.*

    The streets were deserted <u>although she was in the middle of the city</u>.

41. *She waited silently in the shadows <u>until she was sure that the man wasn't coming back.</u>*

    <u>Until she was sure that the man wasn't coming back</u>, she waited silently in the shadows.

42. *She did not see the chain that wriggled across the floor <u>because it was hidden by layers of dust and dirt</u>.*

    <u>Because it was hidden by layers of dust and dirt</u>, she did not see the chain that wriggled across the floor.

43. *She kept looking over her shoulder <u>because in her mind every shadow in the gloom had grown eyes and arms</u>.*

    <u>Because in her mind every shadow in the gloom had grown eyes and arms</u>, she kept looking over her shoulder.

44. <u>*When the truth had finally dawned on her,*</u> *she had been enveloped by a sense of horror and dread.*

    She had been enveloped by a sense of horror and dread <u>when the truth had finally dawned on her.</u>

    She, <u>when the truth had finally dawned on her</u>, had been enveloped by a sense of horror and dread.

45. *After she had turned down the television,* she was sure she had heard footsteps outside the door.

    She was sure she had heard footsteps outside the door <u>after she had turned down the television.</u>

46. *Where the corridor ended,* a padlocked metal gate blocked the entrance.

    A padlocked metal gate blocked the entrance <u>where the corridor ended</u>.

47. *As she tripped over the chain,* her flailing hand sent the suit of armour clattering to the floor.

    Her flailing hand sent the suit of armour clattering to the floor <u>as she tripped over the chain</u>.

48. The hours seemed endless while he waited for the phone to ring.

    While he waited for the phone ring, the hours seemed endless.

    The hours, <u>while he waited for the phone to ring</u>, seemed endless.

49. *If he arrived too late,* everything he had been through would have been for nothing.

    Everything he had been through would have been for nothing <u>if he arrived too late.</u>

50. *It would be dangerous to attempt to cross at night <u>because the ground was covered with potholes the size of bomb craters</u>.*

    <u>Because the ground was covered with potholes the size of bomb craters</u>, it would be dangerous to attempt to cross at night.

18

Relative (adjective) clauses

Relative clauses are sentence parts that:

★ begin with *who, which, that, whose*
★ give **more information about a noun (to the left of the relative clause)**
★ are also called adjective clauses.

FOR EXAMPLE

1. She had a commanding air of someone **who was used to being obeyed**.

1.1 She had a commanding air of someone.
1.2 ~~She~~ was used to being obeyed. (**WHO**)

2. He had wide bulging, frog-like eyes **that stared as if he was in a trance**.

2.1 He had wide bulging, frog-like eyes.
2.2 ~~They~~ **stared as if he was in a trance**. (**THAT**)

3. The warm air, **which was thick with the scent of honeysuckle**, wafted through the open window.

3.1 The warm air ^ wafted through the open window.
3.2 The air **was thick with the scent of honeysuckle**. (**WHICH**)

DOI: 10.4324/9781032662862-21

4. The pungent smell of rotting rubbish, **whose decaying stench wafted through the house**, caught in the back of her throat.

4.1 The pungent smell of rotting rubbish ^ caught in the back of her throat.

4.3 ~~The smell of~~ **decaying stench wafted through the house**. (**WHOSE**)

INSTRUCTIONS

A. **Combine the kernel sentences using the relative pronouns in brackets.**

FOR EXAMPLE

She was lost in an ice-bound wilderness, which cracked and growled under her weight.

1.1 She was lost in an ice-bound wilderness. ,^
1.2 It **cracked and growled under her weight**. (**WHICH**)

B. **Imitate the model sentence using the main clause and substituting your own relative clause.**

She was lost in an ice-bound wilderness, **which stretched in all directions as far as the eye could see**.

EXERCISE

1.1 She was guided down the corridor by the smell of rotting meat., ^
1.2 ~~The smell~~ **drifted out of the shadows. (THAT)**

_____

_____

Imitation:

_____

_____

2.1 She needed to leave the room.
2.2 ~~She needed~~ **to escape the smell of damp and mould.** ^
2.3 ~~It~~ **seeped from the curtains. (THAT)**
2.4 ~~It seeped from~~ **the carpets.**
2.5 ~~It seeped from~~ **the white sheets covering the furniture. (AND)**

_____

_____

Imitation:

_____

_____

3.1 Torrents of water ^ transformed the waterhole into raging, foaming falls.
3.2 ~~The water~~ **plunged over the top of the cliffs in huge clouds of white spray. (WHICH)**

_____

_____

Imitation:

_____

_____

4.1 She edged deeper into the tangled thicket. ,^

4.2 Its **branches twisted together to form a gloomy tunnel**. (**WHOSE**)

_____

_____

Imitation:

_____

_____

5.1 The hunting owl, ^ , suddenly flew above them like a white shadow.

5.2 Its **loud piercing hoot shattered the silence**. (**WHOSE**)

_____

_____

Imitation:

_____

_____

6.1 They waited behind the boulder ^ and watched for any sign of the wolves.

6.2 The boulder **was directly above the trail**. (**WHICH**)

_____

_____

Imitation:

_____

_____

7.1 The two goblins, ^ , sniffed the air and scanned the path.

7.2 The goblins **had stopped metres from where she was crouched**. (**WHO**)

_____

_____

Imitation:

_____

_____

8.1 The sun glinted on the sharp, dagger-like claws. ^
8.2 The claws **sprouted from its ten legs**. (**THAT**)

_____

_____

Imitation:

_____

_____

9.1 She could just make out the hollow cavern. ^
9.2 It **was the entrance to the ancient wood**. (**THAT**)

_____

_____

Imitation:

_____

_____

10.1 The goblin ^ was obviously the leader of the group.
10.2 ~~The goblin's~~ **red beard reached almost to his knees**. (**WHOSE**)

_____

_____

Imitation:

_____

_____

11.1 The moss, ^, crept across the floor and the walls.
11.2 The moss glowed with a phosphorescent light. (**WHICH**)

_____

_____

Imitation:

_____

_____

12.1 Robert looked up and saw a crossbow. ^
12.2 The crossbow was aimed directly at his head. (**THAT**)

_____

_____

Imitation:

_____

_____

13.1 John, ^, forced himself to stay calm and wait for the signal.
13.2 He knew he could not afford to make any movement. (**WHO**)

_____

_____

Imitation:

_____

_____

14.1 His fear, ^, was replaced by a cold hard determination.
14.2 His fear was gradually subsiding. (**WHICH**)

_____

_____

Imitation:

_____

_____

15.1 Rob, ^, was ready to move as soon as the lights were extinguished and the building plunged into darkness.
15.2 Rob had studied the routes and routines of the guards for several nights. (**WHO**)

_____

_____

Imitation:

_____

_____

16.1 Dark clouds were gathering.

16.2 They were gathering above the roofs.

16.3 They cast long shadows down the streets. (**WHICH**)

_____

_____

Imitation:

_____

_____

17.1 A gigantic bank of black clouds blotted out the sun.

17.2 The clouds were amassing above Ann. (**WHICH**)

17.3 They blanketed the city in a gloomy light. (**AND**)

_____

_____

Imitation:

_____

_____

18.1 The storm prevented them climbing any further.

18.2 The storm had churned into a miniature, swirling hurricane. (**WHICH**)

_____

_____

Imitation:

_____

_____

19.1 A funnel cloud snaked its way down the slope like an inky black finger.

19.2 The cloud had swallowed the top of the hill. (**WHICH**)

_____

_____

Imitation:

_____

_____

20.1 The thunder echoed through the city.
20.2 It rumbled and roared. (**WHICH**)

_____

_____

Imitation:

_____

_____

21.1 The lightning blinded him with its dazzling light.
21.2 It streaked like a guillotine blade across the night sky.

_____

_____

Imitation:

_____

_____

22.1 Lightning cut through the darkness like camera flashes.
22.2 It came in bursts of white light.

_____

_____

Imitation:

_____

_____

23.1 The misty haze brought with it a feeling of dread and unease.
23.2 It was like a veil drifting across the sky.

_____

_____

Imitation:

_____

_____

24.1 The wind bent the tops of the trees into arches.
24.2 The wind whistled and sighed through the wood.

_____

_____

Imitation:

_____

_____

25.1 The fierce gales made the branches twist and writhe like a serpent searching for its prey.
25.2 The gales tore through the trees.

_____

_____

Imitation:

_____

_____

26.1 The ferocious wind beat like a fist against the roof.
26.2 The wind was gaining in power all the time.
26.3 It howled around the building. (**AND**)

_____

_____

Imitation:

_____

_____

27.1 The breath of icy wind made his skin prickle with foreboding.

27.2 The wind blew on the back of his neck.

_____

_____

Imitation:

_____

_____

28.1 The fierce wind forced her to take cover behind the rocks.

28.2 The wind swirled around her.

_____

_____

Imitation:

_____

_____

29.1 The blizzard forced him back inside the building.

29.2 The blizzard tugged and shoved at him like a gigantic invisible hand.

_____

_____

Imitation:

_____

_____

30.1 The wind howled and shrieked.

30.2 It grew stronger by the minute.

30.3 It whipped at his clothes and hair. (**AND**)

_____

_____

Imitation:

_____

_____

31.1 The rain blurred the shadow of the building behind it.
31.2 The rain had formed into a misty silvery veil.

_____

_____

Imitation:

_____

_____

32.1 The rain pounded on his skull.
32.2 The rain burst like waterfall from the black clouds.
32.3 The rain soaked his hair.
32.4 It sent a stream of damp down his spine to his waist. (**AND**)

_____

_____

Imitation:

_____

_____

33.1 The waves battered the ship.
33.2 The waves grew monstrous and black.
33.3 The waves sent it rocking and pitching into its heavy swells. (**AND**)

_____

_____

Imitation:

_____

_____

34.1 The river tore whole trees out of the ground and swept them away.

34.2 The river had become a surging current of grey water.

_____

_____

Imitation:

_____

_____

35.1 The huge wall of water came thundering towards the village.

35.2 The huge wall of water had swallowed the trees and the land as it swirled and spread.

_____

_____

Imitation:

_____

_____

36.1 The lake twisted around their legs.

36.2 The lake boiled and churned into swirling currents.

36.3 It dragged them down into its black depths. (**AND**)

_____

_____

Imitation:

_____

_____

37.1 John knew he had to make the most difficult decision of his life.

37.2 He lay awake night after night.

_____

_____

Imitation:

_____

_____

38.1 John worried that he didn't have enough time to prepare.
38.2 John had seen enough to know that he was in grave danger.
38.3 He was worried he was not powerful enough to face it. (**AND**)

_____

_____

Imitation:

_____

_____

39.1 The shadows cloaked the ground with a gloomy light.
39.2 The shadows were now merging into one another.

_____

_____

Imitation:

_____

_____

40.1 John knew it was time to make his move.
40.2 John had been counting the time by the shadows creeping slowly
     across the ground.

_____

_____

Imitation:

_____

_____

41.1 Ann feared she was running out of time.
41.2 Ann could feel the seconds ticking away.

_____

_____

Imitation:

_____

_____

42.1 John ran through his options.
42.2 John knew his next move would be crucial.

_____

_____

Imitation:

_____

_____

43.1 John hadn't noticed the slight rise of her chest or the slight twitching of her fingers.
43.2 John had already turned away.

_____

_____

Imitation:

_____

_____

44.1 In front of him was a huge bronze-bound book.
44.2 The book's cover was carved with mystical symbols and mysterious sigils.

_____

_____

Imitation:

_____

_____

45.1 The pages eventually stopped at a map of the Lost City of Atlantis.
45.2 The pages flicked open with a dry crackle.

_____

_____

Imitation:

_____

_____

46.1 The manuscript had obviously never been opened.
46.2 The manuscript was stamped with a heavy black seal like a hammer.

_____

_____

Imitation:

_____

_____

47.1 He studied the outer circle of the watch.
47.2 It was lined with symbols of towers, spires, minarets and domes.

_____

_____

Imitation:

_____

_____

48.1 The runic symbols lit up when he touched the enormous buckle.
48.2 The symbols were etched on each link of the bronze belt.

_____

_____

Imitation:

_____

_____

49.1 A ring of standing stones were each carved with the pattern of a hand.
49.2 The stones had been sunk deep into the hillside.

_____

_____

Imitation:

_____

_____

50.1 Pentagrams and circles framed the pattern of a doorway.

50.2 The pentagrams and circles had been burned into the grass.

_____

_____

Imitation:

_____

_____

ANSWERS

1. She was guided down the corridor by the smell of rotting meat <u>that drifted out of the shadows</u>.
2. She needed to leave the room to escape the smell of damp and mould <u>that seeped from the curtains, the carpets and the white sheets covering the furniture</u>.
3. Torrents of water <u>which plunged over the top of the cliffs in huge clouds of white spray</u> transformed the waterhole into raging, foaming falls.
4. She edged deeper into the tangled thicket, <u>whose branches twisted together to form a gloomy tunnel</u>.
5. The hunting owl, <u>whose loud piercing hoot shattered the silence</u>, suddenly flew above them like a white shadow.
6. They waited behind the boulder <u>which was directly above the trail</u>, and they watched for any sign of the wolves.
7. The two goblins, <u>who had stopped metres from where she was crouched</u>, sniffed the air and scanned the path.
8. The sun glinted on the sharp, dagger-like claws <u>that sprouted from its ten legs</u>.
9. She could just make out the hollow cavern <u>that was the entrance to the ancient wood</u>.
10. The goblin <u>whose red beard reached almost to his knees</u> was obviously the leader of the group.

11. The moss, <u>which glowed with a phosphorescent light</u>, crept across the floor and the walls.
12. Robert looked up and saw a crossbow <u>that was aimed directly at his head.</u>
13. John, <u>who knew he could not afford to make any movement</u>, forced himself to stay calm and wait for the signal.
14. His fear, <u>which was gradually subsiding</u>, was replaced by a cold hard determination.
15. Rob, <u>who had studied the routes and routines of the guards for several nights</u>, was ready to move as soon as the lights were extinguished and the building plunged into darkness.
16. Above the roofs, dark clouds were gathering, <u>which cast long shadows down the street</u>.
17. A gigantic bank of black clouds, <u>which were amassing above Ann</u>, blotted out the sun and blanketed the city in a gloomy light.
18. The storm, <u>which had churned into a miniature, swirling hurricane</u>, prevented them climbing any further.
19. A funnel cloud, <u>which had swallowed the top of the hill</u>, snaked its way down the slope like an inky black finger.
20. The thunder, <u>which rumbled and roared</u>, echoed through the city.
21. The lightning, <u>which streaked like a guillotine blade across the night sky</u>, blinded him with its dazzling light.
22. Lightning, <u>which came in bursts of white light</u>, cut through the darkness like camera flashes.
23. The misty haze, <u>which was like a veil drifting across the sky</u>, brought with it a feeling of dread and unease.
24. The wind, <u>which whistled and sighed through the wood</u>, bent the tops of the trees into arches.
25. The fierce gales, <u>which tore through the trees</u>, made the branches twist and writhe like a serpent searching for its prey.
26. The ferocious wind, <u>which was gaining in power all the time</u>, beat like a fist against the roof and howled around the building.
27. The breath of icy wind <u>which blew on the back of his neck</u> made his skin prickle with foreboding.

28. The fierce wind, <u>which swirled around her</u>, forced her to take cover behind the rocks.
29. The blizzard, <u>which tugged and shoved at him like a gigantic invisible hand</u>, forced him back inside the building.
30. The wind, <u>which grew stronger by the minute</u>, howled and shrieked and whipped at his clothes and hair.
31. The rain, <u>which had formed into a misty silvery veil</u>, blurred the shadow of the building behind it.
32. The rain, <u>which burst like a waterfall from the black clouds</u>, pounded on his skull, soaked his hair and sent a stream of damp down his spine to his waist.
33. The waves, <u>which grew monstrous and black</u>, battered the ship and sent it rocking and pitching into its heavy swells.
34. The river, <u>which had become a surging current of grey water</u>, tore whole trees out of the ground and swept them away.
35. The huge wall of water, <u>which had swallowed the trees and the land as it swirled and spread</u>, thundered towards the village.
36. The lake, <u>which boiled and churned into swirling currents</u>, twisted around their legs and dragged them down into its black depths.
37. John, <u>who lay awake night after night</u>, knew he had to make the most difficult decision of his life.
38. John, <u>who had seen enough to know that he was in grave danger</u>, worried that he didn't have enough time to prepare and was not powerful enough to face it.
39. The shadows, <u>which were now merging into one another</u>, cloaked the ground with a gloomy light.
40. John, <u>who had been counting the time by the shadows creeping slowly across the ground</u>, knew it was time to make his move.
41. Ann, <u>who could feel the seconds ticking away</u>, feared she was running out of time.
42. John, <u>who knew his next move would be crucial</u>, ran through his options.
43. John, <u>who had already turned away</u>, hadn't noticed the slight rise of her chest or the slight twitching of her fingers.

44. In front of him was a huge bronze-bound book <u>whose cover was carved with mystical symbols and mysterious sigils</u>.
45. The pages, <u>which flicked open with a dry crackle</u>, eventually stopped at a map of the Lost City of Atlantis.
46. The manuscript <u>which was stamped with a heavy black seal like a hammer</u> had obviously never been opened.
47. He studied the outer circle of the watch, <u>which was lined with symbols of towers, spires, minarets and domes.</u>
48. The runic symbols, <u>which were etched on each link of the bronze belt</u>, lit up when he touched the enormous buckle.
49. A ring of standing stones <u>that had been sunk deep into the hillside</u> were each carved with the pattern of a hand.
50. Pentagrams and circles <u>that had been burned into the grass</u> framed the pattern of a doorway.

19

Participial phrases

INSTRUCTIONS

A. Combine the kernel sentences.

For example:

1.1 The forest pressed in on her from all sides.
1.2 ~~The forest~~ trapp**ed** her in its thorny grasp. (**-ING**)
   The forest pressed in on her from all sides, trapping her in its thorny grasp.
2.1 ~~The forest~~ pressed in on her from all sides. (**-ING)**
2.2 The forest trapped her in its thorny grasp.
Pressing in on her from all sides, the forest trapped her in its thorny grasp.

B. Experiment with the position of the participial phrase.
Decide which position is preferred and why.

For example:

1.1 ~~The forest~~ press**ed** in on her from all sides. (**-ING**)
1.2 The forest trapp**ed** her in its thorny grasp.

Pressing in on her from all sides, the forest trapped her in its thorny grasp.
The forest, **pressing in on her from all sides**, trapped her in its thorny grasp.
Note: Present participial phrases (-ING) often describe events that are happening at the same time (as in the example above) and in this case the order of the participial phrases is flexible. However, when they describe events that happen

DOI: 10.4324/9781032662862-22

in a sequence (Question 5) or as result of an action, the order of the participial phrases is important.

C. Experiment with converting the verb in another clause into a participial phrase and combining them. Decide which is preferred and why.

For example

Pressing in on her from all sides, the forest trapped her in its thorny grasp.
The forest pressed in on her from all sides, **trapping her in its thorny grasp**.

D. Experiment with using a coordinating conjunction or past participial phrases and discuss which is the most effective and why.

The forest pressed in on her from all sides <u>and</u> trapped her in its thorny grasp.

E. Experiment with using a past participial phrase and discuss which is the most effective and why.

It swooped out of the trees, <u>plunging like a dart</u> and <u>diving at the tree above their heads</u>.
It swooped out of the trees, plunged like a dart and dived at the tree above their heads.

EXERCISE

1.1   She strode into the room.
1.2   ~~She~~ <u>muttered under her breath</u>. (**-ING**)

_____

_____

Variation:

_____

_____

2.1   A billowing mist spread through the hall.

2.2   ~~It~~ <u>filled the air with its grey tentacles</u>. (**-ING**)

_____

_____

Variation:

_____

_____

3.1   She put a finger to her lips.

3.2   ~~She~~ <u>warned him not to make a sound</u>. (**-ING**)

_____

_____

Variation:

_____

_____

4.1   She jumped up and down on the spot.

4.2   ~~She~~ <u>punched the air with her fist</u>. (**-ING**)

_____

_____

Variation:

_____

_____

5.1   ~~She~~ <u>lowered herself to the ground inside the ditch</u>. (**-ING**)

5.2   She waited a few minutes before peering over the muddy lip.

_____

_____

Variation:

_____

_____

6.1   ~~She~~ <u>kept her back pressed against the wall</u>. (**-ING**)
6.2   Scarlett inched her way up the alley.

_____

_____

Variation:

_____

_____

7.1   He <u>ducked down</u>. (**-ING**)
7.2   He sought cover behind the reeds.

_____

_____

Variation:

_____

_____

8.1   James <u>closed his eyes</u>. (**-ING**)
8.2   He squeezed back the tears that were welling up.

_____

_____

Variation:

_____

_____

9.1   Scarlett edged her way back up the alley.
9.2   She <u>paused every so often to listen for any sounds</u>. (**-ING**)

_____

_____

Variation:

_____

_____

10.1 Rob imagined them lurking in the shadows.

10.2 They <u>waited for him to make a move</u>. (**-ING**)

_____

_____

Variation:

_____

_____

11.1 It <u>hung</u> ominously over the village. (**-ING**)

11.2 The crater and its plume of vapour was a silent menacing reminder of its awesome power.

_____

_____

Variation:

_____

_____

12.1 It <u>whispered</u> as it fell. (**-ING**)

12.2 The waterfall was a silky, watery stairs.

_____

_____

Variation:

_____

_____

13.1 The river hurtled over the edge into the swirling mist below.

13.2 It roared fiercely. (**-ING**)

_____

_____

Variation:

_____

_____

14.1 Spears of dazzling lightning tore through the sky.

14.2 They blinded him as they flickered in and out. (**-ING**)

_____

_____

Variation:

_____

_____

15.1 His wide eyes strained to pierce the darkness.

15.2 They darted wildly from side to side. (**-ING**)

_____

_____

Variation:

_____

_____

16.1 He crawled over the ground.

16.2 He kept low.

16.3 He did not dare to raise his head.

_____

_____

Variation:

_____

_____

17.1 He held his breath.

17.2 He gritted his teeth.

17.3 Rob staggered to his feet.

_____

_____

Variation:

_____

_____

18.1 Kitty staggered to a halt.

18.2 She slumped to the ground.

_____

_____

Variation:

_____

_____

19.1 The ugly little goblin grinned maliciously at Joe.

19.2 The goblin beckoned him to enter the cave.

_____

_____

Variation:

_____

_____

20.1 It swooped out of the treetops.

20.2 It plunged like a dart.

20.3 It dived at the tree directly above their heads.

_____

_____

Variation:

_____

_____

21.1 She held her breath. (-**ING**)

21.2 She waited.

21.3 She was huddled in the shadows.

21.4 She drew her knees up against her chest. (-**ING**)

21.5 She couldn't be seen. (**SO**)

_____

_____

Variation:

_____

_____

22.1 She ran.
22.2 She tried to get out of sight.
22.3 She forced herself to ignore the burning ache.
22.4 The ache was creeping up her legs.

_____

_____

Variation:

_____

_____

23.1 Rob whirled around.
23.2 He saw a crack spreading like a lightning bolt.
23.3 It spread across the ice behind him.

_____

_____

Variation:

_____

_____

24.1 James fought a wave of panic.
24.2 He began paddling wildly with his arms.

_____

_____

Variation:

_____

_____

25.1 James whirled around.
25.2 He searched desperately for the light.
25.3 The light would guide him back to the surface. (**THAT**)

_____

_____

Variation:

_____

_____

26.1 Sizzling embers drifted down.
26.2 It set fire to everything in their path.
26.3 It sent flaming branches crashing to the ground.

_____

_____

Variation:

_____

_____

27.1 Rob forced himself to keep moving.
27.2 He shuffled forward.

_____

_____

Variation:

_____

_____

28.1 He ran.
28.2 He zigzagged through the trees.
28.3 He moved as quickly as he could.

_____

_____

Variation:

_____

_____

29.1 James tore a strip from his shirt.
29.2 He pressed it over his mouth and nose.

_____

_____

Variation:

_____

_____

30.1 Kitty looked over her shoulder at Tom.

30.2 She put a finger to her mouth.

30.3 She warned him to be quiet.

_____

_____

Variation:

_____

_____

31.1 Rob pressed himself against the wall.

31.2 He made his way towards the front door.

_____

_____

Variation:

_____

_____

32.1 She hugged the wall with her back.

32.2 She shuffled sideways.

32.3 One foot crossed the other.

32.4 She reached the front door.

_____

_____

Variation:

_____

_____

33.1 She threw herself against the door.

33.2 She groped for the bolt.

33.3 She breathed a sigh of relief.

33.4 She felt it slide home. (**AS**)

_____

_____

Variation:

_____

_____

34.1 Kitty slipped on the damp floor.

34.2 She almost fell headlong down the stairs.

_____

_____

Variation:

_____

_____

35.1 She sprinted wildly down the corridor.

35.2 Kitty pulled.

35.3 Kitty pushed.

35.4 She tugged at every door.

_____

_____

Variation:

_____

_____

36.1 He screamed at the top of his lungs.
36.2 He ran down the hall.
36.3 He pounded on all the doors.

_____

_____

Variation:

_____

_____

37.1 She grabbed a chair.
37.2 She smashed the window.
37.3 She climbed up onto the sill.
37.4 She stretched out her arms to grab the drainpipe.

_____

_____

Variation:

_____

_____

38.1 Kitty wrapped her arms and legs around the pipe.
38.2 She gradually inched her way down to the ground.

_____

_____

Variation:

_____

_____

39.1 A CCTV camera was pointing straight at her.
39.2 It jerked back and forth.
39.3 It followed her every movement.

_____

_____

Variation:

_____

_____

40.1 She kept her eyes on the flickering light.
40.2 It flashed intermittently in the distance.
40.3 Kitty followed the path.

_____

_____

Variation:

_____

_____

41.1 Rachel darted and dodged through the trees.
41.2 She blundered and slipped.
41.3 She fought her way through the undergrowth.

_____

_____

Variation:

_____

_____

42.1 She stayed close to the walls.
42.2 Kitty edged round the side of the house.
42.3 She paused for a moment.
42.4 She paused to listen for any unnatural sounds.
42.5 Then she moved closer to the main entrance.
42.6 She did this as quietly as she could.

_____

_____

Variation:

_____

_____

43.1 Rachel blew out her cheeks.

43.2 She let out a long rasping breath.

_____

_____

Variation:

_____

_____

44.1 She grabbed her phone.

44.2 Kitty darted down the stairs back into the entrance hall.

_____

_____

Variation:

_____

_____

45.1 She backed away from the mirror.

45.2 Kitty felt behind her for the door.

_____

_____

Variation:

_____

_____

46.1 Kitty clasped her hands in her lap.

46.2 Kitty moved her lips silently in prayer.

_____

_____

Variation:

_____

_____

47.1 The figure had thinned out in a shimmering mist.

47.2 It had disappeared through the locked door.

47.3 This happened <u>before he could cry for help</u>.

_____

_____

Variation:

_____

_____

48.1 Kitty ducked down.

48.2 She sought cover behind the reeds.

_____

_____

Variation:

_____

_____

49.1 Scarlett took off her glasses.

49.2 She leaned back in the chair.

49.3 She stretched her arms behind her head.

_____

_____

Variation:

_____

_____

_____

50.1 Kitty wrapped her arms around her legs.

50.2 Kitty hugged them close to her chest.

50.3 Kitty crouched in the shadows.

_____

_____

Variation:

_____

_____

ANSWERS

1.   *She strode into the room, muttering under her breath.*

Variations:

a.   Muttering under her breath, she strode into the room.

b.   Striding into the room, she muttered under her breath.

c.   She strode into the room and muttered under her breath.

2.   *A billowing mist spread through the hall, filling the air with its grey tentacles.*

Variations:

a.   Spreading through the hall, the billowing mist filled the air with its grey tentacles.

b.   A billowing mist, spreading through the hall, filled the air with its grey tentacles.

c.   A billowing mist spread through the hall and filled the air with its grey tentacles.

3.   *She put a finger to her lips, warning him not to make a sound.*

Variations:

a.   Putting a finger to her lips, she warned him not to make a sound.
b.   She put a finger to her lips and warned him not to make a sound.

4.   *She jumped up and down on the spot, punching the air with her fist.*

Variations:

a.   Jumping up and down on the spot, she punched the air with her fist.
b.   She jumped up and down on the spot and punched the air with her fist.

5.   *Lowering herself to the ground inside the ditch, she waited a few minutes longer before peering over the muddy lip.*

Variations:

a.   She lowered herself to the ground inside the ditch, waiting a few minutes before she peered over the muddy lip.
b.   She lowered herself to the ground inside the ditch and waited a few minutes before peering over the muddy lip.

6.   *Keeping her back pressed against the wall, Scarlett inched her way up the alley.*

Variations:

a.   Inching her way up the alley, Scarlett kept her back pressed against the wall.
b.   Her back pressing against the wall, Scarlett inched her way up the alley.
c.   Scarlett kept her back pressed against the wall and inched her way up the alley.

7.   *He ducked down, seeking cover behind the reeds.*

Variations:

a.   Ducking down, he sought cover behind the reeds.
b.   He ducked down and sought cover behind the reeds.

8.   *James closed his eyes, squeezing back the tears that were welling up.*

Variations:

a.   Closing his eyes, James squeezed back the tears that were welling up.
b.   James closing his eyes, squeezed back the tears that were welling up.
c.   James closed his eyes and squeezed back the tears that were welling up.

9.   *Scarlett edged her way back up the alley, pausing every so often to listen for any sounds.*

Variations:

a.   Pausing so often to listen for any sounds, Scarlett edged her way back up the alley.
b.   Edging her way back up the alley, Scarlett paused every so often to listen for any sounds.
c.   Scarlett, pausing so often to listen for any sounds, edged her way back up the alley.
d.   Scarlett paused every so often to listen for any sounds **as** she edged her way back up the alley.

10.   *Rob imagined them lurking in the shadows, waiting for him to make a move.*

Variations:

Rob imagined them lurking in the shadows and waiting for him to make a move.

11. *Hanging ominously over the village, the crater and its plume of vapour was a silent menacing reminder of its awesome power.*

Variations:

a. The crater and its plume of vapour, hanging ominously over the village, was a silent menacing reminder of its awesome power.

b. The crater and its plume of vapour hung ominously over the village and was a silent menacing reminder of its awesome power.

12. *Whispering as it fell, the waterfall was a silky, watery stairs.*

Variations:

a. The waterfall, whispering as it fell, was a silky, watery stairs.

b. The waterfall was a silky, watery stairs, whispering as it fell.

c. The waterfall was a silky, watery stairs and whispered as it fell.

13. *Roaring fiercely, the river hurtled over the edge into the swirling mist below.*

Variations:

a. The river, roaring fiercely, hurtled over the edge into the swirling mist below.

b. The river hurtled over the edge into the swirling mist below, roaring fiercely.

c. The river roared fiercely and hurtled over the edge into the swirling mist below.

14. *Spears of dazzling lightning tore through the sky, blinding him as they flickered in and out.*

Variations:

a. Spears of dazzling lightning, blinding him as they flickered in and out, tore through the sky.

b. Blinding him as they flickered in and out, spears of dazzling lighting tore through the sky.

c. Tearing through the sky, spears of dazzling lightning blinded him as they flickered in and out.

d. Spears of dazzling lightning tore through the sky and blinded him as they flickered in and out.

15. *His wide eyes strained to pierce the darkness, darting wildly from side to side.*

Variations:

a. Darting wildly from side to side, his wide eyes strained to pierce the darkness.
b. Straining to pierce the darkness, his wide eyes darted wildly from side to side.
c. His wide eyes strained to pierce the darkness and darted wildly from side to side.

16. *He crawled over the ground, keeping low, not daring to raise his head.*

Variations:

a. Crawling over the ground, he kept low, not daring to raise his head.
b. Keeping low, he crawled over the ground, not daring to raise his head.
c. He crawled over the ground, kept low and did not dare to raise his head.

17. *Holding his breath, gritting his teeth, Rob staggered to his feet.*

Variations:

a. Rob held his breath, and gritting his teeth staggered to his feet.
b. Rob holding his breath and gritting his teeth, staggered to his feet.
c. Rob held his breath, gritted his teeth, and staggered to his feet.

18. *Staggering to a halt, Kitty slumped to the ground.*

Variations:

a. Kitty, staggering to a halt, slumped to the ground.
b. Kitty staggered to a halt and slumped to the ground.

19.   *The ugly little goblin, grinning maliciously at Joe, beckoned him to enter the cave.*

Variations:

a.   Grinning maliciously at Joe, the ugly little goblin beckoned him to enter the cave.

b.   The ugly little goblin grinned maliciously at Joe and beckoned him to enter the cave.

20.   *Swooping out of the treetops, it plunged like a dart and dived at the tree directly above their heads.*

Variations:

a.   Plunging like a dart, it swooped out of the treetops and dived at the tree directly above their heads.

b.   It swooped out of the treetops and, plunging like a dart, dived at the tree directly above their heads.

c.   It swooped out of the treetops, plunged like a dart and dived at the tree directly above their heads.

21.   *Holding her breath, she waited, huddled in the shadows and drawing her knees up against her chest so she couldn't be seen.*

Variations:

a.   She waited, holding her breath, huddling in the shadows and drawing her knees up against her chest so she couldn't be seen.

b.   Huddling in the shadows, she held her breath and drew her knees up against her chest so she couldn't be seen and waited.

c.   She huddled in the shadows, held her breath and drew her knees up against her chest so she couldn't be seen and waited.

22. *She ran, trying to get out of sight, forcing herself to ignore the burning ache creeping up her legs.*

Variations:

a. Running, she tried to get out of sight, forcing herself to ignore the burning ache creeping up her legs.
b. Trying to get out of sight, she ran, forcing herself to ignore the burning ache that was creeping up her legs.
c. She ran, tried to get out of sight and forced herself to ignore the burning ache creeping up her legs.

23. *Whirling around, Rob saw a crack spreading like a lightning bolt across the ice behind him.*

Variations:

a. Rob whirling around, saw a crack spreading like a lightning bolt across the ice behind him.
b. Rob whirled around and saw a crack spreading like a lightning bolt across the ice behind him.

24. *Fighting a wave of panic, James paddled wildly with his arms.*

Variations:

a. Paddling wildly with his arms, James fought a wave of panic.
b. James, fighting a wave of panic, paddled wildly with his arms.
c. James fought a wave of panic and paddled wildly with his arms.

25. *Whirling around, James searched desperately for the light that would guide him back to the surface.*

Variations:

a. James whirled around, searching desperately for the light that would guide him back to the surface.
b. James whirling around, searched desperately for the light that would guide him back to the surface.
c. James whirled around and searched desperately for the light that would guide him back to the surface.

26. *Sizzling embers drifted down, setting fire to everything in their path, sending flaming branches crashing to the ground.*

Variations:

a. The sizzling embers drifting down set fire to everything in their path and sent flaming branches crashing to the ground.
b. Sizzling embers drifted down, set fire to everything in their path and sent flaming branches crashing to the ground.

27. *Forcing himself to keep moving, Rob shuffled forward.*

Variations:

a. Shuffling forward, Rob forced himself to keep moving.
b. Rob, shuffling forward, forced himself to keep moving.
c. Rob shuffled forward and forced himself to keep moving.

28. *He ran, zigzagging through the trees and moving as quickly as he could.*

Variations:

a. He ran and, zigzagging through the trees, moved as quickly as he could.
b. He ran, zigzagged through the trees and moved as quickly as he could.

29. *Tearing a strip from his shirt, James pressed it over his mouth and nose.*

Variations:

a. James, tearing a strip from his shirt, pressed it over his mouth and nose.
b. James tore a strip from his shirt and pressed it over his mouth and nose.

30. *Looking over her shoulder at Tom, Kitty put a finger to her mouth and warned him to be quiet.*

Variations:

a. Kitty looked over her shoulder at Tom and put a finger to her mouth, warning him to be quiet.
b. Kitty looked over her shoulder at Tom, put a finger to her mouth and warned him to be quiet.

31. *Pressing himself against the wall, Rob made his way towards the front door.*

Variations:

a. Rob, pressing himself against the wall, made his way towards the front door.
b. Rob pressed himself against the wall and made his way towards the front door.

32. *Hugging the wall with her back, she shuffled sideways, one foot crossing the other until she reached the front door.*

Variations:

a. She hugged the wall with her back, shuffled sideways, one foot crossing the other until she reached the front door.
b. She hugged the wall with her back and shuffled sideways with one foot crossing the other until she reached the front door.

33. *She threw herself against the door, groped for the bolt, breathing a sigh of relief as she felt it slide home.*

Variations:

a. Throwing herself against the door, she groped for the bolt and breathed a sigh of relief as she felt it slide home.
b. She threw herself against the door and, groping for the bolt, breathed a sigh of relief as she felt it slide home.
c. She threw herself against the door, groped for the bolt and breathed a sigh of relief as she felt it slide home.

34. *Slipping on the damp floor, Kitty almost fell headlong down the stairs.*

Variations:

a. Kitty slipped on the damp floor, almost falling headlong down the stairs.
b. Kitty, slipping on the damp floor, almost fell headlong down the stairs.
c. Kitty slipped on the damp floor and almost fell headlong down the stairs.

35. *Sprinting wildly down the corridor, Kitty pulled, pushed and tugged at every door.*

Variations:

a.   Kitty sprinted wildly down the corridor, pulling, pushing and tugging at every door.
b.   Kitty, sprinting wildly down the corridor, pulled, pushed and tugged at every door.
c.   Kitty sprinted wildly down the corridor and pulled, pushed and tugged at every door.

36. *He screamed at the top of his lungs and ran down the hall, pounding on all the doors.*

Variations:

a.   Screaming at the top of his lungs, he ran down the hall and pounded on all the doors.
b.   Screaming at the top of his lungs, he ran down the hall, pounding on all the doors.
c.   He screamed at the top of the lungs, ran down the hall and pounded on all the doors.

37. *Grabbing a chair, she smashed the window, climbed up onto the sill and stretched out her arms to grab the drainpipe.*

Variations:

a.   She grabbed a chair, smashed the window, climbed up onto the sill, stretching out her arms to grab the drainpipe.
b.   Grabbing a chair and smashing the window, she climbed up onto the sill and stretched out her arms to grab the drainpipe.
c.   She grabbed a chair, smashed the window, climbed up onto the sill and stretched out her arms to grab the drainpipe.

38. *Wrapping her arms and legs around the pipe, Kitty gradually inched her way down to the ground.*

Variations:

a. Kitty wrapped her arms and legs around the pipe, gradually inching her way down to the ground.
b. Kitty, wrapping her arms and legs around the pipe, gradually inched her way down to the ground.
c. Kitty wrapped her arms and legs around the pipe and gradually inched her way down to the ground.

39. *A CCTV camera was pointing straight at her, jerking back and forth, following her every movement.*

Variations:

a. Pointing straight at her, a CCTV camera jerked back and forth, following her every movement.
b. Pointing straight at her, a CCTV camera jerked back and forth and followed her every movement.
c. A CCTV camera was pointed straight at her, jerked back and forth and followed her every movement.

40. *Keeping her eyes on the flickering light that flashed intermittently in the distance, Kitty followed the path.*

Variations:

a. Following the path, Kitty, keeping her eyes on the flickering light that flashed intermittently in the distance, followed the path.
b. Kitty kept her eyes on the flickering light that flashed intermittently in the distance and followed the path.

41. *Darting and dodging through the trees, blundering and slipping, Rachel fought her way through the undergrowth.*

Variations:

a. Blundering and slipping, fighting her way through the undergrowth, Rachel darted and dodged through the trees.
b. Rachel darted and dodged through the trees, blundering and slipping, fighting her way through the undergrowth.
c. Rachel, darting and dodging through the trees, blundered and slipped and fought her way through the trees.
d. Darting and dodging through the trees, Rachel blundered and slipped and fought her way through the undergrowth.
e. Rachel darted and dodged through the trees, blundered and slipped, and fought her way through the undergrowth.

42. *Staying close to the walls, Kitty edged round the side of the house, pausing for a moment to listen for any unnatural sounds and then, as quietly as she could, moved closer to the main entrance.*

Variations:

a. Kitty stayed close to the walls and, edging round the side of the house, paused for a moment to listen for any unnatural sounds, and then as quietly as she could moved closer to the main entrance.
b. Staying close to the walls and edging round the side of the house, Kitty paused for a moment to listen for any unnatural sounds, and then as quietly as she could moved closer to the main entrance.
c. Kitty stayed close to the walls, edged round the side of the house, paused for a moment to listen for any unnatural sounds, and then as quietly as she could moved closer to the main entrance.

43. *Blowing out her cheeks, Rachel let out a long rasping breath.*

Variations:

a. Rachel blew out her cheeks, letting out a long rasping breath.
b. Rachel, blowing out her cheeks, let out a long rasping breath.
c. Rachel blew out her cheeks and let out a long rasping breath.

44. *Grabbing her phone, Kitty darted down the stairs back into the entrance hall.*

Variations:

a. Kitty, grabbing her phone, darted down the stairs back into the entrance hall.
b. Kitty grabbed her phone and darted down the stairs back into the entrance hall.

45. *Backing away from the mirror, Kitty felt behind her for the door.*

Variations:

a. Kitty backed away from the mirror, feeling behind her for the door.
b. Kitty, backing away from the mirror, felt behind her for the door.
c. Kitty backed away from the mirror and felt behind her for the door.

46. *Clasping her hands in her lap, Kitty moved her lips silently in prayer.*

Variations:

a. Moving her lips silently in prayer, Kitty clasped her hands in her lap.
b. Kitty, clasping her hands in her lap, moved her lips silently in prayer.
c. Kitty clasped her hands in her lap and moved her lips silently in prayer.

47. *Before he could cry for help, the figure had thinned out in a shimmering mist, disappearing through the locked door.*

Variations:

a. The figure, before he could cry out for help, had thinned out in a shimmering mist and disappeared through the locked door.
a. The figure had thinned out in a shimmering mist before he could cry for help and disappeared through the locked door.

48. *Kitty ducked down, seeking cover behind the reeds.*

Variations:

a. Ducking down, Kitty sought cover behind the reeds.
b. Kitty, ducking down, sought cover behind the reeds.
c. Kitty ducked down and sought cover behind the reeds.

49. *Scarlett, taking off her glasses, leaned back in the chair and stretched her arms behind her head.*

Variations:

a. Taking off her glasses and leaning back in the chair, Scarlett stretched her arms behind her head.
b. Scarlett took off her glasses and, leaning back in the chair, stretched her arms behind her head.
c. Scarlett took off her glasses, leaned back in the chair and stretched her arms behind her head.

50. *Wrapping her arms around her legs and hugging them close to her chest, Kitty crouched in the shadows.*

Variations:

a. Kitty wrapped her arms around her legs and, hugging them close to her chest, crouched in the shadows.
b. Kitty, wrapping her arms around her legs and hugging them close to her chest, crouched in the shadows.
c. Kitty wrapped her arms around her legs, hugged them close to her chest and crouched in the shadows.

20

How to create a sentence combining exercise from a text

CREATING ORIGINAL SENTENCE COMBINING EXERCISES

These can be created from professional texts (fiction and non-fiction) and student-written texts to address problem areas (usually the de-combining process itself reveals where the writing is going wrong).

★ Consider what you want to accomplish.
★ What type of model are you trying to teach?
★ What is the teaching objective or skill focus?
★ What cues, context will be built in?

1. Collect models from class or independent reading and use what you have read and like about a particular piece of writing.
2. De-combine the passage into clusters of kernel sentences.
3. Students combine the clusters into a paragraph.
4. Students compare their transformation with the original composed by the author, discussing the syntactic options chosen and looking for stylistic patterns.
5. Pay attention to the author's language choices and craft techniques.

DOI: 10.4324/9781032662862-23

Emphasising effectiveness helps students understand that there is often more than one right answer in writing, and it is necessary to evaluate the multiple solutions to decide on the best option. Evaluating the effectiveness of a sentence should include discussion in terms of:

1. clarity
2. precision of meaning
3. rhythmic appeal.

STUDENT TEXTS

If using a student text (past or present), make any revisions to that text to correct the initial problem. Using students' own work engages them at their level of need and provides solutions to problems with a current piece of writing.

It also provides an opportunity to teach proofreading and editing skills in a direct but collaborative way. For example, comma splice, run-on sentences, faulty subject/verb agreement or misplaced modifiers.

COLLECTING MODELS

Develop a habit of:

* re-reading interesting sentences
* copying them into a writing journal
* highlighting what about the content, language choices and style interests a reader.

A. *GEORGE'S MARVELLOUS MEDICINE* – GRANDMA

Original text

George couldn't help disliking Grandma. She was a selfish grumpy old woman. She had pale brown teeth and a small puckered up mouth like a dog's bottom.

She squeezed her lips together tight so that her mouth became a tiny, wrinkled hole.

It was her face that frightened him the most of all, the frosty smile, the brilliant unblinking eyes.

CUED EXERCISE: LEVEL 1

1.1   George couldn't help it.
1.2   ~~He~~ dislik**ed** Grandma. (-ING)

2.1   She was an ^ old woman.
2.2   She was <u>selfish</u>.
2.3   She was <u>grumpy</u>.

3.1   She had ^ teeth.
3.2   They were <u>pale</u>.
3.3   They were <u>brown</u>.
3.4   ~~She had~~ a small ^ mouth. (AND)
3.5   ~~It was~~ <u>puckered</u>.
3.6   ~~It was~~ <u>like a dog's bottom</u>.

4.1   She squeezed her lips together tight.^
4.2   Her mouth became a ^ hole. (SO THAT)
4.3   ~~It was~~ <u>tiny</u>.
4.4   ~~It was~~ <u>wrinkled</u>.

5.1   It was her face. ^
5.2   ~~It~~ frightened him most of all. (THAT)
5.2   ~~It was~~ the frosty smile. (,)
5.3   ~~It was~~ <u>the brilliant ^ eyes</u>.
5.4   ~~Her eyes were~~ <u>unblinking</u>.

Original text

He pointed to something, but she couldn't see anything apart from sea spray, rolling, gunmetal waves and a sense they were entering a forbidden part of the universe.

CUED EXERCISE: LEVEL 2

1.1   He pointed to something.

1.2   She couldn't see anything. (BUT)

1.3   There was sea spray.

1.4   There were waves.

1.5   The waves were rolling.

1.6   The waves were gunmetal.

1.7   She had a sense. (AND)

1.8   They were entering a part of the universe.

1.9   It was forbidden.

Original text

Her eyes travelled over the distant mountains, the wild seas to her left and the flat, snow-covered land stretching out ahead. And then she did a double take. There on the horizon, silhouetted against the sun, something moved. It was in the blink of an eye. So rapid she almost missed it. Something big and loping and most unexpected.

OPEN EXERCISE: LEVEL 3

1.1 Her eyes travelled.
1.2 They travelled over the distant mountains.
1.3 Her eyes travelled over the wild seas to her left.
1.4 Her eyes travelled over the flat land.
1.5 The land was snow-covered.
1.6 The land stretched out ahead.

2.1 She did a double take.
2.2 There was something on the horizon.
2.3 It was silhouetted against the sun.
2.4 Something moved.

3.1 It was in the blink of an eye.
3.2 It was so rapid.
3.3 She almost missed it.

4.1 It was something big.
4.2 It was something loping.
4.3 It was something most unexpected.

BOY: TALES OF CHILDHOOD BY ROALD DAHL – MRS PRATCHETT (PAGES 32 AND 33)

Original text

She was a small skinny old hag with a moustache on her upper lip and a mouth as sour as a green gooseberry. She never smiled.

OPEN EXERCISE: LEVEL 3

1.1 She was small.

1.2 She was skinny.

1.3 She was an old hag.

1.4 She had a moustache on her upper lip.

1.5 She had a mouth.

1.6 It was as sour as a green gooseberry.

1.7 She never smiled.

Original text

But the loathsome thing about Mrs Pratchett was the filth that clung around her. Her apron was grey and greasy. Her blouse had bits of breakfast all over it, toast crumbs and tea stains and splotches of dried egg-yolk. It was her hands, however, that disturbed us most. They were disgusting. They were black with grit and grime.

2.1 There was something loathsome about Mrs Pratchett.

2.2 It was the filth.

2.3 It clung around her.

2.4 Her apron was grey.

2.5 Her apron was greasy.

2.6 Her blouse had bits of breakfast all over it.

2.7 There were toast crumbs.

2.8 There were tea stains.

2.9 There were splotches of dried egg-yolk.

3.0 It was her hands.

3.1 They disturbed us most.

3.2 Her hands were disgusting.

3.3 Her hands were black.

3.4 They were covered in grit and grime.

21

Poetry

INSTRUCTIONS

1. Group the lines that are connected. For example, the sentences in cluster 1 which describe the elephant in the first poem.
2. Experiment with different ways of combining them into lines of poetry.
3. Each stanza can be combined separately and then compared with the original, or all the stanzas can be combined before comparing with the original.
4. The main learning takes place through the process of students experimenting with the word order and combinations (through problem-solving) and then discussing how their texts compare with each other's and the original. This will create a discussion about the poets' craft and the effect of their choices on achieving their intended impact on the reader.

Through this exercise, students are processing the poem, constructing it and comparing it, all of which makes the poem more accessible.

DOI: 10.4324/9781032662862-24

BEING BRAVE AT NIGHT BY EDGAR A. GUEST

STANZA 1

1.1	It was the other night.
1.2	It was about two o'clock.
1.3	Maybe it was three.
1.4	There was an elephant.
1.5	It had shining tusks.
1.6	It came chasing after me.

2.1	His trunk was waving in the air.
2.2	His trunk spouted jets of steam.
2.3	He was out to eat me up.
2.4	I still didn't scream.
2.5	I didn't let him see that I was scared.
2.6	I had a better thought.
2.7	I just escaped from where I was.
2.8	I crawled in bed with Dad.

STANZA 2

1.1	It happened one time.
1.2	There was a giant.
1.3	It was horrible to see.
1.4	He had three heads.
1.5	He had twenty arms.
1.6	He came after me.
1.7	Fire came out of his mouths.
1.8	The fire was red hot.
1.9	Every hand was red.
1.91	He declared that he would grind my bones.
1.92	He declared that he would make them into bread.

2.1	I was too smart for him.
2.2	I fooled him mighty bad.
2.3	It happened before his hands could collar me.
2.4	I crawled in bed with Dad.

STANZA 3

1.1   I am not scared of nothing that comes pesterin' me at night.
1.2   It happened once.
1.3   I was chased by forty ghosts.
1.4   The ghosts were all shimmery
1.5   The ghosts were all white.

2.1   I just raced them around the room.
2.2   And I let them think maybe I would have to stop.
2.3   Maybe I would have to rest for a while.
2.6   They could capture me.
2.5   They leapt onto my bed.
2.6   Oh Gee, they were mad.
2.7   They found that I had slipped away.
2.8   They found I had crawled in bed with Dad.

STANZA 4

1.1   No giants have dared to come in there.
1.2   No ghosts have dared to come in there.
1.3   No elephants have dared to come in there.
1.4   Because if they did he would beat them up.
1.5   He would chase them to their lair.

2.1   They just hang around the children's rooms.
2.2   They snap.
2.3   They snarl.
2.4   They bite.
2.5   They laugh if they can make them yell for help with all their might.

3.1   I don't ever yell out loud.
3.2   I'm not that sort of lad.
3.3   I slip from out the covers.
3.4   I crawl in bed with Dad.

ORIGINAL

The other night 'bout two o'clock, or maybe it was three,
An elephant with shining tusks came chasing after me.
His trunk was wavin' in the air an' spoutin' jets of steam
An' he was out to eat me up, but still I didn't scream
Or let him see that I was scared – a better thought I had,
I just escaped from where I was and crawled in bed with Dad.

One time there was a giant who was horrible to see,
He had three heads and twenty arms, an' he came after me
And red hot fire came from his mouths and every hand was red
And he declared he'd grind my bones and make them into bread.
But I was just too smart for him, I fooled him mighty bad,
Before his hands could collar me I crawled in bed with Dad.

I ain't scared of nothin' that comes pesterin' me at night.
Once I was chased by forty ghosts all shimmery an' white.
An' I just raced 'em round the room an' let 'em think maybe
I'd have to stop an' rest awhile, when they could capture me.
Then when they leapt onto my bed, Oh Gee! But they were mad
To find that I had slipped away an' crawled in bed with Dad.

No giants, ghosts or elephants have dared to come in there
'Coz if they did he'd beat 'em up and chase 'em to their lair.
They just hang 'round the children's rooms
an' snap an' snarl an' bite
An' laugh if they can make 'em yell
for help with all their might.
But I don't ever yell out loud. I'm not that sort of lad,
I slip from out the covers and I crawl in bed with Dad.

WIND ON THE HILL BY A. A. MILNE

1.1 No one call tell me where the wind comes from.

1.2 No one call tell me where the wind goes.

1.3 Nobody knows.

2.1 It is flying from somewhere.

2.2 It is flying as fast as it can.

2.3 I couldn't keep up with it.

2.4 I couldn't keep up not even if I ran.

3.1 I stopped holding the string of my kite.

3.2 It would blow with the wind.

3.3 It would blow for a day and a night.

4.1 This would happen when I found it.

4.2 I would find it wherever it blew.

4.3 I should know that the wind had been going there too.

5.1 I could tell them where the wind goes.

5.2 I could not tell them where the wind comes from.

5.3 Nobody knows.

ORIGINAL

No one call tell me,
Nobody knows,
Where the wind comes from,
Where the wind goes.

It's flying from somewhere
As fast as it can,
I couldn't keep up with it,
Not if I ran.

But if I stopped holding
The string of my kite,
It would blow with the wind
For a day and a night.

And then when I found it,
Wherever it blew,
I should know that the wind
Had been going there too.

So then I could tell them
Where the wind goes …
But where the wind comes from
Nobody knows.

THE MOON **BY ROBERT LOUIS STEVENSON**

STANZA 1

1.1   The moon has a face.
1.2   It is like the clock in the hall.
1.3   She shines on thieves.
1.4   The thieves are on the garden wall.
1.5   She shines on streets.
1.6   She shines on fields.
1.7   She shines on harbour quays.
1.8   She shines on birdies asleep.
1.9   The birdies are in the forks of the trees.

STANZA 2

1.1   She shines on the squalling cat.
1.2   She shines on the squeaking mouse.
1.3   She shines on the howling dog.
1.4   The dog is by the door of the house.
1.5   She shines on the bat.
1.6   The bat lies in bed at noon.
1.7   They all love to be out by the light of the moon.

STANZA 3

1.1 All of the things that belong to the day cuddle to sleep.
1.2 They want to be out of her way.
1.3 Flowers and children close their eyes.
1.4 They close their eyes until up in the morning the sun shall arise.

ORIGINAL

The moon has a face like the clock in the hall;
She shines on the thieves on the garden wall,
On streets and fields and harbour quays,
And birdies asleep in the forks of the trees.
The squalling cat and the squeaking mouse,
The howling dog by the door of the house.
The bat that lies in bed at noon,
All love to be out by the light of the moon.
But all of the things that belong to the day
Cuddle to sleep to be out of her way;
And flowers and children close their eyes
Till up in the morning the sun shall arise.

BUDAPEST BY BILLY COLLINS

1.1 My pen moves along the page.
1.2 My pen is like the snout of a strange animal.
1.3 My pen is shaped like a human arm.
1.4 My pen is dressed in the sleeve of a loose green sweater.

2.1 I watch it.
2.2 It is sniffing the paper ceaselessly.
2.3 It is as intent as any forager.
2.3 The forager has nothing on its mind but the grubs and insects.
2.4 The grubs and insects will allow it to live another day.

3.1   It wants only to be here tomorrow.

3.2   It wants only to be dressed in the sleeve of a plaid shirt.

3.3   It wants only to have its nose pressed against the page.

3.4   It wants only to be writing a few more lines.

4.1   I gaze out of the window.

4.2   I imagine Budapest.

4.3   I imagine some other city where I have never been.

ORIGINAL

My pen moves along the page
like the snout of a strange animal
shaped like a human arm
and dressed in the sleeve of a loose green sweater.

I watch it sniffing the paper ceaselessly,
intent as any forager that has nothing
on its mind but the grubs and insects
that will allow it to live another day.

It wants only to be here tomorrow,
dressed perhaps in the sleeve of a plaid shirt,
nose pressed against the page,
writing a few more lines

while I gaze out of the window and imagine Budapest
or some other city where I have never been.

THE DOOR **BY MIROSLAV HOLUB**

1.1   Go and open the door.

1.2   Maybe there is a tree or a wood outside.

1.3   Maybe there is a garden or a magic city outside.

2.1   Go and open the door.
2.2   Maybe there is a dog rummaging.
2.3   Maybe you will see a face or an eye.
2.4   Maybe you will see the picture of a picture.
2.5   Go and open the door.
2.6   If there is a fog, it will clear.

3.1   Go and open the door even if there is only the darkness ticking.
3.2   Go and open the door even if there is only the hollow wind.
3.3   Go and open the door even it there is nothing there.
3.4   Go and open the door.

4.1   At least there will be a draught.

ORIGINAL

Go open the door.
Maybe outside there's
a tree, or a wood,
a garden,
or a magic city.

Go and open the door.
Maybe a dog's rummaging.
Maybe you'll see a face,
or an eye,
or the picture
of a picture.

Go and open the door.
If there's a fog
it will clear.

Go and open the door.
Even if there's only
the darkness ticking
even if there's only
the hollow wind,
even if
nothing
is there,
go and open the door.

At least
There'll be
A draught.

THE RIVER BY VALERIE BLOOM

1.1   The River is a wanderer.
1.2   It is a nomad.
1.3   It is a tramp.
1.4   He never chooses one place to set up his camp.

2.1   The River's a winder through the valley and hill.
2.2   He twists.
2.3   He turns.
2.4   He just cannot be still.

3.1   The River's a hoarder.
3.2   He buries deep down those little treasures that he wants to keep.

4.1   The River's a baby.
4.2   He gurgles and hums.
4.3   He sounds like he's happily sucking his thumbs.

5.1   The River's a singer.
5.2   As he dances along, the countryside echoes the notes of his song.

6.1   The River's a monster.
6.2   He is hungry and vexed.
6.3   He has goggled up trees and he will swallow you next.

ORIGINAL

The River's a wanderer,
A nomad, a tramp,
He never chooses one place
To set up his camp.

The River's a winder,
Through valley and hill
He twists and he turns,
He just cannot be still.

The River's a hoarder
And he buries down deep
Those little treasures
That he wants to keep.

The River's a baby,
He gurgles and hums,
And sounds like he's happily
Sucking his thumbs.

The River's a singer,
As he dances along,
The countryside echoes
The notes of his song.

The River's a monster,
Hungry and vexed,
He's goggled up trees
And he'll swallow you next.

22

Sentence combining using non-fiction fact sheets or texts

Fact sheets and content-centred sentence combining exercises help students learn content and writing skills simultaneously, including the style of writing appropriate to a particular academic discipline, for example, history, geography or science. It is, therefore, a useful exercise not only to develop sentence construction, variety and cohesion for non-fiction, but also to clarify essential facts of an event, process or concept.

It is also a useful technique for summarising (paraphrasing) a non-fiction text: collecting essential facts as a series of predicate phrases, using them to construct kernel sentences and then using these as a basis for constructing a clear, cohesive paragraphs helps to either:

(a) filter out unnecessary information
(b) identify points which require additional detail, explanation or clarification.

As well as improving sentence construction, working on a text in this way also helps to consolidate the main facts and the memorization of important information.

For students working their way through national assessment past papers (including GCSE) and model answers, an effective way to examine the effectiveness of the model answer is by de-combining it into a series of kernel and modification sentences, with the students transforming these into a coherent paragraph. They then compare their transformations with their peers and the original model, discussing the techniques that make the model answer clear, concise and precise.

DOI: 10.4324/9781032662862-25

It also enables students to pick out the essential information and detail that is required.

PROCESS:

1. List facts – written in predicate phrases.
    For example: *raged for four days*
2. Each of the fact phrases can be made into a sentence by adding a topic word (noun).
    For example: **The fire** raged for four days.
3. Select predicate phrases that make sense together.
4. Combine the phrases to form sentences.
5. Combine the sentences into a paragraph.
6. Revise the paragraph by deleting unnecessary words or combining connected detail into fewer sentences, but also giving consideration to areas where a short single-clause sentence would be more effective for clarity and emphasis.

FOR EXAMPLE: GREAT FIRE OF LONDON

Noun topic: Samuel Pepys and John Evelyn

★ were two famous diarists
★ lived in London in the 17th century
★ recorded their eye-witness accounts of the events of the Great Fire of London in their diaries.

1.1 Samuel Pepys and John Evelyn were two famous diarists.
1.2 They lived in London in the 17th century.
1.3 They recorded the events of the Great Fire of London in their diaries.

a. Samuel Pepys and John Evelyn were two famous diarists who lived in London in the 17th century and recorded the events of the Great Fire of London in their diaries.
b. Two famous diarists living in London in the 17th century, Samuel Pepys and John Evelyn, recorded the events of the Great Fire of London in their diaries.

Noun topic: Their diaries

★ are among England's most prized historical treasures
★ provide a first-hand account of this devastating historical tragedy.

1.1 Their diaries are among England's most prized historical treasures.
1.2 Their diaries provide a first-hand account of this devastating historical tragedy.

a. Their diaries are among England's most prized historical treasures because they provide a first-hand account of this devastating tragedy.
b. Their diaries, which provide a first-hand account of this devastating tragedy, are among England's most prized historical treasures.

EXERCISE

1. Use the fact phrases (predicates) to construct a series of kernel sentences.
2. Combine the sentences using coordinating and subordinating conjunctions, relative clauses and participial phrases.
3. Experiment with different ways of combining the sentences.

Noun topic: The fire

★ began in the early hours of Sunday morning
★ began on 2nd September 1666
★ was started by a spark from an oven in Thomas Farriner's baker shop in Pudding Lane.

Kernel sentences

1.1 _____
1.2 _____
1.3 _____

Combined sentences

_____
_____
_____

Noun topic: a. Weather during the summer of 1666

_____

★ was very hot and dry
★ there had been no rain for weeks.

Kernel sentences

1.1 _____
1.2 _____

Combined sentences

_____

Noun topic: b. Strong wind during the four days the fire raged through London

_____

★ blew from the east
★ spread the flames quickly.

_____

Kernel sentences

1.1 _____
1.2 _____

Combined sentences

_____

Noun topic: Buildings in 17th-century London

_____

★   were built of wood and straw
★   were as dry as tinder
★   were packed tightly together
★   were in narrow rows
★   burnt easily
★   allowed the fire to jump from building to building.

Kernel sentences

1.1 _____
1.2 _____
1.3 _____
1.4 _____
1.5 _____
1.6 _____

Combined sentences

_____

Noun topic: Warehouses

★   located around Pudding Lane
★   contained flammable materials like rope and oil
★   caught alight
★   fuelled the spread of the flames throughout the city.

Kernel sentences

1.1 _____
1.2 _____
1.3 _____
1.4 _____

Combined sentences

_____

Noun topic: Battling the fire

_____

★ no fire brigade in London
★ fought by local soldiers and locals with leather buckets filled with water from the River Thames.

Kernel sentences

1.1 _____
1.2 _____

Combined sentences

_____

Noun topic: Fire breaks

_____

★ were created by pulling down buildings with metal hooks
★ created open spaces so that the fire could not spread
★ could not contain the spread of the fire because the wind propelled the flames across the gaps.

Kernel sentences

1.1 _____
1.2 _____
1.3 _____

Combined sentences

_____

Noun topic: People

---

* ★ panicked
* ★ collected all the belongings they could carry
* ★ fled the raging flames in boats across the River Thames.

Kernel sentences

1.1 _____

1.2 _____

1.3 _____

Combined sentences

Noun topic: Navy

---

* ★ ordered by King Charles II to create an even larger fire break
* ★ used gunpowder to blow up some of the buildings.

Kernel sentences

1.1 _____

1.2 _____

Combined sentences

Noun topic: Fire

_____

★ died down as the wind dropped
★ stopped spreading
★ extinguished four days later on 6th September 1666
★ destroyed a third of the city
★ burned to the ground 13,200 houses, 400 streets and 87 churches
★ burned famous buildings like St Pauls Cathedral and the Royal Exchange
★ left 70,000 people homeless
★ resulted in sickness and disease.

Kernel sentences

1.1 _____
1.2 _____
1.3 _____
1.4 _____
1.5 _____
1.6 _____
1.7 _____
1.8 _____

Combined sentences

_____
_____
_____

Noun topic: Results

- ★ rebuilt city in a safer and more organised fashion
- ★ created wider streets
- ★ built buildings of brick or stone
- ★ formed fire brigades.

Kernel sentences

1.1 _____

1.2 _____

1.3 _____

1.4 _____

Combined sentences

_____

Noun topic: a. The monument to the Great Fire of London

_____

- ★ erected near Pudding Lane.
- ★ to commemorate the fire
- ★ to celebrate the rebuilding of the city
- ★ was designed by Sir Christopher Wren.

Noun topic: b. Inscription on the north panel

- ★ records the city's destruction.

Kernel sentences

1.1 _____

1.2 _____

1.3 _____

1.4 _____

1.5 _____

Combined sentences

_____

_____

_____

_____

_____

_____

_____

_____

_____

23

History

The Blitz in World War II

PARAGRAPH A

1.1   There came the drone of airplanes from everywhere.
1.2   They were hidden behind the billows of black smoke.
1.3   The smoke rolled across the sky.
1.4   They were punctuated by a muffled blast.
1.5   This happened occasionally.
1.6   They were punctuated by waves of broiling heat.
1.7   It was as if someone had opened and closed an oven close by.

PARAGRAPH B

2.1   Bright tracer bullets slashed the sky.

3.1   Tom stood silently.
3.2   His neck was craned.
3.3   He watched the sky.
3.4   All he could see were clouds of smoke.
3.5   All he could see was the flickering orange of fires.
3.6   The fires were reflected against the clouds.

DOI: 10.4324/9781032662862-26

PARAGRAPH C

4.1   He heard a single airplane engine.
4.2   He heard it out of the maelstrom.

_____

5.1   It was close and getting closer.

_____

6.1   He watched.
6.2   Panic flooded through him.

_____

7.1   Something parted the clouds.
7.2   It was something small.
7.3   It was something grey.
7.4   It hurtled towards him.

_____

_____

8.1   He hit the grass.
8.2   He threw his arms over his head.

_____

EXAMPLE COMBINATION

From everywhere came the drone of airplanes, hidden behind the billows of black smoke that rolled across the sky, and occasionally punctuated by a muffled blast and waves of broiling heat as if someone had opened and closed an oven close by. Bright tracer bullets slashed the sky.

Tom stood silently, his neck craned, watching the sky, but all he could see were clouds of smoke, the flickering orange of fires reflected against them.

Out of the maelstrom, he heard a single airplane engine. It was close and getting closer. Panic flooded through him as he watched. Something small, something grey parted the clouds, hurtling towards him. Hitting the grass, he threw his arms over his head.

24

Settings

1. THE RUINS

1.1 The ancient city was shrouded by mists.

1.2 It was surrounded by lush vegetation.

1.3 It was surrounded by steep escarpments.

1.4 It was only accessed by diagonal flights of flagstone stairs.

1.5 The stairs were set into the terrace walls.

_____

_____

_____

2.1 The hill was pocked with the remains.

2.2 The remains were of the massive stone doorways.

2.3 The remains had once guarded the city.

_____

_____

3.1 Kitty passed through the west gate.

3.2 She scanned the ruins.

_____

_____

DOI: 10.4324/9781032662862-27

4.1 There was a labyrinth facing her.
4.2 The labyrinth was of crumbling walls and pillars.
4.3 The labyrinth was of courtyards and tunnels.
4.4 They spread out in all directions.

_____

_____

_____

_____

5.1 The air was stifling.
5.2 The air shimmered in a haze.
5.3 It shimmered around the ancient buildings.
5.4 Dark storm clouds were gathering.
5.5 The clouds were in the distance.

_____

_____

_____

6.1 She wanted to seek cover before the storm broke.
6.2 Kitty forced herself to take slow, deliberate steps.
6.3 She forced herself to avoid placing her feet on the sacred stones.
6.4 The stones littered the path.
6.5 They were covered in ancient markings.
6.6 The markings had been carved deep into their surface.

_____

_____

_____

_____

7.1 Kitty couldn't shake off a sense of unease.
7.2 She made her way towards the temple.
7.3 She had a feeling.
7.4 The feeling was that someone or something was watching her.

_____

_____

_____

EXAMPLE COMBINATION

The ancient city was shrouded by mists, surrounded by lush vegetation and steep escarpments, and accessed only by diagonal flights of flagstone stairs set into the terrace walls. In amongst the tussocks of grass and nettles, the hill was pocked with the remains of the massive stone doorways that had once guarded the city.

Kitty passed through the west gate and scanned the ruins. Facing her was a labyrinth of crumbling walls and pillars, courtyards and tunnels that spread out in all directions.

The air was stifling, shimmering in a haze around the ancient ruins and, in the distance, dark storm clouds were gathering. Even though she wanted to seek cover before the storm broke, Kitty forced herself to take slow, deliberate steps to avoid placing her feet on the sacred stones that littered the path and were covered in ancient markings carved deep into their surface. Kitty couldn't shake off a sense of unease as she made her way towards the temple: a feeling that someone or something was watching her.

2. THE FOGGY STREET BASED ON *A CHRISTMAS CAROL* BY CHARLES DICKENS

1.1   The accountant was at his desk.
1.2   He was once again busy.
1.3   His fingers were tapping.
1.4   His fingers were frantic.
1.5   They were on his keyboard.

_____

_____

_____

2.1   It was cold outside.
2.2   It was bitter.
2.3   There was an icy wind.
2.4   It rattled the windows.

_____

_____

_____

3.1   It was only four o'clock.
3.2   The light had faded.
3.3   It had been dimmed by the blanket of mist.
3.4   The mist swirled around the buildings.

_____

_____
_____

_____

4.1   There were lights in the offices.
4.2   The lights flickered.
4.3   The lights were like yellow flames.
4.4   They were fighting off the mist.
4.5   The mist slunk along the pavements.
4.6   The mist crept up the walls.
4.7   The mist shrouded the windows.

_____

_____
_____

_____

_____

5.1   The accountant gazed out of his window.
5.2   He could see little of the street.
5.3   He could see little of the pedestrians and traffic.
5.4   They were like mere ghostly phantoms.

_____

_____
_____

_____

The accountant was once again busy at his desk, his fingers frantically tapping on his keyboard. Outside, it was cold, bitter, with an icy wind that rattled the windows. Although it was only four o'clock, the light had faded, dimmed by the blanket of mist that swirled around the buildings. Lights flickered in the offices, like yellow flames fighting off the mist that slunk along the pavements, crept up the walls and shrouded the windows. Gazing out of his window, the accountant could see little of the street; pedestrians and traffic were mere ghostly phantoms.

3A. THE JUNGLE

1.1 Dark clouds gathered quickly.
1.2 The clouds were above them.

_____

_____

2.1 The clouds released their heavy load.
2.2 The canopy was pounded mercilessly by driving rain.
2.3 It cascaded down into the tangle of undergrowth.
2.4 It hammered down on their heads.
2.5 It ran in rivulets along the tropical rainforest floor.

_____

_____

3.1 Visibility was now restricted to a few metres.
3.2 The track disintegrated.
3.3 It disintegrated into a morass of glutinous mud.
3.4 It gripped their boots.

_____

_____

Dark clouds gathered quickly above them. When the clouds released their heavy load, the canopy was pounded mercilessly by driving rain, which cascaded down into the tangle of undergrowth, hammering down on their heads and running in rivulets along the tropical rainforest floor. Visibility was now restricted to a few metres and the track disintegrated into a morass of glutinous mud that gripped their boots.

3B. THE JUNGLE

1.1   There was no respite.
1.2   The jungle was alive day and night.
1.3   There was a myriad of biting mosquitoes.
1.4   There were crawling insects scuttling unseen.
1.5   They scuttled in the leaf litter beneath their feet.

_____

_____

_____

2.1   Huge bird-eating spiders lurked everywhere.
2.2   They were bigger than a man's hand.
2.3   There were deadly scorpions.
2.4   The scorpions were armed with needle-tipped stingers.

_____

_____

_____

3.1   There were enormous poisonous vipers.
3.2   They were under every twisted lattice of tree roots.
3.3   They were under decaying logs.
3.4   The logs were buried in the leaf litter.
3.5   The viper's skins were tattooed with intricate camouflage patterns.
3.6   They lay silently in wait.
3.7   They waited for any unsuspecting creature.
3.8   The unsuspecting creature blundered within striking range.

_____
_____
_____
_____

EXAMPLE COMBINATION

There was no respite. Day and night, the jungle was alive: a myriad of biting mosquitoes and crawling insects scuttling unseen in the leaf litter beneath their feet. Everywhere lurked huge bird-eating spiders bigger than a man's hand and deadly scorpions armed with needle-tipped stingers. Under every twisted lattice of tree roots or decaying logs and buried in the leaf litter, enormous poisonous vipers, their skins tattooed with intricate camouflage patterns, lay silently in wait for any unsuspecting creature which blundered within striking range.

3C. THE JUNGLE

1.1   Joe hadn't noticed it lying hidden.

1.2   It was amongst the submerged vegetation.

1.3   The vegetation grew abundantly at the side of the narrow stream.

_____

_____

2.1   It lay perfectly still.

2.2   It was inches below the rippling water.

2.3   It was lost from view in a bed of weeds.

_____

_____

3.1   It broke the surface only occasionally to breathe.

3.2   The creature waited patiently for the wild pig or deer.

3.3   It waited for them to abandon their natural caution.

3.4   It waited for them to approach the stream.

3.5   It waited for them to slake their thirst in the waters.

3.6   It was concealed beneath the waters.

_____

_____

_____

_____

EXAMPLE COMBINATION

Joe hadn't noticed it lying hidden amongst the submerged vegetation that grew abundantly at the side of the narrow stream. Lying perfectly still inches below the rippling water, it was lost from view in a bed of weeds. Breaking the surface only occasionally to breathe, the creature waited patiently for the wild pig or deer to abandon their natural caution and approach the stream to slake their thirst in the waters beneath which it was concealed.

4. THE FOREST OF MICE AND MEN

1.1   The sun slides behind the hills.

1.2   The moon rises.

1.3   It washes the forest in its ghostly silver light.

1.4   I hear footsteps.

1.5   The footsteps crunch on the carpet.

1.6   The carpet is of withered autumn leaves.

_____

_____

_____

2.1   There is a screech.

2.2   It slashes through the silence.

2.3   Birds crash through the trees above me.

_____

_____

_____

3.1   The undergrowth is suddenly alive.

3.2   There are scuttling sounds.

3.4   The sounds are of night hunters.

3.5   The night hunters take cover.

3.6   Something moves on the path.

3.7   A twig snaps.

3.8   There were footsteps.

3.9   The footsteps were slow and shuffling.

3.10 The footsteps move closer.

_____

_____

_____

_____

4.1 There was a gusting wind.

4.2 It rattles the branches.

_____

5.1 There were two boys.

5.2 They emerge out of the shadows.

5.3 They move soundlessly.

5.4 They move from tree to tree.

_____

_____

_____

EXAMPLE COMBINATION

As the sun slides behind the hills and the moon rises to wash the forest in its ghostly silver light, I hear footsteps crunching on the carpet of withered autumn leaves. A screech slashes through the silence and birds crash through the trees above me. The undergrowth is suddenly alive: the scuttling sounds of night hunters as they take cover. Something moves on the path; a twig snaps and slow, shuffling footsteps move closer. The gusting wind rattles the branches. Out of the shadows emerge two boys, moving soundlessly from tree to tree.

5. THE ATTIC

1.1 He grasped the handle.

1.2 He grasped it in his right hand.

1.3 He leaned towards the door.

1.4 He listened intently for any sound from inside the room.

_____

_____

_____

_____

2.1   There was not a sound.

2.2   The thumping had stopped.

_____

_____

3.1   He eased the handle.

3.2   He did it slowly.

3.3   He pushed the door open.

3.4   He pushed it a fraction.

_____

_____

4.1   There was a creak.

4.2   It was of the rusty hinges.

4.3   It was the only sound in the house.

_____

_____

_____

5.1   He pushed it open a little wider.

5.2   He peered through the gap.

_____

_____

6.1   The room was dark.

6.2   It took a few seconds for his eyes to adjust.

_____

_____

7.1   Then, he started to make out silhouettes.

7.2   The silhouettes were of furniture.

7.3   The furniture was dotted around the room.

_____

_____

_____

8.1 He moved his left foot into the room.

8.2 He waited for a moment.

8.3 He then took another step.

_____

_____

9.1 The floorboards creaked.

9.2 The floorboards were rotten.

9.3 They creaked as they took his weight.

_____

_____

10.1 Jack swung his torch.

10.2 He swung it around the room.

_____

_____

11.1 It was packed.

11.2 It had all sort of paraphernalia.

11.3 Everything was shrouded.

11.4 Everything had a blanket of dust and cobwebs.

_____

_____

_____

12.1 It happened suddenly.

12.2 Jack had a strange feeling.

12.3 Someone or something was watching him.

_____

_____

13.1 He shone his torch.

13.2 He shone it to the right.

_____

14.1   It was in the far corner.

14.2   It was huddled in the shadows.

14.3   It was hidden behind a veil of cobwebs.

14.4   It was a one-eyed doll.

14.5   The doll was slumped against an old wooden crate.

_____

_____

15.1   His heart thudded in his chest.

15.2   His hand started to tremble.

15.3   He saw SOMETHING in the flickering light.

15.4   The doll had a stitch smile.

15.5   It was a rotten smile.

15.6   The smile seemed to widen.

_____

_____

_____

_____

EXAMPLE COMBINATION

Grasping the handle in his right hand, he leaned towards the door and listened intently for any sound from inside the room. Not a sound. The thumping had stopped.

Slowly, he eased the handle down and pushed the door open a fraction. The creak of the rusty hinges was the only sound in the house. He pushed it open a little wider and peered through the gap. The room was dark, and it took a few seconds for his eyes to adjust. Then, he started to make out silhouettes of furniture dotted around the room.

He moved his left foot into the room, waited for a moment, and then took another step. The rotten floorboards creaked as they took his weight. Jack swung his torch around the room. It was packed with all sorts of paraphernalia, and everything was shrouded in a blanket of dust and cobwebs.

Suddenly, Jack had a strange feeling that someone or something was watching him. He shone his torch to the right. In the far corner, huddled in the shadows, hidden behind a veil of cobwebs, a one-eyed doll was slumped against an old wooden crate. His heart thudded in his chest. His hand started to tremble. In the flickering light, the doll's rotten stitch smile seemed to widen.

25

De-combining to correct errors and confused constructions

Students often struggle to correct complex and confusing sentences which usually emerge during a first draft when they are trying to transcribe the information held in their working memory or from a plan. Revision often results in a few full stops added or even more commas. De-combining the sentence or passage takes it back to its basic form, thus highlighting the information and detail that the student is trying to include. It also helps to bring students' attention to sentence run-ons or fragments.

This enables students to tackle revision in a step-by-step process and to recombine the original sentence into a series of connected sentences to make the information conveyed clearer.

STEP 1

★ Divide the sentence into chunks of meaning.

STEP 2

★ Use the sentence chunks to write a series of base single-clause sentences.

STEP 3

★ Combine the sentences. Experiment with several different constructions and combinations.

DOI: 10.4324/9781032662862-28

FOR EXAMPLE

1. The wind was already starting to grow in ferocity swirled through the trees blustering around the houses.

Step 1 – Chunking into meaningful sentence parts.

The wind was already starting to grow in ferocity,/ swirled through the trees/ blustering around the houses.

Step 2 – Use the sentence chunks to write a series of base single-clause sentences.

1.1   The wind was already starting to grow in ferocity.
1.2   It swirled through the trees.
1.3   It blustered around the houses.

Step 3 – Combine the base sentences.

The wind was already starting to grow in ferocity. It swirled through the trees and blustered around the houses.

Step 4 – Experiment with different combinations.

Already, the wind was starting to grow in ferocity. It swirled through the trees and blustered around the houses.

Already, the wind was starting to grow in ferocity as it swirled through the trees and blustered around the houses.

Already the wind, which was starting to grow in ferocity, was swirling through the trees and blustering around the houses.

EXERCISE

1. Before he could get to the chair his legs buckled under him he fell to the floor.

Step 1 – Chunking into meaningful sentence parts.

Before he could get to the chair his legs buckled under him he fell to the floor.

Step 2 – Use the sentence chunks to write a series of base single-clause sentences.

_____

_____

1. _____

2. _____

3. _____

Step 3 – Combine the base sentences.

_____

_____

Step 4 – Experiment with different combinations.

_____

_____

2. The following morning it was hot and humid, the day turned out to be exciting and unexpected.

Step 1 – Chunking into meaningful sentence parts.

The following morning it was hot and humid, the day turned out to be exciting and unexpected.

Step 2 – Use the sentence chunks to write a series of base single-clause sentences.

_____

_____

1. _____

2. _____

3. _____

Step 3 – Combine the base sentences.

_____

_____

Step 4 – Experiment with different combinations.

_____

_____

3. The day had dawned bright. And warm exceptionally warm and bright. When she emerged from her tent. She searched the shimmering skies the dazzling and sizzling ray blasted westward across the arid merciless desert.

Step 1 – Chunking into meaningful sentence parts.

The day had dawned bright. And warm exceptionally warm and bright. When she emerged from her tent. She searched the shimmering skies the dazzling and sizzling ray blasted westward across the arid merciless desert.

**Step 2 – Use the sentence chunks to write a series
of base single-clause sentences.**

1. _____
2. _____
3. _____
4. _____
5. _____
6. _____

Step 3 – Combine the base sentences.

Step 4 – Experiment with different combinations.

4.   Suddenly everything became blurred as if a misty curtain had descended on the room a swirling billowing icy veil rising spreading, creeping, along the floor, until its grey tentacles filled the room.

Step 1 – Chunking into meaningful sentence parts.

Suddenly everything became blurred as if a misty curtain had descended on the room a swirling billowing icy veil rising spreading, creeping, along the floor, until its grey tentacles filled the room.

Step 2 – Use the sentence chunks to write a series of base single-clause sentences.

_____

_____

1. _____

2. _____

3. _____

4. _____

5. _____

6. _____

7. _____

Step 3 – Combine the base sentences.

_____

_____

Step 4 – Experiment with different combinations.

_____

_____

5. The only light in the attic came from slivers of light, from the tiny sky lights in the roof Jake swung his torch, around the huge room which stretched across the width of the old manor house.

Step 1 – Chunking into meaningful sentence parts.

The only light in the attic came from slivers of light, from the tiny sky lights in the roof Jake swung his torch, around the huge room which stretched across the width of the old manor house.

**Step 2 – Use the sentence chunks to write a series
of base single-clause sentences.**

_____

_____

1. _____

2. _____

3. _____

4. _____

5. _____

Step 3 – Combine the base sentences.

_____

_____

Step 4 – Experiment with different combinations.

_____

_____

Part 4

Sentence expansion

26

Sentence expansion method

Expanding a sentence means adding one or more words to the main clause to provide extra detail. It could be a single word, phrase or clause or multiple elements in a series.

Explicitly teaching students how to expand sentences focuses on one small section of their writing to see how it can be improved. For example, when assessing a first draft, either individually, with peers or a teacher, part of the revision process is to elicit whether the writer has communicated clearly and with all the requisite detail or explanation so that the reader understands and can visualise the description or understand the message. It is closely connected with work on 'Show not Tell'.

One of the vital processes and techniques in teaching the revision step of the writing process is to develop a routine of asking questions. Learning how to expand sentences is a great way of introducing and practising this technique and will pay dividends when it comes to students 're-seeing' their writing, understanding what areas need more detail or explanation, and being able to incorporate these details into the first draft and the original sentence.

NOTE

1. Plan time for students to zoom in and focus on a particular paragraph rather than trying to improve the entire text at once.
2. Highlight sentence types in different colours to see where they over-rely on simple sentences or start each sentence in the same way.

DOI: 10.4324/9781032662862-30

3. Encourage students to choose just one or two sentences they think would benefit from expansion. This prevents students from thinking that every sentence should be long and detailed.

Most students won't naturally expand sentences without support, modelled sentences and direct teaching of how to do it. Working on expanding sentences, demonstrating the options available and providing models for their writing tool-kits will pay off, resulting in students who begin to carefully create effective sentences rather than mindlessly adding additional words: a vital skill to have learned in respect of revising their texts.

Sentence expanding, sentence combining and sentence imitation are inter-related processes. The sentence combining exercises included in this handbook provide an effective scaffold for students to learn and practise how to expand sentences. As with every section, students should be given an opportunity to imitate the sentence construction.

SECTION A – ADDING PHRASES AND CLAUSES

Model how to expand a sentence using different writing craft tools (words, phrases and clauses), demonstrating the possible positions and punctuation as the words, phrases or clauses are added. Initially model this process by revisiting phrases and clauses learned previously.

Teaching any writing effectively involves:

* teacher modelling
* guided practice
* independent practice (individual or pairs).

EXAMPLE: USING 5WS – WHAT, WHERE, WHEN, WHY, WHO AND HOW

1. **The ruins were hidden.**
   What: The ruins <u>of an ancient city</u> were hidden.
   Where: The ruins of an ancient city were hidden <u>behind a dense curtain of tangled vines</u>.
   Why: The ruins of an ancient city, <u>which had been abandoned by the Incas and frozen in time in the centre of the rainforest</u>, were hidden behind a dense curtain of tangled vines.
2. **Vines wound around the trees.**
   What: <u>Wooded vines as thick as a human body</u> wound around the trees.
   Why: Wooded vines as thick as a human body wound around the trees <u>and searched for light and moisture</u>.
   How: Wooded vines as thick as a human body wound around the trees, <u>crept up the trunks, and slithered across the branches, searching for light and moisture.</u>
3. **Dusk shrouded the buildings.**
   What: Dusk, <u>with its long-fingered shadows</u>, shrouded the buildings.
   How/where: Dusk, with its long-fingered shadows, <u>slithered over the ground and shrouded the buildings.</u>

If teaching to expand a sentence using a particular type of phrase or clause, study a model and identify its function, position, construction and punctuation, as demonstrated in the investigation section of this book.

SECTION B – LAYERING

1. Start with a telling sentence.
2. Gradually add layers using phrases and clauses.

a. *The snake/ slithered slowly/ through the tangled undergrowth.*

Ask a series of questions. Each answer will prompt another question until a wealth of extra details have been collected. These can be recorded either as phrases or (as in the sentence combining process) listed as a series of kernel sentences.

Developing detail about the subject	
What type of snake is it?	A cobra
Does it have any markings?	Green, with black and white bands
How long is it?	Over 3 metres
How does it protect itself? What sort of head, eyes, tongue does it have?	When threatened it flares its neck by expanding ribs and muscles on both sides to create a black banded hood that makes it look bigger. Black forked tongue flicking from side to side, tasting the air. Yellow elliptical eyes with keyhole-shaped pupils.
Is it deadly?	Lethal venom causes excruciating pain, vomiting, blurred vision and paralysis of the heart and lungs and ultimately death.
How does it strike prey?	Two needle-pointed fangs. Sweeps its head forward and downward to bite prey and then sinks its venom-filled fangs into its prey. Spits venom into eyes with blinding accuracy for up to a distance of 2 metres. Contracts muscles – squeezes venom gland and shoots venom out of holes in their fangs.
Movement	In an undulating motion
Where is the tangled undergrowth?	Dense rainforest
Who is watching the snake?	Joe
Does the snake spot the narrator?	Yes, senses through flicking tongue from side to side
What does it do?	Rears into the air

LAYERING

A snake/ slithered slowly/ through the tangled undergrowth.

STEP 1 – WHAT/WHERE

    a.   Include more details about the subject and the location of the setting.

        1.   **Specific noun added in a relative clause to expand description.**

        2.   **Prepositional phrase to add detail about the location of the setting.**

An enormous snake,/ **which was a venomous green and yellow cobra / over three metres in length,/** slithered slowly/ through the tangled undergrowth/ **of the dense rainforest**.

Imitation using a Komodo dragon

A lizard waited patiently in the bushes.

A colossal lizard,/ **which was a grey and armour-plated Komodo dragon,/ over two metres in length**,/ waited patiently in the long grass/ **by the side of the trail**.

STEP 2

    b.   Experiment with other tools that can tighten this construction.

For example:

    1)   **Opening and delayed adjectives**
    a.   Enormous and venomous, a green and yellow cobra slithered slowly through the tangled undergrowth of the dense rainforest.
    b.   A green and yellow cobra, **enormous and venomous**, slithered slowly through the tangled undergrowth of the dense rainforest.

Imitation using a Komodo dragon

    a.   **Grey and armour-plated**, /a colossal Komodo dragon/ waited patiently in the long grass for the wild boar.

    b.   A colossal Komodo dragon, **grey and armour-plated,**/ waited patiently in the long grass/ for the wild boar.

STEP 3 – WHAT/HOW

    c.   Add a prepositional phrase to extend the description of the snake.

    d.   Add a relative clause to describe its movement.

An enormous snake, a venomous green and yellow cobra over three metres in length, **with a black forked tongue that flicked from side to side,** slithered slowly through the tangled undergrowth of the dense rainforest.

Imitation using a Komodo dragon

A colossal lizard, a grey prehistoric-looking Komodo dragon nearly 3 metres in length, **with a long stretched neck that peered over the bushes,** waited patiently in the long grass for the wild boar.

STEP 4 – WHAT, HOW, WHY

    e.   Add a participial phrase to add movement and suspense.

An enormous snake, a venomous green and yellow cobra over three metres in length, slithered slowly through the tangled undergrowth of the dense rainforest, with a black forked tongue that flicked from side to side, **tasting the air** and scenting any threats.

Imitation using a Komodo dragon

A colossal lizard, a grey prehistoric-looking Komodo dragon nearly 3 metres in length, waited patiently in the long grass for the wild boar, with a long stretched neck that peered over the bushes, **tasting the air with its yellow forked tongue and dribbling venomous saliva from its open mouth**.

STEP 5 – WHERE

f.   Add a prepositional phrase (adverb phrase) to give more precision about the location of the subject in the setting.

Between Joe and the tree, an enormous snake, a venomous green and yellow cobra over three metres in length, slithered slowly through the tangled undergrowth of the dense rainforest, with a black forked tongue that flicked from side to side, tasting the air and scenting any threats.

Imitation using a Komodo dragon

To the right of the narrow trail, a colossal lizard, a grey prehistoric-looking Komodo dragon nearly three metres in length, waited patiently in the long grass for the wild boar, with a long stretched neck that peered over the bushes, tasting the air with its yellow forked tongue and dribbling venomous saliva from its open mouth.

STEP 6 – WHEN

g.   Add an adverb clause to place the narrator at the scene.

While Joe was following the guide along the rainforest track, out of the corner of his eye he spotted an enormous snake, a venomous green and yellow cobra over three metres in length, slithering slowly through the tangled undergrowth towards him, with a black forked tongue that flicked from side to side, tasting the air and scenting any threats.

Imitation using a Komodo dragon

As Joe watched from high up on the ridge, he suddenly spotted a movement to the right of the narrow trail leading to the group's mud-wallow, a colossal lizard, a grey prehistoric-looking Komodo dragon nearly 3 metres in length, waited patiently in the long grass for the wild boar, with a long stretched neck that peered over the bushes, tasting the air with its yellow forked tongue and dribbling venomous saliva from its open mouth.

STEP 7 – WHAT

Add more detail about the setting to add a cinematic quality to the scene by:

    f.   adding an independent clause using a semi-colon

    g.   expanding it further using a co-ordinating conjunction (*and*)

    h.   add further movement using a participial phrase.

> While Joe was following the guide along the rainforest track, out of the corner of his eye he spotted a flicker of movement, **a glint of green reflected in the shaft of bright sunlight slanting through a gap in the canopy;** he stopped, took a closer look, <u>and</u>, with a lurch of his stomach, realised that it was an enormous snake, a venomous green and yellow cobra over three metres in length, slithering slowly through the tangled undergrowth towards him, with its black tongue flicking from side to side and tasting the air for any threats.

Imitation using a Komodo dragon

> As Joe watched from high up on the ridge, he suddenly spotted a movement to the right of the narrow trail leading to the group's mud-wallow, a long grey neck with a rounded snout visible in the low evening sun shining over the savanna; he adjusted his binoculars, zoomed in for a closer look, and with an intake of breath realised that he had found a colossal lizard, a grey prehistoric-looking Komodo dragon nearly 3 metres in length, waiting patiently in the long grass for the wild boar, with its long neck stretched to peer over the bushes, tasting the air with its yellow forked tongue and dribbling venomous saliva from its open mouth.

EVALUATING AND EXPERIMENTING

Grammar is about how words, phrases and clauses are combined to create meaning. Apart from learning how to expand a sentence, students should also learn that there are many ways of constructing meaning. While learning how to expand a sentence and the tools available, students should also be given the opportunity to play with language to revise and craft a sentence. With the sentences above, at whatever level the student is at, it is important that part of the exercise is to experiment and explore, to evaluate and assess whether the current construction is the best available.

> **For example**, experiment with dividing the following sentence into two, and discussing the effectiveness of both and which is preferred.
>
> a.   While Tom was following the guide along the rainforest track, out of the corner of his eye he spotted an enormous snake, a venomous green and yellow cobra over three metres in length, slithering slowly through the tangled undergrowth towards him, with its black tongue flicking from side to side and tasting the air. for any threats.
>
> b.   While Tom was following the guide along the rainforest track, out of the corner of his eye he spotted an enormous snake, a venomous green and yellow cobra over three metres in length. It slithered slowly through the tangled undergrowth towards him, its black tongue flicking from side to side, tasting the air for any threats.

EVALUATING THE EFFECTIVENESS OF EXCESSIVELY LONG SENTENCES

Students can find it hard to expand sentences effectively if they haven't learned to evaluate their language choices. They end up rushing in to add extra details without considering how they are doing it or the effect they want to create, for example, adding a whole string of adjectives or a fronted adverbial. It is important that students recognise that long complex, multi-clause sentences are not always the best choice.

Teachers model the process, verbalising the decisions they are making to enable students to observe that a sentence is never created with one attempt. It requires crafting. And sometimes brevity is better.

27

Sentence expansion

A writer's lens: 'Show not tell'

What do students do when teachers write next to imprecise sentences that they need to add:

* detail
* description
* an explanation?

Inexperienced writers frequently have an inability to **evaluate** their work with fresh eyes and to make the necessary revisions. Often they simply add a word or two in the belief that they have done what was asked of them, and the sentences become worse after the alteration or addition. This is because the teacher's suggestions did not help the pupils to discover the kinds of details that would add more colour and depth to their writing.

USING QUESTIONS TO DEVELOP DETAIL

When students assess their first draft, they need to consider what information, detail or description would be important to their reader to help them visualise the scene. Reading the text aloud or using a peer as an editing partner can be very helpful. Asking questions is an effective way of drawing attention to where the student needs to include more detail or description.

When you take a close-up photo of a particular part of a landscape, you use a zoom lens to capture the close, physical description. Asking a series of questions is a writer's lens, each question allowing the writer to zoom in on a particular detail.

DOI: 10.4324/9781032662862-31

A writer's lens includes:

* figurative language: similes, personification, metaphors, onomatopoeia
* adjectives
* sensory details – sight, sound, touch, smell, taste.

FIRST DRAFT – TELLING

Joe looked around the attic. It was stacked high with crates and boxes. In the middle of the back wall was a big hole. The creaking was coming from somewhere through the gap. There was a doll in a rocking chair.

Example questions	
Why had Joe gone into the attic. Was he on his own?	He had been woken every night by a rhythmic creaking from the attic.
What was in the crates and boxes?	Pans, ladles, kettles, footballs, tennis racquets
Was there anything else in the attic?	Battered suitcases, wooden barrels, tea boxes, clothes, scrolls, ledgers, notebooks
What was the light like? Where did it come from?	Dark, sliver of light from tiny sky light.
What was the weather like?	Raining – drummed on the roof.
Were there any sounds, smells?	Sound of rain drumming on the roof. Rhythmic creaking Musty and damp.
What was through the hole in the wall?	A large doll sitting on a rocking chair.
How was Joe feeling?	He was curious and excited. This was the first time he had been in the attic. His anxiety had built the longer he was in the attic.

EXERCISE 1 – DEVELOPING A SERIES OF QUESTIONS

From the table below, make a list of any additional questions that could be asked which would provide more detail or information about the setting or the main character and add it to the table.

EXERCISE 2 – CONVERTING THE TELLING SENTENCES

Using the information in the table and any additional detail collected, convert the telling sentences above into a descriptive paragraph.

Telling sentences

Joe looked around the attic. It was stacked high with crates and boxes. In the middle of the back wall was a big hole. The creaking was coming somewhere through the gap. There was a doll in a rocking chair.

EXERCISE 3 – EVALUATION AND IMITATION

Compare the 'showing' paragraph(s) with the model below. Underline or highlight any devices used in the model that can be imitated in the students' first draft.

MODEL

Apart from the slivers of moonlight shining through the tiny sky lights in the roof, the attic was pitch black. James swung his torch around the huge room which stretched across the width of the old manor house. Crates and boxes, chests and suitcases were packed into every available space. From only a quick scan, he could see that the attic was an historical treasure trove. As the clouds parted briefly, the moonlight brightened, and Joe spotted a set of shelves to his left stacked high with row upon row of scrolls, ledgers and notebooks.

Enormous wooden packing cases lay abandoned all over the room, some open with straw spilling over their sides; others had split open to reveal huge copper pans, kettles, pots and ladles packed away from a bygone era. Piled high against each of the walls were battered suitcases, huge trunks, wooden barrels and a collection of tea boxes: everything you would be likely to find in a time capsule.

In another corner, he spotted trophies crammed into an open trunk; abandoned leather footballs and wooden tennis rackets were in another. Just visible beneath their polythene wrappers and hanging on several rails were long ball gowns: dresses from another era. An old school desk, a quill still in the pot, a tailor's dummy. And over everything was a curtain of cobwebs and layers of dust; nobody had been up here for a very long time. With every step he took, clouds of dust and a musty stench filled the air.

A draught, then a rhythmic creaking came from the back of the room. Joe directed his torch to the rear of the attic. Here the boxes and crates had been arranged to create a gap and between that gap was a hole in the wall: a hole big enough for him to climb through.

As James moved towards the back wall, he had a strange feeling that someone or something was watching him. He shone his torch to the right. Through the gap, partly shrouded in the shadows and hidden behind a veil of cobwebs was a rocking chair: slowly creaking back and forth. He moved closer and shone his torch on the chair. Sitting on the chair was a one-eyed doll dressed in a gown of purple silk with wide crimson sleeves and a black fan-shaped hood covering her strands of red hair. In the flickering light, the doll's rotten stitch smile seemed to widen.

James took a step closer and suddenly everything became blurred as if a misty curtain had descended on the room: a swirling, billowing icy veil rising, spreading, creeping along the floor until its grey tentacles filled the room.

COMPARING TELLING AND SHOWING

1. Highlight or underline details in the 'showing' paragraph.
2. Make a note of the use of grammar tools that are effective in expanding a telling sentence and building suspense.

1. THE CURSE OF HESLEY MANOR

a. Telling paragraph

Kitty turned into the drive and stopped by two iron gates. She got out of the car and looked through the railings at the house. There was a camera pointing at her. Her great uncle had died weeks ago, and the building had been empty ever since. She opened the gates.

b. Showing paragraph

When she turned into the drive, Kitty was halted by two huge wrought iron gates. On top of two stone pillars either side of the gates stood huge black marble griffins, clutching the family's coat of arms in their outstretched talons.

Reluctantly, Kitty got out of her car and approached the gates. Arms folded tightly across her chest and her neck disappearing into her hunched shoulders, Kitty peered through the twisted railings, and stared at the ghostly shadow of the house at the end of the long drive. Above her, a camera was pointing straight at her, jerking back and forth, following her every movement. Her great uncle had died weeks ago, and the house had been empty ever since, so who was operating the camera? Kitty looked again at the dark, empty eyes of the house and got the strangest feeling: a sense of unease she couldn't explain; a sudden sense of a threatening malignant presence waiting for her beyond the gates. She shook her head impatiently. 'Your imagination is getting the better of you again,' she scolded herself. Kitty reached out towards the gate, drew back the bolt and eased the gates open wide enough for her car to get through. And that's when it all started to go wrong.

2. THE SWARM

a. Telling paragraph

He was crouched motionless behind the bush. He spotted their giant wasps' heads swarming towards him. He ran down the track towards the river.

b. Showing paragraph

Crouched behind the wall, Rob hadn't moved a muscle for at least ten minutes. He waited. He listened. He watched. Still no sign. Maybe he had evaded them. Eyes darting from side to side, he probed the shadows, searching for the slightest movement. To his left – a flicker of movement. Immediately, he recognised the loud buzzing noise and jerked his head back. His heart skipped a beat. There was another one above him, then another and another. The buzzing got louder and louder until it filled the air. They were coming at him from all directions, their giant wasps' heads plummeting out of the sky, hurtling towards him. He ran, not daring to look back, not daring to stop to catch his breath. With the sound of his breathing roaring in his ears, he hurtled down the track, swung sharp left and scrambled down the slope towards the river.

28

'Show not tell'
warm-up exercises

The following telling sentences can be used as short-burst warm-up activities, which can either be done orally or in writing. The most effective way of converting telling sentences into showing sentences or paragraphs is to ask questions (what, when, where, who, why, how), as outlined in Chapter 20. Each answer will lead to more questions and greater detail. This information can be collated in a writing plan and used at a later stage to develop a showing description.

TELLING SENTENCES

Section A

1. The room was basic.
2. The house was creepy.
3. The garden was overgrown.
4. He explored the city.
5. He got lost.
6. The streets were packed.
7. The hostel was in an amazing location.
8. Her room was a mess.
9. The sea was rough.
10. It was hot.
11. It was cold.
12. It was wet.

DOI: 10.4324/9781032662862-32

13. It was windy.
14. It was stormy.
15. It was dawn.
16. It was dark.
17. It was light.
18. The weather was bad.
19. It was a stormy night.
20. The camping trip was horrific.
21. The journey was a disaster.
22. She made me laugh.
23. He looked guilty.
24. She was really embarrassed.
25. She was determined.
26. He was desperate.
27. He was delighted.
28. She was sad.
29. She was curious.
30. He was furious.
31. He was suspicious.
32. He was tired.
33. He was full of energy and ready to take on the challenge.
34. She sat bolt upright in her chair.
35. The room stank.
36. It had a pleasant smell.
37. It was really quiet.
38. It was very noisy.
39. The meal was delicious.
40. The food was disgusting.
41. He ate his breakfast.
42. He could tell she was really enjoying her chocolate ice-cream.
43. She ate the cream egg delicately.
44. She ate the cream egg quickly.
45. She hated the feel of slugs.

Section B

Using the following prompts, expand the descriptions below.

1. Her trousers were ripped at the knees, her t-shirt torn and dark damp red patches seeped through both.
2. With a squeal of delight, she hopped up and down on the spot and pumped the air with her fist.
3. His face was lit up with a huge smile as he clenched his fist in triumph.
4. He had a mischievous grin on his face.
5. He was burning with rage.
6. He stared at her.
7. The smile suddenly dropped from her face.
8. Her voice dropped to a whisper.
9. She smothered a sob.
10. She slithered to a halt.
11. He crashed to the floor.
12. Sweat poured from his brow.
13. He clicked his tongue impatiently.
14. She bent her head and stared at her feet.
15. His insides shrivelled with embarrassment.
16. She smothered the giggles that were bubbling in the back of her throat.
17. It was a ghost town of deserted houses.
18. The ground was muddy.
19. The sleepy village seemed an unlikely place for an adventure.
20. They were faced with a strange door.
21. The room was a relaxing haven.
22. They had entered a fairy-tale world.
23. She was surrounded by a stormy sea.
24. She knew she would have to confess.
25. She decided to ignore them.
26. Her heart raced.
27. He watched the scenery drift by until the hypnotic rhythm of the train's wheels on the track rocked him into a deep sleep.
28. They looked up and down the street for the hundredth time.

29. Katie warned him to be quiet.
30. Tom gestured for her to get down.
31. He yanked on the handle. It wouldn't budge. It was locked.
32. Katie put her ear to the door.
33. He knocked three times, waited a few seconds, then knocked three times more.
34. She kicked the door shut.
35. She pressed her back against the door.
36. Something was very wrong.
37. It was taking too long.
38. He felt hopeless; it was time to fight back.
39. It was an impossible task, but he refused to admit defeat.
40. She didn't want to look, but she couldn't seem to stop herself.

Bibliography

Almond, D. (1998/2013). *Skellig*. Hodder Children's Books.

Anderson, J. (2005). *Mechanically Inclined: Building Grammar, Usage and Style into Writer's Workshop*: Stenhouse Publishers.

Anderson, J., & Dean, D. (2014). *Revision Decisions*. Stenhouse Publishers.

Bahrick, H. P. (1979). Maintenance of Knowledge: Questions about Memory We Forgot to Ask. *Journal of Experimental Psychology: General*, *108*(3), 296–308.

Bloom, V. (1960/2004). *The River, Many Creeks: Poems from All Around the World*. Macmillan Children's Books.

Collins, B. (2002). *Sailing Alone Around the Room*. Random House.

Dahl, R. (1981). *George's Marvellous Medicine*. Puffin. (pp. 2, 7 and 10)

Doyle, C. (1902/2002). *Hound of the Baskervilles*. Random House.

Gold, H. (2022). *The Last Bear*. HarperCollins. (pp. 29, 42)

Graham, S., MacArthur, C. A., & Herbert, M. (2019). *Best Practices in Writing Instruction*. The Guildford Press.

Graham, S., & Perin, D. (2007). *Writing Next: Effective Strategies to Improve Writing of Adolescents in Middle and High School*. Carnegie Corporation of New York.

Guest, E. A. (1934). *Being Brave at Night*. In *Rhymes of Childhood*. Reilly & Lee.

Hattie, J. (2012). *Visible Learning for Teachers*. Routledge.

Holub, M. (2006). *The Door: Poems Before and After: Collected English Translations*. Bloodaxe Books.

Killgallon, D., & Killgallon, J. (1997). *Sentence Composing for Middle School*. Heinemann.

Killgallon, D., & Killgallon, J. (2000). *Sentence Composing for Elementary School: A Worktext to Build Better Sentences*. Heinemann.

Killgallon, D., & Killgallon, J. (2007). *Grammar for High School: A Sentence-Composing Approach*. Heinemann.

London, J. (1910). *How to Build a Fire*. Lost Face – Macmillan.

Milne, A. A. (1927). *Wind on the Hill*. In *Now We Are Six*. Methuen & Co Ltd.

Noden, H. R. (2011). *Image Grammar: Teaching Grammar as Part of the Writing Process*. Heinemann.

Nold, E. W. (1981). *Revising*. In C.H. Frederiksen & J.F. Dominic (Eds.), *Writing: The nature, development, and teaching of written communication. Vol. 2, Writing: Process, development and communication* (pp. 67–79).

O'Hare, F. (1973). *Sentence Combining: Improving Student Writing without Formal Grammar Instruction*. National Council of Teachers.

O'Hare, F. (1975). *Sentencecraft*. Ginn and Company.

Perry, T., Lea, R., Jørgensen, C. R., Cordingley, P., Shapiro, K., & Youdell, D. (2021). *Cognitive Science in the Classroom*. London: Education Endowment Foundation (EEF). https://educationendowm entfoundation.org.uk/education-evidence/evidence-reviews/cognitive-science-approaches -in-the-classroom

Saddler, B., & Graham, S. (2005). The Effects of Peer-Assisted Sentence-Combining Instruction on the Writing Performance of More and Less Skilled Young Writers. *Journal of Educational Psychology*, *97*(1), 43–54. https://doi.org/10.1037/0022-0663.97.1.43

Saddler, B., & Preschern, J. (2007). Improving Sentence Writing Ability through Sentence-Combining Practice. *Teaching Exceptional Children*, *39*(3), 6–11. https://doi.org/10.1177/004005990703900301

Saddler, B., & Asaro-Saddler, K. (2010). Writing Better Sentences: Sentence-Combining Instruction in the Classroom. *Preventing School Failure*, *54*(3), 159–163. https://doi.org/10.1080 /10459880903495851

Saddler, B., Ellis-Robinson & Asaro-Saddler, K. (2018). Using Sentence Combining Instruction to Enhance the Writing Skills of Children with Learning Disabilities. *Learning Disabilities: A Contemporary Journal*, *16*(2), 191–202.

Smith, F. (1998). *Joining the Literacy Club: Further Essays into Education*. Heinemann.

Stevenson, R. L. (1885). *The Moon*. In *A Child's Garden of Verses*. Underwoods.

Strong, W. (1973). *Sentence Combining: A Composing Book*. McGraw-Hill.

Strong, W. (1996). *Writer's Toolbox: A Sentence-Combining Workshop*. McGraw-Hill.

Strong, W. (2001). *Coaching Writing: The Power of Guided Practice*. Heinemann.

Twain, M. Letter to George Bainton, 15 Oct. 1888. First printed in *The Art of Authorship: Literary Reminiscences, Methods of Work, and Advice to Young Beginners, Personally Contributed by Leading Authors of the Day. Compiled and Edited by George Bainton*. D. Appleton and Company, 1890, pp. 85–88.

Weaver, C. (1996). *Teaching Grammar in Context*. Heinemann.

White, E. B. (1952). *Charlotte's Web*. Harper and Brothers.

Young, R., & Ferguson, F. (2023) *Handbook of Research on Teaching Young Writers*. www .writing4pleasure.com/the-writing-for-pleasure-centres-handbook-of-research-on-teaching -young-writers.

Zinsser, W. (1988). *Writing to Learn*. HarperCollins.

Zinsser, W. (2012). *On Writing Well: An Informal Guide to Writing Nonfiction*. Collins. Ebook, page 9.